WILLIE'S GAME

WILLIE'S GAME

An Autobiography

Willie Mosconi

and

Stanley Cohen

MACMILLAN PUBLISHING COMPANY
NEW YORK

MAXWELL MACMILLAN CANADA
TORONTO

MAXWELL MACMILLAN INTERNATIONAL
NEW YORK   OXFORD   SINGAPORE   SYDNEY

Macmillan Publishing Company   Maxwell Macmillan Canada, Inc.
866 Third Avenue   1200 Eglinton Avenue East
New York, NY 10022   Suite 200
                                Don Mills, Ontario M3C 3N1

Macmillan Publishing Company is part of the Maxwell Communica-
tion Group of Companies.

Library of Congress Cataloging-in-Publication Data

Mosconi, Willie.
    Willie's game : an autobiography/Willie Mosconi
and Stanley Cohen.
        p.   cm.
    Includes index.
    ISBN 0-02-587495-0
    1. Mosconi, Willie.   2. Billiard players—United States—
Biography.   I. Cohen, Stanley, date.   II. Title.
GV892.2.M67A3   1993   92-31181   CIP
794.7'2'092—dc20
[B]

Macmillan books are available at special discounts for bulk purchases
for sales promotions, premiums, fund-raising, or educational use. For
details, contact:

Special Sales Director
Macmillan Publishing Company
866 Third Avenue
New York, NY 10022

10 9 8 7 6 5 4 3 2 1

Printed in the United States of America

For my wife, Flora
WJM

For my granddaughter, Jessica
SC

ACKNOWLEDGMENTS

The completion of this book owes much to many people, and we wish to thank them all.

The late Don Hutter, a perceptive and astute editor, along with Jon Becker, had the foresight to bring us together for a collaboration on this project.

Clyde Taylor, our literary agent, leaped many hurdles to work out the details and proved once again that he has the endurance of the long-distance runner.

Rick Wolff, our editor, was patient and encouraging throughout the term of the project and treated the manuscript with care and delicacy.

Charlie Ursitti was an invaluable asset from start to finish. A walking encyclopedia on the subject of pocket billiards and the keeper of voluminous files, he gave of himself and his accumulation of newspaper clips freely and also contributed many of the photos in this volume.

Linda Cohen Diaz converted many hours of taped interviews into more than six hundred pages of readable transcript, promptly, efficiently, and without complaint.

Flora Mosconi, Bill Mosconi, and Gloria Dickson shared their insights and recollections of life in the home of the world's leading pocket billiards player.

Paul Newman offered some colorful reminiscences from his work on the movie *The Hustler*.

Howard Shaw, Arthur Pincus, and Paul Dickson contributed bits of information, newspaper clips, and other useful items whenever called upon.

The librarians at the Yonkers Public Library were gracious and helpful in providing books on the history of pocket billiards and reels of microfilm of back copies of *The New York Times*. The librarians at the Temple University Library in Philadelphia and at the Martin Luther King Library and the National Geographic Society in Washington, D.C., also supplied us with news clips and articles from their files.

The members of the writer's family, each in his or her own way, leavened the process of preparing the manuscript. Special thanks, therefore, go to Betty, Linda, Steve, Eddie, Michael, and Jessica.

AUTHOR'S NOTE

The autobiographical portion of this book is written in the first-person voice of Willie Mosconi. Other sections of the book, clearly indicated by space breaks, are written in my own voice or in those of other observers. The use of this technique allowed us to re-create the flavor of the times at each stage of Willie's life, sketching in the background and providing a context that gives his story added dimension. It also permitted those who knew Willie well to offer the reader a more balanced view of his nature and personality. Finally, since Willie's pride in his achievements is equaled by his modesty with respect to them, it enabled me to describe his manner and the quality of his performance without offending his sensibilities.

—Stanley Cohen

WILLIE'S GAME

WILLIE'S GAME

CHAPTER

1

One of my earliest memories is of lying in bed at night and being lulled to sleep by the sounds of the game. My room was on the second floor of a small three-story building and underneath was a small pool hall that was run by my father. It was strictly a neighborhood operation, four or five tables, in an old American Legion Hall in South Philadelphia. The clicking of the balls carried well at night, and I used to listen for the muffled thud as one of the balls hit the pocket and then the hum as it rolled down the return chute and clanked into the rack at the foot of the table. I was only a kid then, maybe four or five years old, but that's how it started. You might say I was born into the game of billiards, courtesy of my father. But it was through circumstance, not design, that he became involved.

My father was a professional prizefighter by trade, a bantamweight. His name was Joseph William Mosconi, but he fought under the name of Charlie Russell. He was pretty good, but not good enough. At one time he was ranked third in the world, but he was never able to get beyond that. He couldn't get a shot at the title, and that's where the money was, so he retired from the ring and began training boxers. He opened a gym at Eighth Street and Wharton and installed a couple of pool tables for the fighters. They liked to relax by shooting a game of pool now and then. The tables were in the front and the gym in the back. When the fighters weren't using the tables he opened them up to the public, renting time at a few cents an hour. After a while he closed down the gym, moved to a larger place, and added a few tables. That's how he got into the business. That's how I got into the business, too.

I used to hang around there a lot. I liked to watch the customers play. I didn't understand anything about the game, of course, but I was attracted to it. I think any kid would be; all those colored balls—red, yellow, blue, green—rolling around the table, knocking into each other, falling into a pocket, bouncing off the rails. I especially used to like watching the striped balls, the bands of color twisting this way and that as they spun across the table. At first I used to go down there, pull the balls out of the rack, and just roll them around the table, seeing how many times I could make a ball hit the cushions, how it would change directions when I put a spin on it. I guess this was my initiation into the workings of English, but I'm sure I didn't know it at the time. [*English* is the spin put on the cue ball that causes it to move in a particular direction upon striking another object.]

It wasn't long before I picked up a cue stick and tried to imitate what I saw the players doing. I started pushing the white ball into the colored balls and hoping they would fall into the holes. It was no easy matter. The cue stick was about a foot and a half bigger than I was, and I needed to stand on a box to reach over the table. But I began watching the games closely and picking up some of the techniques—how to hold the cue, how to make a bridge, how to stroke.

My father offered no encouragement. He didn't want me hanging around the place and he didn't want me playing. The fighters and people of that type were there a lot, and he was concerned that I might get mixed up in that sort of element. Pool halls had an unsavory reputation back then, in the late teens, and some of that feeling rubbed off on the game itself. There was also a practical side of the matter. He was worried that I might cut the cloth or spill something on it and he would have to buy a new one. So I was forbidden to play, but that didn't stop me. In fact, I think it made playing all the more attractive. One way or another, I found my way to the table.

My father was a big baseball fan, and he often went to Shibe Park in the afternoon to watch the Phillies and the Athletics play. While he was out at the ball park I used to go downstairs, eat the candy bars and the pies from the concession stand, and play pool. At night, I would sometimes climb down the rainpipe from my room and into the pool hall through the rear window. Finally he caught me and started locking up the balls and the cue sticks when he was out or went to bed. But that didn't stop me either. I went to the pantry, picked out the roundest small potatoes I could find, got a broom handle from the kitchen and an apple crate to stand on, and improvised. My mother was too busy to keep track of such things. We were a growing family at the time. I already had a younger sister and a set of twin brothers, and another set of twins, also boys, was not far behind. So my mother had more to do than count the potatoes. I knocked them all over the table, but of course they left their mark. One time, the skins started peeling and the juice smeared the cloth so bad I couldn't clean it, and boy, did I catch hell. But I still hung around there whenever I could, and I was watching the players more and more intently.

Some of my father's friends who would drop in from time to time would see me around the tables and say, "Hey, Joe, you gonna make little Willie a pool player?"

"No way," he would say. He didn't want me to have any part of billiards or boxing. He wanted something better for me, something a little classier. Actually, what he wanted was for me to become a dancer.

Dancing ran in the family. My cousins Charlie and Louie were part of a vaudeville team known as the Dancing Mosconis. It was no small-time act. They toured with the Ziegfeld Follies and headlined the Palace Theater fifty-eight times. That was back in the teens and twenties, and they were often the featured act on bills that included Fred and Adele Astaire. They got to know one another pretty well, and Fred remained a good friend of the family's until he died a few years ago. I stayed at his house many times when I was out in California. He enjoyed playing pool. He had a table in his home, and when he was feeling particularly frisky he would take me on. He played a fairly good game—for a dancer.

At one time, there were four members of the Dancing Mosconis. Charlie and Louie brought their younger brother, Willie, into the act, along with their sister, Verna. They did all kinds of dancing—ballroom, tap dancing, stunts, anything. But they were known mostly as eccentric dancers, performing all sorts of leaps and acrobatic maneuvers. Louie did most of the spins and twists and Charlie was an accomplished tap dancer. Willie and Verna dropped out after a while, and my father somehow got the notion that I might one day join Charlie and Louie in the act, follow in their footsteps. I don't know what ever gave him the idea that I had a gift for dancing, but I suppose it was like any father's wish that his son might join what he looked on as the family business. I guess he thought dancing ran in the genes. It didn't. I found that out at a very early age.

My father sent me to dancing school when I was six years

old. My uncle Charlie, the father of the dancers, owned the South Philadelphia Dance Academy, and I was enrolled there in the summer of 1919. I had no interest in dancing, and I don't think I was especially good at it. Certainly my dancing cousins, who were at the top of their form at that time, expressed no great interest in my potential as a dancer. It was my father; he thought it would be an easy way for me to get started in a career and keep me away from the pool hall. It didn't work out that way. As it happened, attending dance school was the critical factor that served to get my billiard playing off the ground. It was in dancing school that I really learned to shoot pool.

Uncle Charlie's studio consisted of a cigar store out front and a rehearsal hall in the back. In the rear corner of the rehearsal hall he had a pool table. He liked to play and he kept it there for his own amusement. When I was finished with my lesson I would play while waiting for my father to pick me up. Sometimes he was late and I got to play for an hour or more. I began practicing some of the techniques I had observed in my father's pool hall. I learned how to control the cue ball and play position, looking four or five shots ahead. I also picked up some pointers watching Uncle Charlie; he was a fairly good player. After about a month or so, I was able to run a rack. Then I learned to leave a break ball to break open the next rack. After that, it was just a question of practicing and refining my technique.

One day, Uncle Charlie saw me at the table while I was waiting for my father.

"Let's see what you can do," he said.

So I broke open the balls and ran the table. My uncle couldn't believe it.

"Let's see you do it again," he said, and I ran a second rack.

Uncle Charlie was impressed. He told my father about it, but my father was still not interested. I kept practicing at the studio and Charlie encouraged me. He was the first one to see that I had a kind of talent for the game. It took a chance happening to make a believer of my father.

One day a friend of his came into the pool hall looking for a game, but the place was deserted. He asked my father to play, but he was busy checking the books and didn't want to be interrupted.

"I'll play you," I said to the man.

"Okay, young fella," he said, "let's see if we can find a cue stick that's not too heavy for you."

He broke open the balls, patted me on the head, and said, "There you go, now do your stuff."

I ran off fourteen balls and left one for the break. He called my father over, and my father watched as I ran a second rack and got started on a third. Picking off the balls was easy. The hard part was getting up and down from the box and moving it around the table. My father laughed. He had no idea I could play that well. No one else believed it either until they saw me do it. It was just something that came naturally to me. No one ever taught me anything or gave me any lessons. I just watched other players and copied what they did. Running a rack of balls was nothing to me. I was wondering what all the fuss was about. But I knew better than to ask any questions.

My father gave me permission to practice on his tables, and he also had some ideas of his own. It occurred to him that I had a talent that could earn us some money. Perhaps there were some people out there who were curious enough to come watch a six-year-old shoot pool against some neighborhood hot-shots. He consulted with Uncle Charlie, and Charlie had not spent most of his life in and around show business without developing some of the instincts of a promoter. He suggested that we have posters printed up declaring me a Child Prodigy and try to book a few exhibitions. The poster came out reading "protege" instead of "prodigy" but no one seemed to mind. At first, my father put the posters in the window of his own pool hall in order to draw some customers. When he found I was a marketable commodity, he got me appearances in other rooms at twenty-five dollars apiece. A family could live for weeks on that kind of money in those days. My share of the take was usually an ice cream soda and a pat on the back. But my career was under way, and from that point on my father was my biggest supporter.

There were a lot of neighborhood billiard parlors in Philadelphia in those days, and the proprietors began calling my father to arrange matches for me. They would put me up against one of the better local players, and we drew pretty good crowds. It was a novelty to see a six-year-old kid standing on a box shooting pool against a grown man. No admission fee was charged, but it was still a good deal for the owner of the room. The people who came to watch the game would often stay and play themselves, they would patronize the concession stands, and it was a way of building a clientele. The owner's only expense was the twenty-five dollars he paid my father. The guys I played got nothing but free time on the table and some local notoriety, which was no small thing in the pool-hall culture of South Philadelphia.

After I won the first few games, I became even more of an attraction. Top players in other rooms wanted a chance to play me; they wanted to be the one who beat the Child Prodigy. They couldn't believe they could lose to a six-year-old, but most of the time they did. We built up a real following, and when none of the locals was able to beat me, some interest developed in seeing how I would do against a more established player.

Around the time I turned seven, a match was set up between me and a guy by the name of Joe Angelo in Asbury Park, New Jersey, which was not far up the road from Philly. Angelo played professionally, but he was not among the top tournament players. To make the show more attractive, the game was scheduled as part of a double-header. Before playing me, Angelo went up against Andrew Ponzi, another Philadelphia kid, who was about ten years older than me. Ponzi was on his way to a great professional career in which he won the world championship three times in the thirties and forties. He and I became good friends and fierce competitors in later years, and neither of us had any trouble beating Angelo.

When he saw how easily I won that match, my father began taking me to some of the better pool halls in town, like Allinger's at Thirteenth and Market, to watch the top pros. I saw guys like Alfredo De Oro, who won the world championship thirteen times beginning in the 1880s, and Frank Taberski, who was undefeated between 1916 and 1918, and the greatest of them all, Ralph Greenleaf. Greenleaf was the current champion and he held the title for six straight years without losing a match. They all lived in the Philadelphia area at one time or another, and among them they represented half a century of pocket billiards champions.

Watching them play really opened my eyes. They did things I never saw before. They made shots I didn't believe could be made. They played position that made it look as though the cue ball were controlled with a string. I never dreamed the game could be played that way. All at once, I realized that there were things I'd never done and was not able to do. It was a real education. I watched them closely—every move, every subtle bit of strategy—and I tried to copy what they did. I began to get a bit of an idea of how complex this game was and how difficult. I was still only seven years old, and I hadn't understood before that natural ability was not enough; you had to really know what you were doing and be able to plan what you were going to be doing by the end of the rack.

Most of the great players are naturals. They pick up a cue stick and it just feels right, they have an intuitive sense of what to do with it. You can tell just by the way they hold the stick, how they make a bridge, the rhythm of their stroke. That's the way it was with me. I could set up shots and make them, whereas if I set up the same shot for someone else and told him exactly what to do, he still might not be able to make it. I don't think you can teach someone to be a great billiard player. I never heard of any of the top players taking lessons, the way you do in golf or tennis. Most of them started out young and picked it up by playing and observing. So natural ability is essential, but it won't take you to the top. Just as in any other pursuit, you have to put in the time. It takes hours of practice, day after day, and right about the time you think you're as good as you can ever be, you see another player do something you never even thought about—a new way to make a shot or play position, or a defensive strategy that can change the momentum of a game. There is almost as much strategy in this game as there is in chess, and you never stop learning. I got a firsthand education not long after my match with Joe Angelo.

It occurred to someone that if I could attract a crowd playing local favorites, we might really pack them in for a match between me and Ralph Greenleaf. Greenleaf was then in the second year of his reign as champion, but even more than that he was a magnificent personality, a crowd-pleaser like few others. A fellow by the name of Tom Gilchrist, I think they called him English Tommy, owned a local pool hall, and he set it up. Greenleaf wore a tuxedo for the occasion, and I was outfitted in a shirt and tie, which was what I usually wore when I played in public, and people really jammed the place. The Child Prodigy versus the World Champion. Greenleaf was a wonderful, friendly guy, but not so friendly that he was going to let a seven-year-old beat him. He won the game, but they tell me I gave a pretty good accounting of myself. I don't know whether Ralph looked upon me as future competition at the time, but we would play each other hundreds of times in the years ahead.

After I played Greenleaf, they started referring to me as the Juvenile Champion. But there was another child prodigy around at the time, and if I was going to be Juvenile Champion I would have to prove it. The other young whiz happened to be a girl, which gave the match between the two of us an added bit of glamour. Her name was Ruth McGinnis, and she came from Honesdale, Pennsylvania, which is a town near Scranton. She was ten years old at the time and I was seven, but in later years she somehow got to be younger than me. She went on to become the ladies' billiard champion, and she held the title for quite a few years. She was one of the best women players I ever saw. But I ran forty balls in the first inning and won the match easily. She didn't take losing very well. She wouldn't speak to me, her father wouldn't speak to me, they were in a real huff.

We played in English Tommy's place. I think it was called National Billiards, and we were supposed to play for four or five days. But so many people came out to see us that it attracted the attention of the director of public safety, James T. Cortelyou, and on the second day he stopped the match because we were minors. Under Pennsylvania law, you were not allowed in a pool hall until you were eighteen years old.

After the game with Ruth, my activities were pretty much restricted. Besides, the novelty of it was beginning to wear off. There were no other juveniles to challenge me, I had played most of the locals, I was not nearly ready to take on the top pros, and I was getting tired of it myself. I gave a few more exhibitions now and then, but by that time I was really sick of the whole routine. First my father tried to stop me from playing, then he went overboard in the other direction. I was disenchanted and confused, and I just didn't feel like playing anymore. My father didn't push it, and I guess you can say I retired as Juvenile Champion. It was an early age at which to retire and the wrong time, I suppose, because in the twenties pocket billiards was at its peak and growing more popular every year.

▲ ▲ ▲

The decade of the twenties lingers in memory and folklore as the Golden Age of Sports. It was a time when athletes were truly heroes, their feats embellished by a collective imagination that craved nothing so much as an incursion into the grand and spectacular. The Great War was not long ended, and the new decade had burst upon America with the flourish and sizzle of champagne-pop and the feel of soft velvet on every surface. It was the Roaring Twenties, the Jazz Age of Fitzgerald, flappers bouncing and strutting to new rhythms, speakeasies humming with a wink and a nod. A whole generation, it is said, got lost in its fold and then found itself.

In the world of sports, mere excellence was taken for granted in the twenties; greatness was considered routine. The mood of the time demanded no less than that the limits of possibility be extended and, as chance would have it, the field was crammed with personalities able to oblige. Right from the start, the decade seemed to breed heroes of a broader dimension, of proportions vast enough to embody the myths of an age—Babe Ruth and Walter Johnson, Red Grange and Bronco Nagurski, Jack Dempsey, Bill Tilden, Bobby Jones, Man o' War. These were names invested with a species of magic, woven into legends that grew with each telling until the records of their deeds seemed no more than footnotes to the aura that enveloped them.

Upon just such a scene, his entrance timed to perfection and executed with flair, strode Ralph Greenleaf, a tournament pool player who could orchestrate the movement of a cue ball like few before him and who did it with a style that was the measure of his era. Greenleaf was tall and handsome and he dressed to the nines. He sported a bearskin coat on his way to matches and performed in formal attire, diamond cufflinks glistening from beneath the sleeves of his tuxedo. He was married to a "princess," traveled in lofty social circles, moved in the fast lane, and was never unaware of the crowds he attracted. Greenleaf won his first world championship in December of 1919 and prepared to stake his claim on the decade of the twenties. He defended his title successfully nine straight times before relinquishing it, briefly, in 1925. He was referred to frequently as the Babe Ruth of his sport, setting new records and then breaking them, winning title matches by margins that looked like typographical errors in the morning papers.

Pocket billiards, or pool as it is colloquially called, was

a big-time sport in the twenties, and the daily press gave prominent coverage to championship tournaments. Title matches drew crowds that filled the ballrooms of large hotels. Greenleaf was paid two thousand dollars a week—a sum that, on an annual basis, would have exceeded the earnings of Babe Ruth and the president of the United States at the time—for giving exhibitions at the Palace Theater in New York.

Pool was a game whose popularity grew out of a grassroots appeal. It was played, at varying levels of efficiency, by millions of citizens in pool halls that studded the neighborhoods of big cities and the streets of small backwater towns. Every major city had a showcase billiard parlor that exuded class and refinement—Allinger's in Philadelphia, McGirr's in New York, Bensinger's in Chicago. The more intimate rooms ranged from modest respectability to gritty little dungeons in which money changed hands quickly and reputations were made or lost on the stroke of a cue.

Pool had always been a pastime that thrived at both ends of the social spectrum. It was, at the same time, a pursuit of elegant grandeur played by men of breeding and character, and a seamy ritual indulged in by small-time hoods and quick-buck con-men hungry for an easy score.

The origins of the game are as elusive and difficult to identify as the roots of most other sports. Some attest that an incipient form of the game was played more than two thousand years ago in ancient Greece. But its current form, most believe, evolved in France, the name "billiards" itself deriving from the French word *bille*, meaning ball. It was, at the time, an aristocratic diversion.

The first known billiard table was purchased by Louis XI in the fifteenth century. In later years, Parisian courtiers sat on couches of green velvet and watched Louis XIV play under twenty-six chandeliers on one of his two tables.

The game was given fresh impetus in a Paris jail during the French Revolution when a political prisoner named Captain Mingaud discovered that it was possible to exercise a degree of control over the position of the cue ball. When he had served his sentence, Mingaud asked for and received an extension of his term to allow him to perfect his technique. He then took his show on the road, attracting large crowds with a dazzling display of trick shots.

In the United States, the game quickly took root and, in true democratic fashion, soon cut a wide swath across disparate segments of the population. It was played frequently in the drawing rooms of the rich and influential. George Washington owned a table and was known to match strokes with Jefferson, Hamilton, and Lafayette. At the same time, a subterranean mystique surrounded the sport and seemed to nourish its growth. Pool halls sprouted up in small towns and the working-class neighborhoods of big cities. An association with gambling developed and would never quite be shed. Increasingly, the pocket variety of billiards was referred to more commonly as "pool," a term derived from the betting pool spectators would wager on the outcome of a game. In the election campaign of 1828 President John Quincy Adams was attacked by his opponents for keeping "gaming tables" in the White House. The Brunswick company, the nation's leading manufacturer of billiard equipment, began calling the game "pocket billiards" in an effort to sanitize its reputation.

But the term pool could not easily be shaken, and as the cities of the East grew and the country moved west, the popularity of the game continued to flourish. The first world championship tournament was held in New York in 1878. It was won by a man named Cyrille Dion. Samuel F. Knight finished second in the ten-man field. The tournament became an annual event and further nourished the public appetite for the sport. Its own roster of heroes began to emerge—Alfredo De Oro and Thomas Hueston at the turn of the century, Bennie Allen and Frank Taberski in the teens. By the early twenties, there were some forty thousand pool rooms—about ten times the current number—in the United States. Ralph Greenleaf was the newly crowned champion. And in South Philadelphia, Willie Mosconi, erstwhile Juvenile Champion, sick of the game before he turned ten, was laying up his cue stick. For all he cared, he might never play this game again.

CHAPTER

2

When I quit playing pool it was like having a weight lifted from my shoulders. It was a relief just to be able to go to school and have a normal youth, like the other kids in the neighborhood. I liked other sports better than pool. I enjoyed playing baseball and stickball. Every chance I got, I would get hold of a stick, an old broom handle, and we would use that as a bat. The ball was a pink, rubber high-bouncer that we used to call a Spaldeen, which was just our way of pronouncing Spalding, the name of the manufacturer. We played mostly in the streets, with makeshift bases, and we devised our own ground rules. The fire escape on the front of some tenement would be the foul pole and a ball hit over the roof of a particular building might be a home run or an automatic double. We measured the length of our hits by the number of telephone poles the ball would pass. A two-pole shot was pretty good; a three-poler gave you major-league status. Stickball was an urban form of baseball. We couldn't afford real bats and balls and gloves, and there were no ball fields we could play on. This was long before the days of organized Little Leagues, when kids were given uniforms and equipment and real baseball diamonds to play on. But we all wanted to play baseball, so we had to improvise and make do with what we had.

Baseball and boxing were the big sports in our neighborhood. We played touch football once in a while, but football was chiefly a college game then, and there weren't any teams or players that we could identify with. It was strictly baseball and boxing. I went to school with a kid by the name of Frankie Caras, who later became a professional fighter. He started out as a featherweight and grew into a welterweight, and I think he fought for the title at one time. He was a local hero, and so was Don Battles, another boxer. Battles later became a promoter of some note, and he either owned or managed a well-known Philadelphia night spot. He was like the Big Mahah in our section of town. [Big Mahah is a street term for a man of influence and renown. Mahah is believed to be a shortened form of Maharajah].

But our biggest heroes were baseball players, especially the home run hitters like Babe Ruth and Lou Gehrig. We didn't have much to root for in Philadelphia at that time. Both the Athletics and the Phillies were horrible in the early twenties, probably the two worst teams in baseball. The A's became a powerhouse a few years later, but I was always more of a Phillies fan, bad as they were. I never could warm to Connie Mack. He always seemed more interested in making money than anything else. But we all followed both teams. We couldn't often afford to go to a game even though admission was only about thirty-five cents in those days. We read about it in the papers every day, and we knew the records and batting averages of all the players. So after I was finished with playing pool, my school years were pretty much the same as those of most other kids. We had our fun, but life wasn't always easy.

I grew up in a tough area of South Philadelphia and I often had to fight my way to and from school. I still have a scar on my forehead and one on my chin from boyhood fights. Of course it was not like it is today; no one used guns or knives. But bricks and clubs were not uncommon. These were not ethnic battles. I don't remember there being much prejudice in the neighborhood, but times were hard, and if you had a few cents in your pocket or were carrying your lunch you might have to fight to keep it.

Once you were in school, everything settled down. No one acted up too much in the classroom. I went to the local public school, then to Barrett Junior High School and South Philadelphia High. About halfway through high school my father took me out and enrolled me in Banks Business College. I had no interest in business and I certainly didn't want to go to a specialized school, but my father had his own ideas. His sister's husband was in the shoe-binding business, and my father was hoping to get me some training so that I could join him in the business. But it didn't work out that way. I completed enough courses to receive my high school diploma, but about halfway through I had to leave and go to work.

Both my parents had fallen ill. My father contracted pneumonia, which was a serious illness in the days before antibiotics, and he closed up the pool hall. He worked at odd jobs for a while, then he had a heart attack and was unable to work at all. My mother in the meantime was suffering from cancer. So there was no money coming in, there were medical bills to be paid and six children to feed. Since I was the oldest, it fell to me to get a job and support the rest of the family. This was in 1930, the Depression had just hit, and getting a job that would put bread on the table for a family of eight was no easy matter, especially if you were only seventeen years old.

We were fortunate in that my father had a good friend in the upholstery business, and he got me a job in his factory. I think the place was called Beifield's Upholsterers. I was hired as an apprentice and taught to put the outside on the frame of the chair. I was paid eight dollars a week, which in our family amounted to one dollar a person, and that made things really tight. But I soon discovered that other employees were being paid on a piece-work basis, getting thirty-five cents for every chair and fifty cents for a sofa. So I got myself put on piece work and in no time at all I was making thirty-five to forty dollars a week. Now that was pretty good money at a time when millions of people were out of work, but in order to make it you had to turn out a hell of a lot of chairs. I held that job for close to two years, and then something happened that cost me the job and changed the course of my life.

My uncle Johnny, my father's brother, had gotten a couple of tickets for the 1931 World Series between the A's and the Cardinals. It was a Saturday game and since I worked only a half day on Saturdays I didn't think I would have any problem. I worked like a beaver to get my work done early and then I started for the door. When the boss's son saw me leaving he called me back.

"Where to you think you're going?" he said.

I told him I had finished my work and was going to the ball game.

"You're not going to any ball game," he said. "There are some other things I want you to do before you leave."

"Well gee, Larry," I said, "I already finished my work. I did everything I was supposed to do and now it's quitting time."

"I don't give a damn what time is," he said. "You get yourself back in here and do your job or you won't have any job to do."

Well, I got pretty hot, and I told him what he could do with his job. He didn't like the way I put it. We exchanged a few unpleasantries, and the next thing I know he throws a punch at me. Lucky for me, he missed. He was a big son-of-a-bitch, over six feet and about 220 pounds, while I was around five-seven and maybe eighty pounds lighter. But I could move pretty fast. When I saw him still coming after me, I threw some tools at him to slow him up and ran out the door as fast as I could, and I never went back. I went to the game with my uncle, and it wasn't until the game was over that what I had done really sank in.

▲ ▲ ▲

The latter part of 1931 was a poor time to be out of work. The fizz and bubble of the twenties had dissolved with the end of the decade and the shadow of the Great Depression covered the landscape like a shroud. Times were already harder than they had ever been and the bottom had not yet been hit. Within a year, more than one-fourth of the nation's work force was unemployed. While no section of the country was spared, the urban centers suffered the greatest losses. The financial markets had collapsed, manufacturing plants had closed, service industries were offering services that few could afford.

The Golden Age of Sports had ended just as abruptly. Attendance was down at big-league ball parks, and the gate receipts for other major sporting events were counted in smaller denominations. In a curious fashion, the dramatic change in the style and tempo of the country seemed to be mirrored on the playing fields. The carefree elegance and breakneck power with which the Yankees roared through the twenties had given way to a new style of play that more closely reflected the mood of the times. The St. Louis Cardinals' Gas House Gang—the team

of Dizzy Dean, Pepper Martin, and Leo Durocher—
approached their work with a sullen desperation which
declared that survival was the first imperative. In a hard-
scrabble world, an unblinking toughness would carry
you further than a flair for the critical moment. Other
sports had undergone similar transformations. Dempsey
was gone now and so were Nagurski and Grange. And
Ralph Greenleaf, who had straddled the field of pocket
billiards for more than a decade, was nearing the end of
his reign.

The Depression had cut into professional billiards as
it had most other sports. The big-time rooms, the classy
halls in which the championship tournaments were
played, were all hurting. The business clientele to which
they catered was not doing much business. The crowds
that paid to watch the title matches were in short supply.
With rentals remaining high in the better neighborhoods
of the cities, the big billiard parlors struggled to ride out
the crunch.

Ironically, however, the local pool halls prospered.
The streets of the cities were filled with men out of work
and pool rooms became a popular gathering place, a
shelter of sorts for those with no place to go. Time at the
tables was measured in small change, there was protec-
tion from the elements, and the common feeling of despair found its balm in the ease of good fellowship. So
the Depression, in its way, nourished the neighborhood
pool halls, and they became a breeding ground for new
talent. Many of them sponsored amateur tournaments
with cash prizes for the winners. They were open to all
at a modest entry fee, and who could tell but that one of
them might someday produce a future world champion.

▲ ▲ ▲

On my way home from the ball park I passed Frankie Mason's
billiard hall at Seventh and Morris. There was a sign in the
window advertising a pool tournament with a first prize of
seventy-five dollars. I thought, "I used to play this game,
maybe I still can." When I got home and told my father that
I lost my job he gave me all kinds of hell.

"What are you going to do now?" he asked me.

"Well, Pop," I said, "they're running a pool tournament
over at Seventh and Morris and the winner gets seventy-five
bucks."

"Okay, go ahead and try it," he said.

So I paid the entry fee, it was just a few bucks, and damned
if I didn't win it. I won it easy, too. It was a two-week tournament, but the prize money was about the same as I would
have made working at the upholsterer's and the hours were a
lot better. I came home and handed my father the money. He
gave me about three dollars for myself and said, "Now go out
and find yourself another tournament." And that's exactly
what I did. They were holding them all over town. It was
a good deal for everyone. The proprietors brought in new
customers, and the players had a chance to pick up a few
bucks. Those were tough times—no jobs, no money—and no
one passed up the chance to earn a few dollars.

I entered one tournament after another, and to be truthful,
I don't remember losing any of them. The other players were
not very good at that level, and I didn't have much trouble.
So for a while I supported the family with the prize money
from these tournaments. Not all of them paid as well as Mason's. There was one guy, Phil Longo, who ran a room at Fifth
and South, and he was as cheap as they came. The top prize

in his place was only thirty-five dollars, but anything was welcome in those days, and I took the money and ran. I played in every tournament I could find, and after a while I began to think that maybe I could make a living at this game.

I began hanging around Frankie Mason's place when there was no tournament in progress. He liked having me there because I attracted customers, and he paid me to help out. I would work behind the desk and punch the time card when players rented a table, give them a rack of balls and some chalk, and then clock them out and collect the fee when they finished playing. When Frankie had to leave for a while, he asked me to run the place for him. He paid me according to the amount of work I did each week, so I always had some money coming in. But the real money came from playing the hustlers who walked in the door.

There were a lot of top players in the Philadelphia area—Andy Ponzi, Jimmy Caras, Greenleaf lived there at one time—so it attracted a lot of out-of-town hustlers. People often asked why one city produced so many billiard champions in a short period, and someone once answered it was because there was nothing else to do in Philadelphia. But good players tend to attract other good players—I think that's true in any sport—and when they play one another they become even better. You can't improve your game unless you play with people who are better than you are; you learn from them. So the hustlers would come into Philadelphia looking for pigeons, and very few of them ever left with any money in their pockets.

They came from all over, a lot of them up from the South, and they all had their own approaches. Some would just come in, all full of bluster, and ask, "Who's the best player in the house?" Their technique would be to win and lose a few until the stake grew large enough and then they would show their true speed. Sometimes they'd come in in pairs and play each other for a while. Neither of them would play particularly well, and of course other people would be watching. Then the guy who was losing would quit.

"Come on, one more game," the other would say.

"You got me beat," he would answer. "I'm busted."

So the guy who had won would look around the room. He would pick out someone who looked like a pigeon and say, "How about a game, kid, there's still some time on the table." His idea was to play below his ability, even lose a few games, until he worked the bet up high enough, and then blow the kid away.

Sometimes I was the kid they picked. I was only eighteen or nineteen at the time and I looked even younger and a lot of them took me for an easy mark. But I had them spotted the minute they walked in the door. After a while, you were just able to pick them out. It was as if they were wearing a sign on their chests. But none of them got very far in Philadelphia. They had to get by me before they could even think about taking on Caras or Ponzi, and I left them slim pickings. They used to get mad as hell at me because I was stopping all the action before it got to them. They called me every name in the book, but that was all right with me as long as I got the money, and I usually did.

Even the most skilled hustlers often had trouble when they came to town. We always played on tournament-size tables, which were five by ten feet, while in a lot of small towns around the country they used the four and a half by nine tables, and the pockets were about half an inch wider. The change in size made a tremendous difference. The angles were sharper on the cut shots, and an extra foot means a lot when

you're shooting from one end of the table to the other. So
they were at a disadvantage no matter who they were playing.
But even the ones who were used to playing on the five-by-
tens were in for a tough time.

Some of them came to town with reputations that preceded
them. You would hear that Rags Fitzpatrick was in town or
Cue Ball Kelly or Boston Shorty. But they were all pretty
much the same; they could play just well enough to lose.
Hustlers are a sleazy bunch of bastards. They would take your
last dime if they could. They were a blessing to me, though.
My family ate pretty well on their money.

▲ ▲ ▲

The pool hustler is a part of America's informal mythol-
ogy. He is a quixotic figure, a man who stirs the imagination and inspires a magical mix of fear and respect. He
is, in a sense, the urban counterpart of the Old West
gunfighter. His name is uttered in awe by those who
have never seen him, who wonder in fact whether he
really exists or is the product of homespun legends that
have been passed along from one to another, growing
brighter with each translation. Hustlers were rarely
known by their full names, and they seemed to have no
addresses. They were mainly referred to by aliases as
descriptive and colorful as Billy the Kid: Cornbread Red,
Tuscaloosa Squirrel, Weanie Beanie, Daddy Warbucks,
Abraham Sunshine. The goal of the pool hustler, one of
them said, was "to lift people up by their pockets."

America has always treated such types with an uncer-
tain conscience, its moral outrage tempered by a primi-
tive lust for independence and adventure. A curious
fascination was reserved for the hunter who chose his

prey with discernment. Jesse James, Legs Diamond, Willie Sutton were never objects of the disdain reserved for the common criminal. They were a part of Americana, condemned for their deeds but treasured for their style and their daring. They were, in their way, too large, too complex to be subject to the strictures that measured their value. Like the practiced pool hustler, they approached their business with a dedicated indifference to consequence. They were impelled by a romantic vision that courted danger and thrived on the prospect of sudden endings.

▲ ▲ ▲

You can live for just so long off the people who happen to wander into your room. After a while, the word gets out that that Mosconi kid is no soft touch. You begin to attract a better class of player, which was all right with me, but I needed the action. I was not playing the walk-ins for the glory of it. I was trying to feed a family of eight. So I started going to other rooms around town. I would go as far as Camden, New Jersey, on occasion. But one of the best money rooms around was the Fox Billiard Academy. It was a much bigger room than Frankie Mason's. Mason's was a neighborhood place, a storefront that you would just walk into off the street. It used to be a dance hall at one time. Fox was more than twice the size. It was located in the basement, underneath the old Fox movie theater in North Philadelphia, about eight miles from where I lived. But I started going there a lot. The Fox attracted good players from all over the area, and we would play one after another as long as the money held out.

Sometimes I would start out with no more than fifty cents

in my pocket and play in Mason's or some other small room until I worked it up to a couple of bucks. Then I would go to the Fox, looking for bigger fish to fry. I never hustled anyone. I played everyone straight. What I had working for me was my youth and the other guy's ego. A lot of these guys had been around a while, and they had taken money from some pretty good players. They considered themselves big-time and they didn't think that a baby-faced kid who hardly looked old enough to enter the room could beat them. When I did, they still couldn't believe it and they wanted to play me again. They felt their reputation was on the line and they were willing to risk their money to salvage it. One time I went downtown with a stake of two and a half bucks, and the manager of the pool hall challenged me to a game. We started at about eleven o'clock at night and played through until ten the next morning. By that time I had won everything he had in his pockets and the entire contents of his cash register. If he could have laid his hands on some more money we might still be playing.

Not all of them were that compulsive. There were some quality players who knew about me or Ponzi or Caras and wanted to try their luck against us. One fellow, Harry Hallman, used to come down to Fox's from Northeast Philadelphia and he would challenge us to a game now and then. Hallman was a legitimate player. He won the city championship a few times, but he was never able to get beyond that. He gave us a good game once in a while, but Hallman knew when he was beaten. A lot of those guys just never knew when to quit.

One of them was a neighborhood character by the name of Fatty Pincus. He owned a cigar store and they say he made a little book on the side. He wore a lot of expensive jewelry and was always flashing big rolls of cash, and for some reason, he fancied himself a pool player. One night he was feeling particularly good and he asked me to play. We played a few games of straight pool, but there was no way he could beat me; he just wasn't much of a player. So then he figured he might get lucky at some of the quick, short-rack games like nine-ball and rotation. We played well into the night, but he still couldn't win.

"Is that it, Fatty?" I said.

"How about giving me a little spot?" he said. "Give me a chance to get some of my money back."

So I spotted him a couple of balls. We played a variation of nine-ball, where I had to make the nine to win, but he could win by making the five, the seven, or the nine. It proved no help to him at all. By the time morning came, I had beaten him out of all his cash, about nine hundred dollars. That was a fortune in those days, half a year's salary for many people.

"Okay, Fatty?" I said. "Had enough now?"

But he still wasn't ready to quit. He started inventing games that he thought he couldn't possibly lose, betting his jewelry against its cash value. We played a rack in which I had to make the one ball in the side pocket to win and all he had to do was hit the one with the cue ball. The first game cost him his watch, the next one his diamond ring.

"That's it," Fatty said finally. "That is definitely it."

He broke the cue stick over his leg and walked out. We had been playing for about twelve hours, but at an hourly rate I had done pretty well.

Of course it wasn't always that easy. I didn't always win. As my reputation spread, I was forced to play better competition, and there were some damn good players working the area.

There were some nights when I left broke, my hands thrust into my empty pockets, and I had to walk home because I couldn't afford the carfare. It was like going to work and not getting paid. And I hated to lose; I couldn't afford it. I was hungry back then. My whole family was hungry. Winning was everything to me because we needed the money. That's exactly how it was. All I wanted was to get the money. If you don't win, you don't eat. You want to know what pressure is like, try it some time.

On the nights I came home broke I was very depressed. I felt as though I had let my whole family down. But my father always tried to pick me up. He encouraged me.

"You can beat anybody, Willie," he would tell me. "Anybody, anyplace, anytime."

I would go back to the same place the next night, and if the guy who beat me was there I would play him again, and more often than not I would win back what I lost and then some. It was like the old saw about getting right back up on the horse that threw you. I couldn't tolerate the thought that this guy could beat me, that he was walking around with my money. I wanted the money back and I wanted to take his. I wanted every cent he had. He might be a nice enough guy, but when I was playing him he was the enemy and I wanted it all. You need to have that attitude in order to survive in those circumstances. That kind of competition is trial by fire, and it steeled me. It made me that much tougher when I got to tournament play. I don't think a pool player can rise to the top and show championship mettle unless he has sharked bets in his youth. During those years, I learned to shark bets with the best of them, but I never hustled anyone. I always declared myself and I never played anything less than my best game.

▲ ▲ ▲

Willie draws the distinction between the pool shark and the hustler with scrupulous care. It is a distinction worthy of note, and being able to distinguish one from the other can save a man a lot of money.

The shark—as good as his name—has a quick nose for blood and an instinct for making the kill. He is schooled not only in his game but in the fine art of winning. He plays all the angles and has cultivated a sense that will detect the first crack in the composure of his opponent. He does not conceal his identity; others seek him out. He enlists their vanity as a confederate of his own. He allows their ambition to betray them. He nourishes their confidence. They believe that with a good run or two they can beat him; they can't. When they lose, it is with the conviction that their luck has run out; it is more often their bankroll.

The hustler lives in the shadows. Anonymity is an ally that he guards with resolve. He weaves a fabric of deceit, creating an illusion that others take for reality. It is his art to be able to play well enough without looking too good. He will make a difficult shot but leave himself with poor position. He engenders the notion that he is dangerously adept but careless of detail. He encourages the belief that pressure unnerves him. His intent is to lose until the other man's greed drives the stakes higher. Then, with the big money finally on the table, he somehow manages to put it all together. He makes it appear that luck has kissed his cue stick. If he plays it just right, the sucker, the mark, might be inclined to try him again: Once more under pressure and he'll crack; he won't.

The hustler, of necessity, lives out of a suitcase. He travels from city to city, state to state, making his temporary home in out-of-the-way places like El Dorado, Kansas, or Amarillo, Texas, searching out backwater towns in which his reputation is unknown. At each stop he plays for one big score, then is obliged to leave quickly. He is a man of the road, and he lives that way until his skill fades or he runs out of geography. Occasionally, a very good hustler will test himself as a professional. He will sign up for a tournament or two and perhaps make the circuit. But rarely is he good enough to make it to the top. His pulse is timed for the quick kill. Few hustlers possess the patience and the stamina that are the coin of world-class tournaments. Many of them sneer at such endeavors. They prefer to perpetuate the fiction that they are the true money players and are nourished by the tainted but curiously romantic image of desperadoes who live their lives close to the edge.

Willie understood the difference at a rather early age. He had learned to spot the hustlers at a glimpse, and he had proven he could beat them all day and all night. He also nursed the recollection that when he was just seven years old he had played with Ralph Greenleaf, the billiard champion of the world. He was nineteen years old now. It was 1932, and he had cause to wonder whether he was good enough to play with the pros.

▲ ▲ ▲

Just before Christmas in 1932 my father took me to Allinger's to watch a session of the world pocket billiards tournament. I had played in Allinger's from time to time but not too often. This was not your ordinary pool hall. Allinger's was a palace,

the Palace of Pool, someone once called it. It had opened in
1906 at 1307 Market Street, not far from City Hall, and right
from the start it was a national showcase. It catered to an elite
clientele, mostly businessmen. The hustlers who frequented
the other rooms around town were not welcome in Allinger's.
If they came in and played someone they knew, that was all
right, but they were not permitted to approach the customers.
Strangers were watched very closely. Anyone who came in
looking to pick up a game was shown the door in a hurry. If
they were reluctant to leave, there were always a few big guys
in the place to offer some gentle persuasion.

Allinger's was strictly a gentleman's establishment. It was
run like the Urban League. If you spoke above a whisper you
were asked to lower your voice. It was a huge place. It occupied three full floors, and there was a glass-enclosed room on
the second floor that was reserved for only the top quality
players. That's where the world tournaments were held, with
the players wearing black tie and tuxedo.

On the night my father took me there, we arrived early and
I went into the practice room to watch the players warm up.
There was one guy from California who looked terrific. He
was running rack after rack and he seemed to be in dead
stroke. He made some nice combination shots and he played
good position. I said to myself, "This guy could be hard to
beat."

When tournament play started, this fellow was matched
against Greenleaf, and all of a sudden he looked like an amateur. Greenleaf left him tied up and he couldn't run more
than three or four balls. He was pathetic. I watched him and
I thought, "Hell, if a guy like that can play in a national
tournament, why shouldn't I?"

CHAPTER

3

Getting to play in the world championship tournament was no easy matter if you had not been there before. The tournament was sponsored by the Billiard Association of America, which is now called the Billiard Congress of America, and the guidelines varied from year to year. Usually, it was played as a round-robin, with each contestant playing a 125-point match against every other player, and the championship was decided on the basis of best overall record. In the event of a tie, a playoff was held to determine the winner. There were rarely more than ten or twelve players competing, and being included in that elite cadre was already an accomplishment worthy of note.

The recognized world-class players—the current champion, recent champions, and runners-up in the previous tournament—received automatic invitations. The balance of the field was made up of the survivors of a series of elimination tournaments that were held around the country. These were also sponsored by the BAA, which was looking to attract new faces and stimulate interest. Local competitions, called divisionals, sent players to one of four sectional tournaments, and the top three or four players in those qualified to play for the national championship. The winner, and as many runners-up as were needed to fill out the field, played in the world championship tournament.

Ironically, the U.S. national billiard champion was rarely the best player in the country, since the top players never had to compete in the national, which was strictly a qualifying tournament. George Kelly, a quality local player, won the national championship many times but he never won a world title. He was a tough competitor; he just couldn't break through into the top echelon, but he went to the nationals almost every year.

For a new player, it was difficult even getting into the city competition. You couldn't just decide you wanted to enter; you had to be sponsored by one of the participating billiard halls. I got to play in the 1933 tournament by a quirk of fate. Izzie Goodman, the owner of Fox Billiard Academy, was sponsoring a player by the name of Eddie Brown. Eddie was considered one of the best amateurs around at the time. I had played him when I was about sixteen years old and at least held my own against him, but he was a few years older than me and had established more of a reputation. However, Eddie suddenly fell ill. He had an appendectomy, developed peritonitis, and the poor guy died just a week or two before the tournament was to start. Izzie had already paid the entry fee, so he asked me if I would take Eddie's place. I said, "Sure." The winner would get seventy-five dollars and move on to the sectionals. So this was my initiation into tournament billiards.

Before the divisionals even began, I learned I would have to overcome an unexpected obstacle. I was acquainted with the competition around the Philadelphia area. Players of the caliber of Ponzi and Caras—experienced professionals— would not be competing at the city level. I had played most of the other guys at one time or another, and I thought I had a pretty good shot at winning the tournament. But the brain trust of the Billiard Association had ideas of their own. They wanted a name player from Philadelphia to go to the sectionals, so they performed some minor geographical surgery. They decided that Lowell, Massachusetts, was in the general vicinity and shipped in a seasoned pro by the name of Andrew St. Jean to mop up the competition. St. Jean was one of the better players in the country and one of the most popular. He had given Ralph Greenleaf a tough game for the title in 1928, and he was also a colorful character, a real crowd pleaser.

▲ ▲ ▲

There were many who believed Andrew St. Jean to be one of the most versatile pool players in the nation during the twenties and thirties. He never quite made it to the championship, but then he was not strictly a tournament player. St. Jean was a hustler of some repute, known variously as the Lowell Kid, the Saint, and occasionally as the Coca-Cola Masked Marvel. The Masked Marvel was a promotional gimmick instituted by the soft-drink manufacturer in the twenties. A number of good amateur and professional pool-shooters played the role at one time or another. Wearing a black hood over his head, he would walk into a neighborhood pool hall and take on the local talent. No one knew who the Masked Marvel was, but he was always a top player who put on a good show. When the show was over, Coca-Cola would be served on the house, and the masked man would leave as quietly as he had entered. His appearance was always anticipated but never expected, even by the proprietor of the pool hall.

St. Jean was a man who favored such escapades. Even when he was hustling, he often seemed more committed to the style and flavor of the action than to taking the

other guy's money. He would offer huge spots and flaky
propositions that could rarely be covered. One contemporary of his suggested that if he wanted the action badly
enough the Saint might bet you it was Christmas Eve
when it happened to be Easter Sunday. But he thrived
on the pulse of the challenge and the spectators loved it.
And when he played straight pool, tournament-style, he
was a formidable opponent.

▲ ▲ ▲

The divisionals were supposed to be a freebie for St. Jean, an
automatic pass to the sectionals. But he never made it. The
tournament was set up as a double round-robin, which meant
that each player played every other player twice. As it happened, I beat St. Jean both times, by scores of 100–8 and
100–20, and won the tournament undefeated. So St. Jean
went back to Lowell, Massachusetts, and I went to New York
City to try my luck at the next level.

There were four sectional tournaments, with the top two or
three finishers from each moving on to play for the national
championship. In New York, we played at the Strand Academy, which was the best billiard room in the city. It was
located right in the center of the Theater District, underneath
the Strand Theater, and it was every bit as classy as Allinger's
in Philadelphia. There was a separate room for championship
matches, with bleachers surrounding the tables, and they really packed them in. There must have been a couple of hundred paid admissions, and I remember being nervous as hell.

My cousin Charlie had a ticket agency in New York; he
knew a lot of show business people, and it seemed as though
he brought them all to watch me play, and that made me even
more nervous. At twenty years of age, I was by far the youn-

gest player in the tournament, and I was up against some real old pros. But once the games started my competitive instincts took over and I felt fine. I won my first two matches. One of them was against Onofrio Lauri, an old-timer from Brooklyn who was as bald as a cue ball and as explosive as a firecracker. He'd sometimes get so angry when he lost that he would break his cue stick or even ram his head into a wall. But our game was not close enough to set him off. I won it pretty easily but then suffered my first loss, 100–76, to Charlie "Chick" Seaback, another veteran, from Astoria, Queens. I lost only one other game and won the tournament by a narrow margin over Seaback and a player by the name of Arthur Church. All three of us qualified for the nationals, which were scheduled to begin two weeks later, on October 30, in Minneapolis. The sectional championship was worth $250, which brought my earnings to $325 so far, not bad for two weeks' work during the depth of the Depression.

Minneapolis was as far as I had ever been from home. New York was less than one hundred miles from Philadelphia and I had been there many times before, so it was not really like being out of town. But Minneapolis was like another country. It took an overnight train ride to get there, and from the minute we arrived I was looking forward to leaving. It was cold; boy, was it cold! It was still October and I wasn't prepared for that kind of weather. To this day, all I can remember about Minneapolis was damn near freezing to death.

There were ten players in the tournament. The winner and the two runners-up would qualify for the world competition in December. I always felt it was important to get off to a good start in that kind of competition. Each of us would be playing nine games, and you knew you could not afford to lose more than twice and still have a chance to win it.

My first opponent was Harry Wood, so I knew I was in for a long afternoon. Wood was a defensive specialist. He wouldn't take a chance on a shot unless he could see it right into the pocket. That was not my kind of game. I always liked to shoot fast and play quickly—break open the balls and look for a long run. I never spent much time studying the lay of the table. I felt it threw my rhythm off. But you couldn't play that way against Wood. He played safety after safety, and the game dragged on. I finally won it 125–102, but it took fifty-three innings and I had a high run of only thirty-three. A 125-point game usually takes no more than fifteen or twenty innings and very often a lot less. (An inning is completed when each player finishes a turn at the table.)

In the final game of the tournament, George Kelly set a tournament record when he ran 125 balls in a match with Seaback. That was one ball short of the world's record set by Ralph Greenleaf in the 1929 world championship in Detroit. Kelly had opened the game by playing safe on the break. Then, after Seaback missed, George made his unbroken run, also tying a tournament mark by completing the game in two innings. One of the interesting things about that run is that it took an hour and twelve minutes, which was very slow time. In the years to come, I often made runs of that length in less than half an hour. But Kelly played a very deliberate game. He looked the table over closely and sized up his shots with meticulous care. It was his style of playing and it worked well for him. He was never in better stroke than he was in that tournament. His win over Seaback gave him a 7–2 record and left the three of us tied for first place.

The three-way tie necessitated a round-robin playoff. Kelly and I each handled Seaback easily and then played each other for the title. I started out hot and led 84–27 after fourteen innings, but then Kelly took control. He tied me up with some good defense, and as I said, he was at the very top of his game. He tied me at 98 and ran out with an unfinished run of twenty-seven after twenty-nine innings.

While I hated losing, I was not altogether displeased with my performance. I received second-place money of $450. Kelly got $550 in prize money and a diamond medal emblematic of the national title. Most important, all three of us qualified for the world championship tournament, which was to open on December 4 in Chicago. At this point, I had won a total of $775, and professional billiards was looking like a pretty good way to make a living. I sent most of the money home. My father had been feeling better in recent months, but he needed a new start. Prohibition had just been repealed, and I sent him enough money to get a beer license and open a tavern in Barrington, New Jersey, which was just up the turnpike from Philadelphia. I held out enough money to pay my expenses in Chicago and another $27.50 to buy myself a formal suit. Tuxedos were required dress for evening matches in the world tournament. Now, I was headed for the big time.

▲ ▲ ▲

The format for the world pocket billiards championship was a carbon copy of that used in the national tournament. Each of the ten players would play the other nine in a round-robin, and the man with the best record would win the title. The tables were a tournament-standard five feet by ten. The rules were fundamental. Players had to call each shot—which ball in which pocket—and they continued to shoot until they missed. The first to score 125 balls won the game. This form of play, called straight pool, or 14.1 continuous, had been in vogue for just over twenty years. It did not become the official championship game until 1912, when the term "pocket billiards" was formally introduced.

The earliest championship game was called "61-pool." It was a single-rack game played with fifteen numbered object balls. Each ball was worth its numerical value, and the first player to reach the total of sixty-one or more was the winner. A match consisted of a race to a specified number of games, usually twenty-one. This was the manner in which the world championship was decided from 1878 until 1888. However, this style of competition was inherently flawed. Under the numerical scoring system, the five highest-numbered balls had a greater total value than the other ten; therefore, a player could win a game, and a match, while scoring far fewer balls than his opponent.

To correct this inequity, the game of "continuous pool" was developed in 1889. The players still played individual fifteen-ball racks, but each ball counted for only one point, and the first player to reach a predetermined total, generally one hundred, was the winner. The player who sank the last ball of a rack would break the new rack of fifteen. But he was not required to call a shot on the break. Any ball that fell into a pocket counted toward his total, so extended runs over many racks became fairly common. The record run in this form of continuous pool was ninety-six, achieved by Alfredo De Oro in a non-championship game in 1911.

In championship play, however, players tended to be a bit more cautious. They were reluctant to break open the full rack on the chance that one or more balls would drop, possibly leaving their opponent with an easy run on an open table. It became customary, therefore, to begin each new rack with a safety, a defensive maneuver designed to leave one's opponent without a clear shot. When playing it safe, a player does not attempt to make a ball. Instead, he announces his intent and then must drive two object balls and the cue ball against the rail. An accomplished player can often leave the pack frozen solid, with the cue ball flush against the rail at the opposite end of the table. His opponent, rather than taking a chance on scattering the balls while missing a difficult shot, would likely play another safety. This technique made for prolonged, uneventful championship matches, much like early-era basketball games in which a jump ball followed every basket.

The remedy was fashioned by Jerome Keogh, the 1910 champion. Keogh suggested that the last ball of each rack remain on the table as a target ball. The other fourteen balls would be racked in the standard triangular configuration, with the front position left open. The shooter would then attempt to make the loose ball while using the cue to shatter the pack, allowing him easy access to extend his run. Keogh proposed that the newly structured game be called "14 racked, 1 ball free," which soon became known as "14.1 continuous," and more commonly as straight pool. The new game was adopted as the championship form for the tournament in April 1912, which was won by Edward Ralph. It immediately became the standard competition by which champions were measured and gave the game a popular appeal by speeding the action and creating the likelihood of longer, unbroken runs. It was also sweet meat for the gifted player, who learned to structure his whole strategy around leaving a break ball that would be an open door to the next rack of balls.

Straight pool was, of course, nothing new to the ten players who gathered in Chicago in 1933 in quest of Ralph Greenleaf's title.

▲ ▲ ▲

Chicago was almost as cold as Minneapolis. I got there a few days before the tournament was scheduled to begin so I could acclimate myself to the surroundings. I also wanted to get a cue stick custom-made to my own specifications. Until then I had always used a stick from the rack in whichever room I was playing, just like any other customer would do. But all the professionals had their own cues. I knew that Greenleaf and Rudolph and some of the others had theirs made by Herman Rambow in Chicago so I went there to get one made up before the tournament began. Rambow worked for Brunswick; he had his shop in the basement of their office building. I had smaller hands than some of the other players, and Rambow cut the stick to fit me. It was fifty-seven inches long and weighed about nineteen ounces. Rambow had it ready in time for me to use it in my warmup sessions.

The tournament was being held at Bensinger's Recreational Amphitheater on Randolph Street, the best-known billiard parlor in the country. Bensinger's was the model for the room in which Fast Eddie Felson played Minnesota Fats in the movie *The Hustler*. It was a magnificent place, with velvet curtains and original oil paintings on the walls. An open, wrought-iron cage elevator took you up to the second floor where the tournament games were held. At night, you were surrounded by the glow of neon lights from Chicago's Loop until the games were ready to begin. Then the curtains were drawn and you felt yourself isolated, like gladiators ready for combat.

The top seeds in the tournament were Greenleaf, the defending champion; Erwin Rudolph, the previous champion; Frank Taberski, another former champion; Andrew Ponzi; and Jimmy Caras. Kelly, Seaback, and myself, who had gotten in through the qualifying tournaments, were placed in the lower bracket. I drew Rudolph in the opening round and, as it happened, the tournament turned for me on that game.

I knew Rudolph would be a difficult opponent; he was the last player to beat Greenleaf in a championship match. But I didn't feel intimidated. I never feared another player. I always felt that when I was shooting all the other guy could do was sit in the chair and wait for me to miss. It didn't matter who it was. Rudolph was an excellent defensive player, but I was a better shot-maker than he was, and I was feeling pretty confident. During the early stages of the match I had things much my own way.

Rudolph ran twenty-one balls in his first inning, but when he missed he left more than he meant to, and I ran sixty-five. That put me in command. I already had more than half of what I needed to win, and I continued to stretch my lead. I was ahead 112–67 in the fourteenth inning, when Rudolph ran sixteen and then missed. I don't remember the shot he missed, but I know he left me in pretty good shape. I needed thirteen balls to win the match. I made twelve and then played a shot down the side rail into the corner pocket. I guess I hit it a little too hard because it jawed back and forth and then hung on the lip. Rudolph then picked up his cue and ran forty-two and out to win the game 125–124. It was frustrating as hell, just sitting there watching while he made shot after shot. In other sports you can do something to try to stop your opponent, but in pool you're helpless. All you can do is sit in that chair and hope that he misses. In this case, he didn't.

Looking back on it, missing that shot might have been the best thing that ever happened to me. It taught me not to be careless. I was a cocky kid back then and I shot very fast and didn't think I could miss. So I learned a valuable lesson but at a very high price. As things developed, that game cost me the tournament. I won six of my next eight games, which left me in a four-way tie with Ponzi, Kelly, and Caras, all with records of 6–3. Rudolph won the title with a 7–2 record. So if I had won that game, I would have been 7–2 and won the world championship on my first try, at the age of twenty. Instead, I wound up fifth and out of the money after a playoff with the other runners-up.

Still, it was a good experience for me. It was, after all, my first professional tournament, and I had gone pretty far. You could say that I came within one shot of winning it all. Now I knew that I could hold my own with the best players in the world, but I also knew that winning a championship in that company was no easy matter. When you compete at the highest level in any sport, talent is never enough. Knowing how to win is a skill all its own, and it takes time, and experience, and there are no shortcuts. The 1933 tournament provided me with an essential step in my education. But that was not the only benefit I derived from it.

Right after the tournament ended, I was approached by Clyde Storer, who was president of the Billiard Association of America and the promotional director of the Brunswick Corporation. Brunswick, which was then called Brunswick-Balke-Collender, had been the leading manufacturer of billiard tables since 1845, and they maintained a stable of pool and billiard players who used to tour the country promoting their products. Storer offered me six hundred dollars a month to join their staff, and I wasted no time in accepting. Six hundred dollars a month was all the money in the world to me in those days, and I was just beginning to understand how much money could be made at this game. I suppose it was at that point that I chose billiards as my life's work.

Brunswick kept twenty-one players under contract in what they called their Better Billiards Program, and they included some of the best in the country—Greenleaf, Rudolph, Caras, and Willie Hoppe, the three-cushion billiards champion. I was the youngest player in the group, but they were always looking for new talent, possibly a future champion, and in this instance my youth worked to my advantage. The other runners-up in the tournament were a good deal older than me, and I guess they thought I had the most potential.

The program was divided into three geographical regions— the East, Midwest, and Pacific—with seven players in each area. Brunswick would set up the exhibitions, and pay all our expenses, but we were at their beck and call. The phone would ring and Storer or one of his associates would say, "Willie, we've got a tour for you starting Sunday," and you packed your bags. Sometimes a tour would last a few weeks, other times you would be gone for months. When you took the monthly stipend it was under a one-year contract, and being ready to travel was part of the deal. It was not uncommon to spend three hundred days a year on the highway. There was no conflict when tournament time rolled around because the Billiard Association was a subsidiary of Brunswick, and they cleared time for you to compete for the championship.

It was a tough grind living out of a suitcase most of the time, but what were the alternatives? It was certainly a lot better than stalking the pool halls at night risking your own money while hoping for an easy score. And where was a twenty-year-old kid going to find a job worth $150 a week in 1933? So I was happy to sign with Brunswick, and my first assignment did nothing to change my mind. I was sent on a 112-day, two-man tour with Ralph Greenleaf.

CHAPTER

The Greenleaf tour was conducted at a whirlwind pace. Brunswick assigned one of its top booking agents, a man by the name of Edgar Spears, to make the arrangements, and he traveled ahead of us booking the rooms and scheduling the matches. We often played in cities I never heard of and whose names I couldn't even spell. I always kept a hundred-dollar bill stashed in my watch pocket so that if something went wrong I would be able to get home. I was just a kid and I wasn't going to let myself get stranded in some godforsaken place. I don't know how many cities we covered, but we definitely spent more time traveling than playing. All told, we played 107 games in 112 days, and we rarely spent more than a day or two in the same place. Wherever we were, we packed them in. Of course Greenleaf was the principal attraction. He was not only a great player, he was great to watch. He had looks and style, a theatrical flair, and a shooting touch so soft that only a connoisseur could fully appreciate it.

I had played Greenleaf just once since I was seven years old. That was in the recent tournament, and I had beaten him 125–55. But I knew from the start that this tour would be the opportunity of a lifetime for me. The 1933 tournament had convinced me that I had all the talent I needed to compete with the best in the world. But it also taught me that I had a

lot to learn. Now, I was being given the chance to learn it at
the side of the greatest pool-shooter who ever played the
game. I watched him like a hawk. I learned all the little tricks
and profited from the tremendous hoard of knowledge he had
accumulated in his career. I also watched for his mistakes. We
traveled together for almost four months, but during all that
time Ralph never took me aside to offer any instruction. He
was cordial enough when we were away from the table, but
when the matches began he was a fierce and friendless competitor.

One of the first things that impressed me about him was his
intense desire to win. It didn't matter to him that these were
just exhibition games, that there was no money at stake, no
title to be won. He didn't care that we were, in a sense, part
of the same team, working for the same employer. He wanted
to beat me; he wanted to beat me every game and by as big
a score as possible. And during the first few months he won
a substantial majority of the games. But then I started to hold
my own. I began to apply the lessons I was learning.

Greenleaf and I were essentially the same type of player.
We both played a fast game, looked for long runs, and played
defense only when necessary. But at that time, Ralph had the
smoother shooting stroke. He had the softest touch I ever
saw. Even on long shots he seemed to be able to feel a ball
right into the pocket, to shoot it just hard enough without
banging away. It was a beautiful thing to watch; it was like
watching a virtuoso playing the violin, just beautiful. Fast
players have a tendency to shoot hard, and I was no exception.
I used to bang away and assume the ball would hit the cushion
and drop into the pocket. Now I knew better. I realized that
if I had used a softer stroke in my match with Rudolph I would
have made that last shot and won the championship. So I

began to ease up, and as I developed more touch I started to win a little more often.

I had always thought I was a better shot-maker than Greenleaf. Actually, I believed I could make any shot that any other player could make. But the reality is that the best players don't often have to make difficult shots. The key to pocket billiards is the playing of position, controlling the cue ball so that you leave yourself with an easy shot every time. A lot of people don't know that. They are impressed by what appear to be trick shots—kisses, bank shots, combinations. Of course sometimes you have to be able to make those. But shot making is not what wins games; position play is. And Greenleaf played position like no one else; there was no other player in his league. He would sometimes play whole racks without having to make a long shot.

The rule of thumb for the average player is that you want to leave yourself within one to two feet of the ball you want to make, the object ball. But Ralph cut that distance in half. He shortened his shots so that most of the time he would be shooting no more than six to twelve inches. He was usually able to leave the cue ball within two inches of where he wanted it. Once in a while, when he was cutting the pie during an exhibition, he would mark a spot on the table and indicate to the audience that that's where he would leave the cue ball. Then he would make his shot and the cue would wind up within a dime's width of the spot he had marked, and he would bow to the applause. It was like Babe Ruth pointing to where he would hit his next home run. He was quite a showman, but it wouldn't have been much of a show if he didn't deliver, and he rarely missed.

I understood that the basic difference between his game and mine was that he played closer position. So I made up my mind to learn it. I watched his every move, the way he got around the balls, his selection of shots calculated to bring him closer to the next object ball, always playing around his break ball. I began figuring his sequence while he shot, guessing which ball he would make next, which he had selected as the break ball. I began playing the game the way he did and then trying to improve upon it by adding my own embellishments.

Instead of playing around one break ball, I started playing around two, so that if I got out of position for the first one I had the other to fall back on. I would also try to leave myself a target ball, which I would use to get in position to make the break ball. I began setting up my shots further and further ahead. I had always seen six or seven shots in advance, but that wasn't enough. You had to see as many shots as there were balls open on the table. You could never calculate where the balls would end up when you broke a rack or a cluster, but if the whole rack was scattered, you had to see all fourteen shots in sequence, including the break ball and the target ball. Now, I could tell you within an inch or two where the cue ball would be after I made thirteen straight.

Once I felt I was able to do that, I said to Ralph, "You belong to me now." He just laughed. After all, he was about fifteen years older than I was, a nine-time champion, and I had just completed my first tournament and finished fifth. He thought I was a brash kid blowing smoke, and he took my remark in good humor. But I was dead serious, and I proved it. I began beating him with increasing regularity. By the end of the tour, he had won fifty-seven games and I had won fifty, but most of my wins came during the final month. I guess I had learned my lessons well.

Ralph was pretty gracious about losing at the end, but then

what else could he do? Besides, there was nothing really at stake. We were both doing it for the money. It was a professional venture in which we worked together. There was nothing more to our relationship than that. Even through four months of traveling together Ralph and I never became particularly friendly. Most of the time we spent together, I felt that I had to stay with him to keep him sober. Ralph had a serious drinking problem, and it cut short his career and probably his life. I'm not giving away any secrets here. Greenleaf never made an attempt to hide it, and everyone knew about it—the promoters, the proprietors of the rooms, the other players, even the public. He carried a flask with him wherever he went, and he often showed up drunk for one of his matches. The amazing thing was that he could play better drunk than most players could sober. I don't know how he did it.

When I was on tour with him, I tried to keep him away from the booze because if he was not able to make one of the exhibitions the money would go down the drain. But it was an impossible task. He seemed to have friends in every town, and somehow or other they managed to get the booze to him in the hotel. Sometimes, if he hadn't had too many, you couldn't tell that he had been drinking; other times he'd come into the room staggering but still manage to play a good game. He depended on that booze; he needed it to firm up his nerves. But there were times when it got out of hand. Some years he had to pass up the world tournament because he couldn't stay sober long enough to play.

His wife did everything she could to keep him on the wagon, but she was overmatched. She was a beautiful part Chinese and part English woman and a prominent vaudeville star. In the twenties, she sometimes sang on the same bill with my dancing cousins. She performed under the name of Princess

Nai Tai Tai, and no one ever called her anything else, but she certainly had her hands full. She kept Ralph sober as much as she could, but it was a losing battle. The bottle was Greenleaf's toughest opponent, and unfortunately it was one he did not seem to care to defeat.

▲ ▲ ▲

Ralph Greenleaf had flashed upon the scene from out of Monmouth, Illinois, in 1916 and immediately made his presence felt. That year, at the age of seventeen, he challenged Frank Taberski for his title and lost 450–407. Two years later, he again lost a head-to-head championship match to Taberski. But in 1919 Greenleaf became the youngest player ever to win the title, and he proceeded to defend it successfully nine times without a defeat over the next six years before surrendering it, briefly, to Taberski again.

Taberski's deliberate style of play and his low-key disposition were of a type to unnerve the flamboyant Greenleaf. Greenleaf performed with a hurried efficiency, an aggressive precision that could leave an opponent in shock as the balls cascaded into the pockets. Taberski, by contrast, studied the lay of the table with the care of a general pondering the most likely point of invasion.

"He used to drive Greenleaf crazy," Willie recalls. "It would take him ten minutes to shoot a shot. He'd walk around the table and look at it from every angle, measure the distance from the cue ball to the object ball, from the object ball to the pocket. That was the way he normally played, but against Greenleaf he slowed it down even more. Ralph was a fidgety type of guy who wanted to play fast and get it over with, and Taberski used to drive him nuts, really upset him. That's why Greenleaf had so much trouble with him."

Nonetheless, Greenleaf finally accommodated himself to Taberski's tempo, and he rewrote the record books during the twenties and thirties. But gradually, his taste for liquor began to undermine his effectiveness. He took to carrying a pint bottle in his alligator bag. He became what is sometimes referred to in the world of the renowned as a legendary drinker. He would appear for a match reeling from booze and still dazzle his opponents with brilliant shooting. Once, asked to explain how he played so well when he appeared to have trouble standing, he replied, laughing, "I just shoot at the ball where the light shines brightest."

In his autobiography, *McGoorty: A Billiard Hustler's Life*, Dan McGoorty, a world-class billiard player and a self-acknowledged alcoholic, describes his own experience with Greenleaf's dependence on booze:

In 1922 Greenleaf was playing in the world's pool tournament in the Auditorium in Chicago. . . . About thirty minutes before one of Ralph's games he came busting into the shithouse looking like hell. I was always hanging around, so he knew me.

"Danny," he said, "you gotta get me a mickey. I need a mickey awful bad." A mickey was a flat pint.

"I will have to go all the way to Clark and Lake to get it, Ralph, and I don't know if I can make it in time, the weather the way it is."

"You'll make it . . . you've got to make it. Here's the money."

"I'm on my way."

"Don't let me down, kid." He called me "kid" even though he was only twenty-three himself at the time.

In heavy weather in the Loop cabs are no help, so I hustled both ways on foot through the snow and slush and shit. When I got back to the Auditorium I gave him the high sign and he followed me into the shithouse. He uncorked the bottle and, holy Christ, he started *draining* it. I grabbed his arm.

"Wait a minute," I said. "Not so fast."

"What's the matter? I need a drink . . ."

"You've *had* a drink. Worst thing you can do is to drink a whole mickey all at once. It might knock you out. Besides, I ran all the way . . . *I* need a drink."

"Yeah, but you don't need it like I need it."

"Listen, I *need* it. I'll keep the bottle. You get one break during the game. Meet me here then and take the rest." That's all the refs gave you in those days—one break during a game. They didn't care if you had *diarrhea*.

Knowing there was a bottle waiting for him was all Ralph needed. He went out under those lights and played the most beautiful pool you can imagine. A big five-by-ten table with small pockets, but he still got off a run of ninety. It was the greatest shooting I've ever seen.

By the time they made their tour in 1933, Greenleaf was still of championship caliber, but his was the light of a dying star, while Willie's had just begun to shine. He had acquitted himself well during a long and arduous campaign. He had learned what he could from the former champion and shown that he could put it to immediate use. But there were yet other lessons to be learned, and Willie would soon take the next step in his education.

▲ ▲ ▲

After one of my exhibitions that year, 1934, a stranger came up to me from out of the crowd and said, "My business is arranging financially productive exhibitions for *artistes* like yourself, Mr. Mosconi. Here's my card; call me one day." He was a short, rather stout man of middle years, I would say in his forties, but he was well-groomed and dressed exceptionally well, and he spoke smoothly, with a sense of ease and assurance in his manner. From his card I learned that his name was Sylvester Livingston, a well-known booking agent who, from time to time, represented some of the best billiard players in the country, including Greenleaf and Willie Hoppe. He also handled more than a few not-so-good players, but he had a knack for convincing pool-room proprietors that these guys would be good attractions for one reason or another, and he managed to get them enough bookings to keep them working. I called him a few days later and he explained his terms:

"I get 25 percent," he said. "You get 75, out of which you must be prepared to meet any and all expenses."

I was still under contract to Brunswick, but that didn't seem to pose a problem. Livingston had his own program, which he had sold to Brunswick but operated himself. I'm not sure exactly what the relationship was, but I signed up with Livingston and traveled his path for the next eight years. He was a tireless worker and an astute businessman, and he looked the part, too. He was a dapper guy, with a great deal of polish, but what was most important was that he knew his business. He knew what it took to draw a crowd, he understood the psychology of winning and losing, and he had all the right connections. He and his wife lived in an apartment right off Central Park in Manhattan, but he didn't spend much time there. His annual itinerary had him leaving New York City in the fall, weaving his way through the southern coastal states, spending a good part of the winter in Florida, then working his way up through the interior states to Chicago, and back to New York in the spring. He traveled ahead of his players, booking games in advance, and somehow he managed to line up a full slate of games for every member of his stable. Occasionally, he attended one of our matches, but mostly we followed in his wake. He would notify us of our schedules about a month in advance and it was up to us to keep the dates. I had my own car, and I was out on the highway about ten months of the year.

▲ ▲ ▲

Sylvester Entwhistle Livingston was the most famous pool-hall impresario of his time. He booked dates for the reigning champions in both pocket and three-cushion billiards, and it was widely believed that he also booked bets on the horses for Frank Erickson, a nationally known bookmaker, who lived not far from Livingston's West Side apartment. In fact, Livingston's travel route, not coincidentally, was tuned to the rhythms of the thoroughbred racing season. He left New York when the big northern tracks closed and remained in Florida for the winter meetings before heading north again.

But he did not allow his racing activities to interfere with his efforts in behalf of his cadre of billiard players.

He kept in close touch, attended some of their exhibitions, and followed their fortunes with more than a passing interest. He also had an eye for spotting young talent and an instinct for nurturing it. In Willie, he found all the ingredients of both the pool champion and the showman.

"He has the soft touch of a baby," he said when he first saw Willie play. "He plays position by instinct. He knows what his shots will be clear into the next rack."

Livingston also discerned other attributes he found to his taste. He liked Willie's easy grace as he moved around the table, his cocky self-confidence, his good looks, and a somewhat boyish charm that would warm the heart of an audience. And he liked Willie's style of play.

"He shot fast and he was daring," Livingston said. "He was not afraid to take a chance. He was precisely the type of player that people were ready to pay money to watch."

▲ ▲ ▲

The entire country was in the full grip of the Depression back then, and the pickings were sometimes lean. We'd be lucky to get fifty dollars for an exhibition, and many times it was a lot less. So Livingston would pack our schedule as tight as he could. I sometimes played as many as four exhibitions a day in four different towns if they were not too far apart. That meant that you spent more time on the highway than you did playing, and we were not exactly going first class. I spent many nights in rundown hotels, ate my meals on the fly, and often ended up playing in shabby rooms, before hostile crowds, on tables that should have been scrapped long ago.

It was a tough, grinding life on the highway. I never kept track, but I would guess that I traveled more than twenty thousand miles a year and would give as many as five hundred exhibitions. After a while I got to know my way around, and I would stay at hotels where you could get a decent room for two–three dollars a night. It wasn't elegant by any means, but I knew that I would at least have a clean bed to sleep in. I was paying all my own expenses and the fees weren't that high, so I tried to conserve as much as possible and sent most of my earnings home.

I could usually count on one square meal a day, because the owner of the room at your last stop would often take you to a restaurant and pick up the tab. The rest of the time I would just grab a bite on the highway wherever I could and keep going. Getting your laundry done was also a hassle. I used to look forward to hitting a big city, like Kansas City or Chicago, because you were able to send out your dirty clothes and get them back the next day. Otherwise, you would have to do it yourself, and you really didn't need another job to do when you were making three or four appearances a day and driving hard to try to stay on schedule. Besides, you knew when you arrived at your next destination that you were not likely to be greeted with open arms.

At each stop I played the local favorite, the Big Mahah in that town, and he almost always had the audience on his side. But the worst part of it was playing on some of those tables. A lot of them had bad slates, torn cloths, cushions with an uneven bounce, and pockets as tight as a Scotchman. The local guy, of course, was familiar with the peculiarities of the table, but if you were just coming in to play that exhibition there was no time to adjust. It was just one of the hazards of the trade, what today is called the home field advantage. Most of the time I was able to overcome that edge, but occasionally I got clipped.

One night, up in the Bronx, I played on a table with the most peculiar corner pockets I ever saw. The jaws at each end were parallel instead of being placed at angles so that it was next to impossible to make a shot down the rail. If you tried it, the ball would jaw back and forth and just hang there, leaving an easy shot for your opponent. The only way you could make a shot was to center the ball perfectly and split the pocket. I finally adjusted to it, but it was too late. The local guy knew that table like the palm of his hand. He shot slowly and with a very soft roll and he closed out the game with a long run.

Some of those local players were damn good. It was not as if you were playing a pigeon every night, and pool is a game where you are absolutely helpless when the other fellow is shooting. So if a man is on a run, all can do is sit in your chair and watch him. I got beat that way one night in Upstate New York, I think it was in Binghamton. I was playing a guy who didn't look too good at the start—he seemed a bit nervous and unsure of himself—and I eased up a little after making a long run. After all, this fellow was playing in front of his neighbors and friends, and I didn't want him to look too bad. I tried a difficult shot that I would not normally have played and opened the balls for him and he ran out before I ever got to the table again.

The usual routine on these tours was to play a 100- or 125-point game and then do ten or fifteen trick shots. The trick shots were an integral part of the show. Sometimes the game was over very quickly, and you wanted to give the people their money's worth. An exhibition that ended too soon could create problems, as I found out one night in Pittsburg, Kansas.

Pittsburg was my fourth of five stops that day, and the towns were about sixty miles apart. The weather was atrocious. The

Kansas flatlands were deep in snow and the wind was piling it in drifts, and I was running behind schedule. My contract called for me to play a 125-point game and do fifteen trick shots. Since I was in a hurry, I wasted no time with my opponent. I ran out the game in about twenty minutes, did the trick shots and was on my way to my next destination. The owner was mad as hell. He felt the exhibition was too short, and he wrote to Brunswick saying he would never allow me or their equipment in his pool hall again. And he didn't. It was hard to keep everyone happy. If you played too well, the owner felt he had shortchanged his customers; if you did not play well, he felt the same way.

It was a tough way to make a living and certainly no way to get rich. After expenses and Livingston's 25 percent cut were paid, there was barely enough left to tide me over during the summer months when there was very little action. But those tours were an invaluable experience for me. I learned to play before all kinds of audiences, on all kinds of tables, and to perform even when I wasn't feeling up to it. In tournament play, you had to be able to adjust to all situations, and there was virtually no hazard I didn't encounter while touring the highway.

I also learned a lot from Livingston. In fact, he taught me the most valuable lesson of my young career. During my first year on tour I had developed the tendency to ease up when I thought I had the game in hand. I would throw my opponent a few shots to let him save face and sometimes to prolong the match for the benefit of the proprietor. But Livingston warned me off that practice. He took me aside one day and told me not to concern myself with my opponent or the owner.

"Habits are hard to break," he said. "You play anything less than your best and pretty soon you'll be doing it with everybody and they'll be beating your brains out. Willie," he said, "if there is one thought I want to leave you with when I'm no longer here, it is this: When you have the knife in, *twist* it."

That is the best advice anyone ever gave me. You've got to hate the man you're playing, and he's got to hate you. If you don't, you can't play your best game. From that point on, I never let up. If I could beat you 125–0, I would do it; I didn't care who you were. I developed the killer instinct until it got so that I hated to lose, *hated* it. And I carried that feeling with me into every tournament I ever played in.

CHAPTER

Over the next five years I began to understand the meaning of frustration. In 1933, I had come within one game—I guess you might even say one shot—of winning the championship and came up empty. In my next four tournaments, although I was not always at my best, I continued to stay close to the lead but each time fell a game or two short of winning it. There are many ways to lose, but only one way to win, and it can take a long time to find it.

There was no world championship tournament in 1934. The weight of the Depression had taken its toll and not much money was being spent on diversions. It took substantial funds to run a tournament. In addition to the prize money, players' expenses had to be paid, there were travel costs, and the room had to be rented. The promoters and the proprietors had become exceedingly cautious. They were concerned that they might make their investment and then find that not enough people showed up to cover the costs. So they skipped a year and set up a tournament for 1935 in precisely the same format that was used two years earlier.

I won the eastern sectional competition but finished behind George Kelly and Jimmy Caras in the nationals. The world tournament was held in New York on the Roof Garden of the Pennsylvania Hotel, across the street from where Madison

Square Garden now stands. It was a magnificent location, with Manhattan all lit up and shining, the bright lights of Broadway and the Theater District just a few blocks to the north, and the entire city alive with the glow of the Christmas season.

We were scheduled for a ten-man, thirteen-day round-robin, and I was optimistic going in. The defending champion, Andrew Ponzi, who had won the title from Erwin Rudolph in a challenge match in 1934, had just gotten married and was away on his honeymoon, and Greenleaf was in the second year of a four-year period of recuperation and retrenchment. Their absence thinned the field a bit and gave the rest of us a better shot at winning.

Rudolph proved to be in championship form again and so was Caras. Jimmy, who worked in Allinger's, had been coming on strong in recent years. In 1932 he had finished second to Greenleaf, and that seemed to be a springboard that launched his career. For some reason, he never had much trouble playing against Rudolph. He beat him 125–21 in the regularly scheduled match, and after they finished in a tie for first place he beat him again 125–53 to win the title. Kelly and I tied for third with records of 5–4, two games behind the leaders, and I lost to him in a close playoff, 125–114.

During the tournament, I had handled Caras easily but lost badly to Rudolph. I always seemed to have a difficult time with Rudolph and would have preferred to play Caras even when Jimmy was at his best. Pool, like most other one-on-one competitions, is very much a matter of styles. The way players match up against one another often determines the outcome. Caras was basically a shot-maker, and when he was on stroke he was capable of making very long runs. But he was patient. He did not hesitate to play safe when he didn't have a high percentage shot, and you needed that kind of discipline when

you played against Rudolph. Rudolph was one of the best
defensive players in the game. He would tie you up in a dozen
different ways, rarely leave you anything good to shoot at, and
he played a very methodical game. At that stage of my career,
I did not have the patience for that kind of game. I liked to
shoot fast and get it over with. After a few safeties I was ready
to shoot at anything that had a chance to go, and too often I
would miss the shot and leave my opponent with an open
table. You couldn't play that way against Rudolph; he counted
on the other guy's impatience, it was one of his weapons.

▲ ▲ ▲

The frenetic haste with which Willie shot, his impatience, the throbbing edginess of his manner did not go
unnoticed. Covering the tournament for the *New York
Herald Tribune*, Al Laney described it this way:

> Under the bright lights that hung low over the bil-
> liard table on the roof garden of the Pennsylvania,
> a nervous young man raced about as though in a
> desperate and losing battle against time. . . . The
> young man down below was Willie Mosconi. He
> was playing a match in the world pocket billiard
> championship and he was in a hurry. Where other
> billiard players walk slowly around the table, mea-
> sure their shots carefully and sometimes wiggle
> their cues for what seems an interminable period,
> this young man can scarcely permit himself time
> enough to leap from one shot to another.
>   He is the fastest billiard player of all time and
> he uses up energy at an alarming rate, his fingers

grinding the chalk viciously into the cue after each shot so that he has to pause frequently to tamp down the tip, attacking it as though he would drive the cue through the floor.

He is small, dark and of Italian ancestry. He is dapper. His dinner jacket fits him perfectly. When he must wait while the balls are being racked he does it with impatience, screwing up his face in an expression of concentration that conceals for the moment a pair of soulful eyes whose softness is striking in one so intense.

Every emotion that passes through his brain is immediately reflected on his handsome features, for Mosconi is a Latin and restraint is not in him. If his cue ball does not come to rest exactly at the spot his eye has marked out, he raises his eyes to Heaven, slaps his thigh and an expression of despair spreads over his face. If a ball is slow in moving into place, he helps it along with a frantic little hop and a prayer on his lips.

And when at last he misses a shot his eyes widen in an expression of amazement that such a thing could happen, and he throws himself into a chair with dejection, there to squirm and fidget while his opponent has an inning. But when his turn comes again he is out of his seat like a runner off the mark. You wonder how this jumpy little man can possibly excel at a game calling for such delicacy of execution, but when he bends over the table all nervousness suddenly leaves him. Hand and eye are steady. Here, obviously, is a high degree of skill.

▲ ▲ ▲

After the 1935 tournament I knew that I still had a lot to learn. Caras was three or four years older than I was and he was the second-youngest to ever win the title. There's a lot more to this game than being able to control the balls on the table; that's just the mechanics of it. A lot of players are able to do that. But there are other things you have to know as well— strategies that the average player never even thinks about, techniques that go unnoticed by most observers—and they can be acquired only with experience.

Now I had played in two tournaments, two years apart, and I had shown no improvement. If anything, I had taken a step in the opposite direction. I was beginning to understand that you cannot advance your game playing on the highway. You think you're staying sharp because you're playing three hundred days a year, but actually you're becoming stale. In order to improve your game, you have to play against players who are better than you; that's true in any sport. When you're touring the country, going from room to room, it's like boxing's bum-of-the-month club. You're not going to learn anything playing the best amateur in Topeka, Kansas. In fact, the opposite is true. You develop a tendency to get careless. You rush the game so that you can move on and get to the next stop on your schedule. The owners of those rooms are looking for you to put on a show, that's why they booked you. They don't want you coming in there and playing safe for two hours. So you begin to take chances and try shots that you would never think of playing in championship competition. Sometimes I would even call a shot on the break. If I made it, it was a great show for the customers. If I missed, there was not much chance of the other guy running out on me. Out on the highway, you're nothing but a showman, and showmen don't win world championships. I knew that I needed to practice more and to play against better competition. When I got back to Philadelphia, I made it my business to play with people like Caras and Ponzi as often as possible.

Early in 1937 (no tournament had been scheduled in 1936) I played both of them in long exhibition matches and was fortunate enough to win each time. The games with Caras attracted particular attention. Jimmy was, after all, the world champion, and although his title was not at stake, the crowds turned out in large numbers and the match was given considerable space in the press. We played in the top rooms all over Philadelphia—Allinger's, Phil Longo's, and Herb Ramsey's place on Thirteenth and Market—through a good part of January and February. It was a thirteen-hundred-point match, and I beat Jimmy by only fifty-six balls. But it's interesting to note that had we been playing in a championship tournament, Caras would have been the winner because he won two more blocks than I did. In tournament play, the score of a game is irrelevant; the winner is determined, as it is in most sports, by won-lost record. But in head-to-head competition it's strictly a race to a prescribed point total. Theoretically, it's possible to win twice as many blocks, or games, as your opponent and still lose the match if he beats you by lopsided scores.

Against Ponzi, in a similar exhibition, I managed to win on both points and number of blocks. That match ended just a week or two before the 1937 world championship tournament was to start, and given my recent performances, I was feeling rather confident; maybe too confident, for I lost some games in the early rounds that I was expected to win quite easily.

The tournament, a twelve-man round-robin, was held in Ponzi's Academy in the Bond Building in New York. It was a less glamorous setting than the Roof Garden of the Pennsylvania Hotel, but it was also less costly. If an additional touch of glamour was needed, it was supplied by the presence of Ralph Greenleaf, who was returning to competition after a four-year absence. Greenleaf had retired as champion in 1933, and in his comeback he was not as sharp as he might have been, but he was good enough to win seven of eleven games and finish in a tie for first place with Ponzi, Caras, Rudolph, and a newcomer to the tournament by the name of Irving Crane. I fell one game short, with a record of 6–5. I defeated three of the five players who tied for first, losing only to Greenleaf and Ponzi. But I lost three out of four to the tail-enders, including Joe Diehl and Bennie Allen, who finished tied for last place.

Diehl and Allen each had won only two other games and neither had beaten a contender other than me. You might say that losing those two games cost me the championship and touched upon an old shortcoming of mine: I still had a tendency to get careless against opponents I thought I should beat. It was not so much a matter of easing up as it was of losing concentration. It is not an uncommon failing in sports. Athletes tend to play up to their competition and to look past a lesser opponent, particularly when they know their next game is likely to be a tough one. The loss of concentration is the stuff of which upsets are made. This is especially true in a game like billiards, where there is no defense when the other man is shooting. Any professional is capable of running one hundred balls or more, and once he gets on a roll there is no way to stop him. All you can do is hope that he misses. So it is a good idea to bear down against such players and put them away as quickly as possible. If you look at the long-term champions in any sport, you will find that they devour the also-rans; they rarely lose a game they should win. Greenleaf played that way and it served him well. He beat the bottom four players in the tournament by scores of 125 to 6, 37, 1, and 75. He never let them in the game. Then he went on to capture the championship in a five-way playoff.

If there was any doubt that Greenleaf was back, at least for a while, he erased it later that year when a second tournament was held, in Philadelphia, with much the same cast of characters. Ralph retained the title, beating Crane in a playoff by the one-sided score of 125 to minus 1 after losing a long, defensive struggle to Crane in their regularly scheduled match. I fared somewhat better this time around, finishing third, one game behind, and earning an extra one hundred dollars for the tournament's long run of ninety-eight. But it seemed that I had found a new way to lose. I cleaned up in the early rounds on the players at the lower end of the standings and built up an early lead. I headed the field with a record of 6–1 but then lost three of my last four matches, to Greenleaf, Caras, and Rudolph. I turned the tables on Caras in a playoff for third place, but third place was not what I wanted. I was growing weary of being a perennial contender.

In 1938, Greenleaf was once again absent from the tournament. After winning it a year earlier, he had defended his title successfully against Crane and then apparently fell off the wagon again and moved to California. He would never win another championship. With Greenleaf in retirement and the title vacant, Caras and Ponzi were the clear favorites to win the crown. Andy had won it in 1934 and Jimmy in 1935, and the only other ex-champion in the field was an aging Erwin Rudolph. I was, of course, quite familiar with the top two contenders. We had played one another many times, and I had proven that I could win about as often as they could. And that was precisely the way things worked out. The three of us tied for first place with 9–2 records, necessitating a playoff for the fourth straight time. I had beaten Ponzi in the round-robin, but in the playoff he broke on top and never let up, winning 125–3. Against Caras, I reversed the procedure, avenging an earlier loss with a 125–65 victory. Since Jimmy had beaten Andy in their match, the three of us ended up tied again, each with one win and one loss. There would not be a subsequent playoff, however. The rules dictated that in the event of a second tie the winner would be determined on the basis of total points scored. That gave Caras the title and left me in third place for the second straight year.

Now, in my last three tournaments, I had finished one game shy of the lead twice, tied for first once, and with nothing better than two third-place finishes to show for it. I had, it seemed, found every way to lose that one could imagine. Yet, I knew I could play with anyone, and they knew it, too. I had beaten Caras in an extended, head-to-head match, but he had held the championship three of the last four years, and in billiard circles he was being hailed now as Greenleaf's heir apparent.

▲ ▲ ▲

Jimmy Caras learned to shoot pool on the tables of the YMCA in his hometown of Wilmington, Delaware, but it was not long before he began making the trip across the river to Philadelphia. Caras was good and he knew it, and by the time he reached his teens he was on the prowl for money games in the rooms that lined the streets of the big city. He earned his reputation early and was launched into prominence in 1926 when, at the age of seventeen, he beat Ralph Greenleaf in an exhibition match. It was then that he became known as the Boy

Wonder of pocket billiards, though he was neither the first nor the last to wear that title.

Caras continued to live in Wilmington, but he soon became an integral part of Philadelphia's pool culture, where he became known as a cool and unforgiving money player. He attached himself to Allinger's, performing the same functions there that Willie did at Frankie Mason's. He was, in a manner of speaking, the middle man in a triumvirate that had Andrew Ponzi as elder statesman and Willie Mosconi as enfant terrible. They constituted a trio that made Philadelphia a nightmare for vagabond hustlers, and as they matured they dominated the professional billiard circuit. One or another of them held the world title at some point every year from 1938 to 1956. Ponzi was the first to win the crown, in a challenge match with Erwin Rudolph in 1934, but Caras captured the title three times in the next four years. It appeared for a while that he might put the same kind of stranglehold on the championship that Greenleaf maintained in the twenties.

Caras, at least at that time, was considered the best and most daring shot-maker of the three. He shot hard, in bang-bang fashion, and could often split the rack wide open on a break shot. He was undaunted by long, cross-table shots, sighting the ball with the unblinking gaze of a diamond-cutter and firing with a cool and deadly precision. Though not a slow player, he was somewhat more methodical than either Ponzi or Mosconi, and he lacked their fire and flair. He approached the table with a solemn assurance, shot until he missed or played safe, then took his seat and quietly, with the ease of a man anticipating the arrival of his next course at dinner, waited for his turn to shoot.

"Jimmy was a cool customer," Willie recollects, "but he was not very colorful. Ponzi and I were always kicking up a storm, sometimes talking to the crowd, sometimes to ourselves when we missed a shot or fell short of position. But Jimmy just kept his mouth shut. He could play a whole tournament and never say a word. And you would never learn anything from his expression either. He wore the same deadpan look whether he was in control of the match or the other guy was in the process of running 125 and out."

When Caras won his first title, at the age of twenty-five, he became the second-youngest player to win a world championship. But his early prosperity did not faze Willie.

"He was about four years older than I was," Willie says, "and he was that much ahead of me. The years of playing had taught him to be patient, and patience was a virtue that did not come naturally to me."

A month after Caras won the 1938 tournament, he defended it successfully against runner-up Ponzi. Ponzi would turn the tables the next time around, and it was beginning to appear as if Willie was the odd man out in what was becoming an intracity tug-of-war. But by that time Willie was in California, hoping to pursue another line of work. At age twenty-six, for the second time in a career that had started two decades earlier, Willie Mosconi had decided to retire from the sport of pocket billiards.

▲ ▲ ▲

There was no tournament scheduled in 1939. The owners of the billiard rooms were still playing it close to the vest, and the Brunswick people, never the biggest of spenders, were not ready to put up the big bucks with the economy still depressed and public interest apparently on the wane. I was still on the highway, playing some exhibitions, but even those were becoming fewer, and I was fed up with the whole routine. I had been playing professionally for six years and had nothing much to show for it and I was beginning to think that maybe it was time to just get the hell out and try something else. So I canceled my contract with Brunswick, got in my car, and took off for California, for Hollywood actually. I figured I was starving to death in the East, I might as well starve where it's warm. I chose Hollywood because my cousin Louie was living out there.

The Dancing Mosconis had broken up their act years earlier and Louie moved out to the Coast. Charlie had settled in New York. He ran a theater ticket agency, and there were those who said that he occasionally booked a bet or two. Charlie was a typical Broadway type who would not have been out of place in a Damon Runyon story. He dressed well, was always carefully groomed, and he loved the night life and the show business crowd. He was a member of the Lambs Club, which catered to theater people, and he got me to join. You could rent a room there for seven dollars a week and I used to stay there whenever I played in New York. Charlie had a beautiful apartment on the West Side, and he knew everyone in show business. For a while he was married to Margaret Whiting's aunt. Louie was a somewhat different type. He was a pure dancer; he looked like a dancer, had the legs of a dancer. He could run right up the wall, right to the ceiling, and come down in a split. When he was finished in vaudeville, he went out to California and opened a dance studio in Hollywood.

California was a nice change for me but there were no more

opportunities out there than there were in the East. I really had no idea what I wanted to do. I suppose I was hoping that something unexpected would come out of the blue and fall into my lap, but nothing did. When my money started to run out I began playing some exhibitions. In the end, it seems, you always come back to what you know best, and playing pool was the only way I knew to make a living. So when Sylvester Livingston offered to book some matches for me I was quick to accept. Ralph Greenleaf was living in Los Angeles at the time, and Livingston suggested that we might all be able to make some money if he scheduled another tour for us. Our first tour, in 1933, had helped launch my professional career. Now, I needed another shot in the arm, and playing with Ralph, I got it.

Over the next three or four months we played exhibitions all over the state of California. No one was keeping score this time. This was not a prearranged tour like the last one when our schedule was set in advance and we knew from the start how many matches we would be playing and where. Livingston booked us whenever and wherever he could, and we kept the date. So I have no idea how many games I won or lost, for it was of little consequence to me at the time. I played because I needed the money, but as it turned out I got a lot more than cash from that tour.

The first time I traveled with Greenleaf I studied his mechanics—the smooth, soft stroke, the meticulous manner in which he played position, particularly on the break ball. By 1939, I felt that my mechanics were as good as his. At the table, I was able to do everything Ralph did; everything, that is, but win the games I had to win when a tournament was at stake. Now, I watched Greenleaf even more closely, but I was looking for other things. It was his demeanor that captured my attention—his even temperament, his attention to detail, the way he mixed a quiet reserve with the flair of showmanship, the steadiness of his nerves, the feeling he communicated that he was in control and that no matter how well you were playing he was going to beat you and you knew it. You could make a beautiful run against Greenleaf, have him down by fifty or sixty balls, and you would look over at him sitting in the chair and he was calm and unruffled. He might even smile at you as if to say, "Nice shooting, but you know how this is going to end, don't you? Deep down, you know you can't beat me." It was like a boxer allowing his opponent to take his best shot and just shaking it off. Greenleaf made you *expect* to lose, and when you expect to lose you usually do.

There is a lot of psychology to this game, as there is in any sport, but the psychological aspects are always more critical when the competition is one-on-one. It begins with one's own temperament, and my natural disposition was to be impulsive, impatient, and emotional. I would get angry with myself when I missed a shot and left my opponent in good position. Then I would sit there and watch him put in forty or fifty balls and tell myself I was unlucky. But it wasn't luck; it was often my own fault. The shot I had taken might have been too risky. Maybe I should have played safe. I allowed situations like that to distract me, to undermine my concentration. I had to learn to control myself, to keep my balance; I had to acquire maturity. These are not easy lessons to learn. It is easier to learn how to play position, how to make a difficult shot, than it is to change your nature. If the truth be told, I never really did change. Throughout my career I remained impatient and emotional, but I acquired a degree of control and learned not to allow the distractions of competition to break my concentration. These, I knew now, were the missing ingredients I needed to play championship pocket billiards. But it would be a while before I had the chance to put them into practice.

When I returned East early in 1940, a championship tournament was being arranged under a slightly different format. Brunswick-Balke-Collender was initiating a new style of play to determine the championship. It was called an Intercity League tournament, with the proprietors of six billiard halls in various cities each sponsoring a player. Caras, the defending champion, was sponsored by Allinger's, and Julian's in New York backed Ponzi. I don't recall which other rooms were involved, but the other players invited were Rudolph, Irving Crane, Onofrio Lauri, and Joe Procita; no Mosconi. I don't know why, but I was passed over. Maybe it was because I had dropped out of competition for a while and spent a year in California. I just don't have the answer, but that kind of arrangement is tough on an outsider. There are no qualifying tournaments that you can use to get into the competition. If you're not invited, you're out and that's the way it was for me in 1940. The tournament was played in late winter and early spring, and Ponzi won his first title, with Caras finishing second.

Ponzi hardly had time to savor his championship when plans were under way for yet another Intercity League tournament. The proprietors apparently had fared well the first time around, because now they were planning a whopper. This was going to be the longest tournament in billiard history, and none since has come close. It would be played over a six-month period, beginning in November 1940 and ending in May 1941, in six different cities. The field was to be expanded to eight players, with each playing 224 games—thirty-two against each of his seven opponents. Every entrant would play two games a day, five days a week except for holidays, for twenty-four consecutive weeks. Nothing of this scale had ever been attempted before. To win would take not only skill but stamina, durability, and fierce concentration.

I knew that the tournament was being planned, but I was not sure whether I would be invited to compete. Then, about a month before it was to start, I got a call from Bob McGirr, who ran McGirr's Academy in the Roseland building on Broadway. Roseland was a popular dance hall at the time, and McGirr's, which was located above it, was an equally well-known billiard hall. I had known Bob McGirr for years, and he asked me to represent his establishment. I agreed, and we negotiated the terms. Each player and proprietor cut their own deal. For the duration of the tournament, you were an employee of that room and were paid a monthly salary. The owners made their profit by charging admission for the games, fifty cents for day games and a dollar at night. I don't remember how much I was paid, but it came to at least one hundred dollars a week. That was pretty good money back then, and I was looking forward to earning a regular paycheck for six straight months.

The tournament was scheduled to open in New York on November 26, just after Thanksgiving. It was two years since I had competed in championship play, but I had been playing regularly and I spent the next few weeks getting myself ready for the long grind. I was twenty-seven years old now; I had been playing professionally for more than seven years. If I was ever going to put my stamp on this sport, this would be as good a time as any.

CHAPTER

A few months after I returned from California, I played an exhibition at McGirr's with Jimmy Caras, which, in retrospect, set the tempo of my play for the next six months. Caras ran 120 balls from the break, but he left himself without a shot and played safe. I'm not sure why, but at that moment, although I had nothing to shoot at, I felt I was going to win that game. I took three straight scratches, which cost me eighteen points. (A player loses one point on a scratch, but he is docked an additional fifteen points if he scratches three times in a row.) So when I got back to the table I was trailing 120 to minus 18, but unaccountably I still felt in control of the game. I quickly got the eighteen points back plus four more to make the score 120–4. I don't know whether Jimmy sensed my confidence or not, but he missed a shot he would ordinarily have made three times out of four. It was a tough shot, and I believe most players would have played safe in that spot, especially with such a commanding lead, but Caras was an extraordinary shot-maker and if he had made that ball, the game would have been over. But he missed, opened the pack, and I ran 121 and out. Jimmy never moved from his opening run of 120.

A few weeks later we were playing again, and this time he ran 112 from the break before he missed. As Yogi Berra said

some years later, "It was déjà vu all over again." I could not
help but laugh when I stepped to the table. I knew Jimmy
had to be thinking of the last time we had played, and I said
to myself, "This guy is beat." I ran sixty-five balls, we each
played safe, and then I ran sixty and out.

Coming back from deficits of that size was not unheard of.
Billiards is different from other sports in that you can only
play defense when you are on offense—when you're shooting.
Once the other guy makes his first ball, there is nothing you
can do to stop him, and any professional player is capable of
running out a game. The reason I remember those games with
Caras is that even when I trailed by 138 points I felt I was
going to beat him. And in that second game I sensed that
Jimmy felt it, too. So as we approached the start of tournament
play, I was feeling pretty good about myself. It had been two
years since I played in championship competition, but I had
all those games with Greenleaf under my belt and I had been
playing regularly since returning from California. I felt well
rested and ready. You might say that I was like a racehorse
who was freshened but sharp.

Getting ready for the start of a tournament of those dimensions—224 games in six cities over a span of twenty-four
weeks—is a little bit like preparing to run a marathon. You
cannot really envision it as an entity because you are unable
to see the course as a whole; the beginning seems to have no
direct connection to the end. At the start of such a test there
is an inevitable shuffling and jockeying for position. Rarely
does the eventual winner break from the pack and take immediate control of the race. There are usually some early sur-
prises, and this tournament was no exception.

Johnny Irish, who was representing O'Brien's Academy in
Syracuse, took the early lead with seven straight victories,

while Erwin Rudolph, a former world champion playing for Doyle's Academy in New York, dropped his first seven decisions. I started out indifferently. Playing my first six games in New York, I opened against Joe Procita (Schenley's Academy, Boston), and we divided our afternoon and evening matches. The next day I split with Ponzi, who represented Julian's Fourteenth Street Academy. Then I took two straight from Rudolph before moving on to Philadelphia and some home cooking, and that's where I started to hit my stride.

I defeated Caras in his home room at Allinger's twice, and after another split with Procita, I took two straight from both Irish and George Kelly. At that point, I had won seven of my last eight matches and moved into first place with a narrow lead over Ponzi. Johnny Irish, following his seven-game win streak, was now in the process of losing his next eleven matches and slipping from contention. Caras had moved into third place, so we three Philadelphians found ourselves locked in a struggle for the lead.

On December 7, just two weeks into the tournament, I defeated George Kelly, another Philadelphia product, who was representing the Four Corners Academy in Newark, by the score of 125–0. I believe it was only the third shutout in tournament history. Two days later, against Ponzi, I did it again, this time in the first inning. Ponzi broke, left a little too much, and I ran out in my first time at the table. If a 125–0 victory might be looked upon as the equivalent of baseball's no-hitter, a first-inning run-out would be comparable to pitching a perfect game. Onofrio Lauri was the only other player to have accomplished that feat. The following day, I beat Ponzi twice more, and a week later I again won two games from the defending champion and opened a six-game lead. I maintained that margin through the end of December, the first full month of play, and celebrated the New Year with a record of thirty-six victories in my first forty-six games.

After a brief break for the holiday, play resumed, and it was during January that I pulled far ahead of the pack. I ran 120 balls against Procita and took advantage of a brief slump that Ponzi had fallen into to open a comfortable lead. By the middle of the month I led by ten games; then I beat Ponzi twice to stretch it to twelve; a day later it was thirteen. The following day I set a new tournament record, running 126 balls in the fourth inning against Procita. Finally, Ponzi turned his game around, and although I went 20–4 over a two-week period, I was unable to add to my lead. Still, with the tournament almost half over, I had won close to 80 percent of my games and led by a substantial margin.

At this point, a number of newspaper reporters who were covering the tournament were prepared to declare me the winner. The press was following the competition daily, and the Philadelphia papers, with four of their own involved, were running feature-length articles complete with interviews and quotations. They were writing things like "Mosconi has taken control of the tournament" or "Mosconi appears to have it all wrapped up." But I knew better. There were well over one hundred games still to be played, and I knew how quickly the complexion of things could change. I had come close before only to see victory slip away, and I was determined to leave nothing to chance. I brushed aside any suggestion that I had the title within my grasp. I kept thinking of what Sylvester Livingston told me eight years earlier: "Willie, when you have the knife in, twist it." And that's exactly what I did; I turned everything up a notch.

On February 10 I pitched another perfect game, defeating Kelly 125–0 in the first inning. It was my fifth run of 125 or more, and in the process I set a tournament record by completing the game in thirty minutes flat, the shortest game in history. The next day I ran 113 against Procita. I won fourteen straight before Ponzi stopped me, then picked up again and ran 113 against Caras and 112 against Kelly. By the latter part of February, I led Ponzi by twenty games, with a record of 100–28.

With fewer than one hundred games to play, a twenty-game lead seemed fairly secure, but I was determined to keep up the pressure, and I had one of my hottest months in March. I ran 125 against Rudolph in the second inning on March 11 and followed that up with a first-inning run of 125 the next day. It was my seventh shutout and fourth perfect game of the tournament. In the nightcap I ran 101, and now the press was all over me. One reporter told me that my long runs were beginning to unnerve my opponents. Another said that one of the players told him he became punchy watching the speed with which I made my shots. They wanted me to comment, but what could I say? I just shrugged it off. If I was getting on their nerves, so much the better. I told the newspapermen that I didn't even want to discuss it until the tournament was over. I wanted to avoid all distractions.

When March ended, I led Ponzi by twenty-five games and it was all but over. Now, I could taste my first championship and was eager to wrap it up. I ripped off nine straight victories. On April 2 I beat Caras twice, once with a run of 120. The next day I took two from Rudolph and followed that with two more wins over Caras, including my eighth shutout of the tournament, and then three in row over Lauri to clinch it. It was April 7, and there was still almost a month to go, but with a record of 142–40, I had a lead of twenty-eight games and Ponzi, still the runner-up, was mathematically eliminated.

Although the tournament was essentially over, I sustained my winning pace over the next four weeks, even increased it a shade, taking thirty-four of my final forty-two matches. On the way, I completed my fifth perfect game and ninth shutout, playing against Lauri at McGirr's. The final standings showed me with a record of 176–48, thirty-three games ahead of Ponzi. Caras finished third, fifty-two games behind. An interesting sidelight to the tournament was that four other players—Ponzi, Caras, Lauri, and Rudolph—all had runs of 125 or more (Lauri, in fact, set a new record by running 127 in a row), while in past years this had been accomplished only twice. But their feats were largely overlooked in the rush of attention bestowed upon me for my performance. I was not simply heralded as the new champion, I was extolled as a hero of sorts. Writers and reporters wanted to interview me, photographers were popping flash bulbs at me, all the quiet corners of my life were being examined. Out of nowhere, it seemed, quite suddenly, I had become a public figure.

▲ ▲ ▲

Nineteen forty-one was a year of glittering achievements on the sports beat. Ted Williams became the first .400 hitter in more than a decade and the last for at least the next half century. Joe DiMaggio hit safely in fifty-six consecutive games, still perhaps the most cherished and enduring record in sports. Willie Mosconi's performance in the 1941 tournament was no less stunning. His thirty-three-game margin of victory was comparable to a baseball team winning its pennant by more than twenty games. He ran one hundred or more balls more times than all the other players combined. Ralph Greenleaf had run 125 balls from the break in 1929; Onofrio Lauri duplicated the feat in 1940; Willie did it five times in one tournament and had four other runs of 125 or more. His perfect game against Kelly has been referred to as the best game of pool ever shot, the most perfect of perfect games. Kelly's safety on the break had been well played, leaving the cue ball close to the rail at the foot of the table. Willie gambled on a long shot, which shattered the pack. It was the only difficult shot he made. He played position so precisely that the cue was rarely more than eighteen inches from the object ball. He did not have to make a single combination. His break shots were planned to perfection. In completing the game in thirty minutes, he had averaged a shot every fourteen seconds, which includes the time it took to rack the balls eight times.

It was, all told, an astonishing performance and it propelled Willie onto the center of a stage reserved for only a handful of sports celebrities. Every crease and crevice of his past was scoured for the telling detail that would illuminate the secret of what was now being described as a supernatural gift. The public was informed of how he had learned to shoot pool with round potatoes and a broomstick; his brief tenure as child prodigy; his match with Ralph Greenleaf, with whom he was now being compared; his days of shuffling through the pool halls of South Philadelphia looking for a score that would put food on his family's table; the years of touring the highways, scrambling to keep dates in towns that only the atlases remembered; the disappointing tournaments in which he often flashed brilliantly but never managed to win. The entire chronicle was laid out, again and again, in newspapers and periodicals. His audience was wider than those who followed the sports pages. National magazines like *Time* and *Newsweek* were interested. And always there was the accompanying photograph, his cleanly chiseled features bearing no small resemblance to those of George Raft, the movie star. There he was, leaning over the edge of a pool table, his jaw set hard, his hair well groomed and swept back from an incipient widow's peak, his clear gray eyes sighting down the shaft of a cue stick with the fierce concentration of a sniper drawing a bead on his target.

He had exploded on the scene as a fully crafted hero, and he had all the ingredients to satisfy the image. There had been several world champions since Greenleaf had surrendered the crown but none possessed the star quality of Willie Mosconi. Willie combined a mechanical efficiency with the style and flair of a showman. His hard-edged intensity was leavened by an ease of manner that suggested a core of vulnerability beneath the impregnable shell of his desire to win. He could be both volatile and serene, street-tough yet gracious. He made his shots with the clattering speed of a Gatling gun and the studied precision of a fine rifle. He was as impatient while waiting to shoot as he was at the table. He would lean back in his chair, his legs crossed, the heel of his cue resting on the ground, as relaxed, it would seem, as a man making conversation at a cocktail party. But as the run proceeded, his face would turn florid and his jaw muscles could be seen working hard on stick after stick of spearmint gum. When he stepped to the table he moved briskly and with an athlete's grace, the heels of his highly polished shoes clicking against the floor. He would make a quick study of the table and then proceed to shoot.

"Three ball, fifteen ball . . ." Once started, he would seem to gather speed, like a car rolling downhill, moving so fast that at times he appeared to be trotting, the clicking of the balls coming in rapid-fire succession. When finally he missed he might turn to the crowd, shrug his shoulders, and extend his hands, palms up. The crowd loved it. But if the game was close and the shot he missed was an easy one, he might as readily display a bit of temper, pounding the side of the table with his fist or hammering the butt end of his cue against the floor. The crowd loved that, too, and so did the press.

Willie was like a media event that had been waiting to happen. He fit precisely the mold of other sports heroes of his time. If Greenleaf—swaggering, flamboyant, and hard-drinking—was, like Babe Ruth, tuned to the tempo of the twenties, Willie was cut to the fashion of a more sedate era. Like DiMaggio and Joe Louis, he carried himself with a courtly dignity. Friendly but formal, he wore a suit coat or a sports jacket even when playing in exhibitions. At five-foot-seven and 140 pounds, he was trim and well-proportioned. His hair, which would soon turn prematurely gray, was always freshly barbered, his fingernails manicured, his clothes finely tailored. He was soft-spoken and courteous, and when asked to discuss his gift he did so with great respect and even a touch of wonder.

▲ ▲ ▲

When the tournament was over, I seemed to have become an instant celebrity. Frankly, I didn't mind the attention. It was a lot better trying to explain why you won than why you lost, but it wasn't any easier. I thought that the format of the tournament helped me a great deal. In a round-robin, when you play each player once or twice, there is an element of unpredictability. Someone gets hot and beats you and you have no chance to recover. One bad game, even one bad shot, and you're out of it. But when you meet every other player thirty-two times there's no luck involved. I had a tough time with Procita in the early rounds, but I ended up beating him twenty-four times. Still, Procita beat me more often that any other player except Ponzi. I went 19–13 against Ponzi and 26–6 against Caras and Rudolph, the other former champions in the competition. A tournament of that length is like playing a baseball season; luck tends to even itself out over the course of play.

People don't always think of pocket billiard players as athletes, but they are, and pocket billiards is a sport like baseball or any other. Talent is the key. If not for talent, how come there have been so few players like Jack Nicklaus, Mickey Mantle, or Babe Ruth? They had that little something extra, that drive. We have to have it, too. But it's easier for people to understand the talent that's involved in playing sports where size, speed, and power are important. In pocket billiards, it's feel, touch, and control of speed, and that's harder to explain. Many seem to believe that there's a lot of mathematical figuring to it, as though you step up to the table and start to compute the angles. That's not it at all. It's mostly a mind's eye picture of each shot as a whole—the cue stick, the cue ball, the object ball, the rails, and the pocket. All of these blend into one and each shot becomes a picture. You learn the different pictures by playing each shot over and over again.

That facility came naturally to me. But you must still study the game. You can't play this game one shot at a time. You have to be able to vizualize the rack, to see as many shots ahead as there are balls open on the table. If all the balls are open, I can look at the table and tell you within an inch or two where the last object ball and the cue ball will be at the end of the rack. But you rarely get the opportunity to play a completely open rack. If there are seven or eight balls open, you still have a cluster that you will have to break before you get down to the last ball. You have to set up your shots so that you can break that cluster as soon as possible. Those are the pictures that are most difficult to envision, and it takes some time to learn to do it.

It also takes time to learn how to play defense properly. It's a part of the game that is often overlooked because it's not very glamorous and because you don't have to do it that often. Out of well over one hundred shots in a game, you might play defense only five or six times. But the irony is that if you don't play defense well you don't get to play offense. Leave too much on a safety and you might never get to the table again. You also must learn to play careful defense no matter who your opponent is. In fact, defense can be more important against an inferior player. I often had more trouble with poorer players because I didn't leave them safe enough when I missed. A player who has only an outside chance of winning is more likely to gamble on a difficult shot. You figure he's going to have to play safe, but he's thinking he has nothing to lose. He ends up making the shot, scattering the balls, and the next thing you know he runs out on you.

I tried to play the same game no matter who my opponent was. You had to respect everyone. Pocket billiards is a game of concentration, and you must concentrate on your shots. The cue ball is going to end up in the same place no matter who you're playing, and you can't concern yourself about try-ing to make adjustments. The other players all looked alike to me. I just said to myself, "The hell with him; let him worry about me."

But the best lesson of all in pool is a simple one: Don't miss! If you don't miss you don't have to worry about anything else. I always kept that rule in mind when I shot, and I left many a son-of-a-bitch sitting in that chair a long while waiting to shoot again.

When the rush of publicity trickled to a stop and the afterglow of victory had faded a bit, I was ready for a rest. The tournament had been a grind, what with the travel, the uneven schedule, playing days and nights; even your days off are tough because you're thinking about the next day's games and who your opponent is. The tension is always with you and it wears on your nerves. After about three months it feels as though you've been at it for a year and you cannot foresee its ending. So when it was finally over I headed for the Jersey Shore. With the first-place prize money, I was earning about ten thousand a year, which in 1941 dollars was a pretty comfortable living, and I could afford to indulge myself for a month or so. I just relaxed—took in the sun, did a little swimming, played some golf. I shot a fairly good game for a duffer. In those days, I was probably shooting in the high eighties. I eventually got down to an eight handicap, but rarely did I ever break par. People often compare golf with billiards, thinking there might be a transfer of skills, but aside from the need for a shooting touch on the green, they're very different games. I liked them both, but I didn't know many other pool players who had a taste for golf. Most pool players learn their game in the big cities, and you don't find many golf courses in South Philadelphia or Upper Manhattan.

After three or four weeks at the shore, I was ready to return to action. I would be called upon to defend my title sooner than I might have expected. The 1940–41 tournament seemed to revive interest in the game. For spectators and fans, it was like following a baseball season. They could pick up the paper each morning and look at the scores and the standings, and if they happened to miss a day or two they could still come back to it and get caught up without feeling that the season had passed them by. Also, it was a great tournament for individual accomplishments. Five of the eight players ran 125 or more, there were many runs of over a hundred, and the fact that a new champion was produced didn't hurt any either. Every sport is freshened by the emergence of a new hero, and the publicity I had attracted drew attention to the game itself. The Depression had eased somewhat, too, and the Billiard Association of America decided to take advantage of a favorable climate and run another championship tournament in the fall of 1941.

They returned to the old round-robin formula, with twelve contestants playing each other once and the best record determining the winner. The entire tournament was played in Philadelphia's Town Hall in late October and early November, with an all-star cast that included four former title-holders and generous prize money of ten thousand dollars. The most notable of the onetime champions was Ralph Greenleaf. Greenleaf, who had returned to action in 1937 after a four-year retirement, had retired again in 1938 and was now making yet another comeback. Somehow, Ralph was a presence that seemed to appear at every critical juncture of my life. He was the reigning king who took me on when I was the Child Prodigy back in 1920. I had toured with him for four months after losing my first tournament in 1933 and again in 1939 when I dropped out of competition for a while. Now, six months after I had won my first title, here was Ralph once more, back on the trail, and his name, added to a roster of challengers that included Ponzi, Caras, and Rudolph, made for an enticing series of matchups and the most extensive press coverage in some years.

Town Hall, of course, accommodated many more spectators than even the most spacious billiard academy, and it was filled every night for more than two weeks. The promoters knew how to get the most out of it, too. They scheduled Greenleaf to open the tournament against Dan Tozer, the champion of Chicago but not much else, while I played the nightcap against George Kelly, whom I had beaten thirty times in the previous tournament. We both won easily and remained undefeated through the first week of competition. After four straight wins, I lost a match to Onofrio Lauri, of Brooklyn, and Greenleaf led the field with a record of 5–0. But then the top players started playing one another, and Ralph's rustiness began to show. He dropped his next three decisions and was no longer a factor, finishing with a mark of 6–5.

A relatively new player to the field, Irving Crane, of Livonia, New York, emerged from the pack and took the lead with a record of 6–1. A tall, wiry gent of high seriousness and little color, Crane had come upon the scene in 1937, when he lost a challenge match to Greenleaf. But he was young and just reaching his peak, and I discovered he was a formidable opponent. We were each 5–1 when we met, and he opened up early leads of 83–8 and 108–16. I got back into it with a run of fifty-one but left a hanger and lost the match 125–75.

Crane lost his next two games, and the race really tightened up. With one game to play, five of us—Caras, Rudolph, Crane, Ponzi, and myself—were tied with records of 7–3, assuring a playoff for the title. My final opponent was Greenleaf, and I wasted no time, opening with a first-inning run of 113 and closing out with a final score of 125 to minus 13. The following day, Rudolph beat Caras and Crane topped Ponzi to set up a three-way playoff. The playoff also ended in a deadlock. I defeated Crane but lost to Rudolph, who, in turn, was beaten by Crane. The championship was decided on the basis of total number of points and that placed Rudolph first and Crane second.

It was not the first time that I lost out in a total-point tie-breaker, but it is a dispiriting way to surrender your title. Of course the case can be made, in Rudolph's behalf, that he had defeated me twice, by almost identical scores of 125–70 and 125–69, and therefore had earned the crown in direct compe-tition. But it was nonetheless difficult for me to rationalize my disappointment. I had, after all, won the title in a grueling six-month trial that encompassed 224 games, and I had lost it in a flash on a score count, a system that was not used in any other sport.

Nonetheless, I did not spend much time licking my wounds. The tournament had ended on November 7, 1941, and exactly one month later the country was at war. For the next four years, nothing would be as it had been. My personal life was being transformed as well.

CHAPTER

The war, of course, changed everyone's life drastically and suddenly. Mine was no exception. In the spring of 1942, I left the Philadelphia area and took a job in a defense plant in Jackson, Michigan. The choice of Michigan as my residence was not an arbitrary one. I had gotten married shortly before the start of the 1940–41 tournament and three months after my victory we celebrated the birth of a son, William Mosconi, Jr. My wife, Ann Harrison, was a native of Michigan and, with a newborn baby in tow, she wanted to be near her family. We lived in a town called Leslie, and I worked in the Goodyear factory in Jackson, which was just a few miles away. I was a lathe operator, and it was the dullest, most tedious job I ever had. The machine I ran produced grinding wheels, which, in one manner or another, helped to shape the weapons of war. I worked ten hours a day, often seven days a week, and the shifts changed, from day to night, just about every month. For me, the long hours and the monotony of the work were aggravated by the fact that I was unaccustomed to a regular work schedule. I had not held a conventional job since I was a teenager, and it was not easy to make the adjustment. But the work was essential to the war effort and it earned me a deferment from the draft. With a young baby at home, even the long hours were preferable to being away at an army camp.

During my first three or four months in Michigan, I hardly touched a cue stick. I was often too tired to stand when I got home from the defense plant and days off were few and far between. What free time I had, I spent with the baby, trying to relax and gather my resources to return to my shift the next day. Strangely enough, I didn't miss playing very much. To some degree, it was refreshing to be away from it for a while. But in the fall, plans were being made for a championship tournament, and I was invited to compete. It was to be a tournament like no other before or since—a double round-robin among the six top-ranked players in the world, all of them champions or former champions.

In May of 1942, Irving Crane had taken Rudolph's title in a challenge match, and his first defense would pit him against Rudolph, Greenleaf, Ponzi, Caras, and me. It was the only time that a tournament was made up exclusively of players who had held the title, and it was billed, of course, as the Tournament of Champions. The competition was scheduled for the first week of December in Detroit. The location was chosen to accommodate me since I was the only player, at the time, engaged in full-time employment. Goodyear gave me the week off, I squeezed in a few hours of practice, and I was as ready as I was going to be when the tournament opened on December 1 at the Recreation.

I suppose that when you put six such players in the same room at the same time some fireworks might be expected, especially when one or another of us had held the title since 1928. In this instance, the first explosion occurred before we even got started. Ponzi and Greenleaf got into some kind of dispute, and Old Ponzola could really get Ralph's goat. Although they were both extroverts, their personalities were quite different, and when they rubbed up against each other you could hear the sound of the friction. Ponzi was excitable and he could lose his composure from time to time, but he was basically a fun-loving type of guy who did not take himself too seriously. Greenleaf, on the other hand, took himself quite seriously indeed. For all his theatrics and his showmanship, he was, at bottom, a prima donna who was quick to take offense when he thought he was not being treated with proper deference.

I don't recall what the initial argument was about, but Ralph took umbrage at something Ponzi said and he had one of his tantrums. He was shouting and swearing, and Old Ponzola, in that impish manner he could affect, took note of the dinner jackets we were all wearing and said, "Come on, Ralph, we're all dressed like gentlemen here, let's try to act like gentlemen." It wasn't so much what he said as the way he said it. The idea of a rather earthy, off-the-cuff fellow like Ponzi lecturing the stately Ralph Greenleaf on decorum was more than Ralph could handle and he blew sky-high. He raged and roared, while Ponzi just turned and walked away with a shrug and a sly grin on his face. I don't know how lasting the effect was on Greenleaf, but he was in a huff throughout the tournament and I had never seen him play with so little concentration.

Ponzi, by contrast, was at the top of his game, opening the tournament with a convincing win over Crane, the defending champion. But I cooled him off a bit that night. After we each played safe in the first inning, I ran twelve in the second frame, then took a deliberate scratch and closed out the contest 125–0, with an unfinished run of 114. The following day, Tuesday, I topped Caras and Crane with successive runs of ninety-eight and ninety-four. On Wednesday, I ran eighty-eight to beat Greenleaf and then was forced to earn a more difficult victory against Rudolph, who twice in the past had cost me a championship. So I had defeated each of my five opponents in the first round of games and was somewhat surprised to find myself so sharp after a long layoff. But I had little time to savor my success. Caras brought me back to earth by the score of 125–43. I rebounded against Crane with another high run of eighty-four, extending my record to 6–1, but Ponzi was right on my heels at 5–2 with three games still to be played. My next opponent was Greenleaf, and he gave me one of my toughest and most memorable matches of the tournament.

Ralph had been in a sour mood all week and the fact that he was already out of contention only served to irritate him further. We had played each other many times in the past, of course, and our games were always briskly paced. But this time Ralph slowed things down to a crawl. He played a lot of safeties, and even when he shot he was moving deliberately, taking uncharacteristically long periods of time to study the table. He kept the game close that way, but it dragged on, an hour and a half, and we still weren't even close to completion. Ralph and I normally played two games in that time. I don't know whether he slowed down for strategic purposes or whether he was just feeling a little unsure of himself, but I was growing increasingly impatient. I had been on a roll all week, finishing my games quickly and usually with a long run, but Ralph was leaving me little to shoot at and throwing my rhythm off.

Finally, after more than two hours of play and trailing 98–73, I had what looked like an open table and a chance to make an extended run, and I blew the shot. At that point, two hours' worth of frustration overflowed and I couldn't contain it any longer. I reared back and fired my cue stick across the room and cursed myself out in the king's best English. Now it was Greenleaf who had the open table, and he couldn't wait to get at it. He chalked his cue quickly, stepped up to the table, took dead aim, and miscued. The cue ball just squirted off the tip of his stick, rolled about six inches and came to a halt. In the years I had watched him play I had never seen Ralph hit a ball so poorly. It was like watching a great punter swing his leg full-force and barely graze the football. I could not keep myself from laughing out loud, and now it was Ralph's turn to explode. He started storming and stomping about the room, shouting that I had broken his concentration and that he could no longer play championship pocket billiards if he was not permitted to concentrate. I didn't say a word. I just chalked up and ran fifty-two and out. My final run took no more than ten or fifteen minutes, but the game had lasted two hours and thirty-five minutes, the longest match of the tournament.

Now, I had a record of 7–1 and a one-game lead over Ponzi. The following day I clinched the title with a little help from Irving Crane. I defeated Rudolph 125–32, closing out with an unfinished run of seventy-one. Then I sat back and watched Crane win a close one from Ponzi. In my final match, I topped Ponzi 125–17 for a 9–1 record and a three-game margin of victory. My second title earned me a championship trophy and fifteen hundred dollars in war bonds, which was more than half a year's wages at the defense plant.

My performance in the tournament surprised a lot of people, myself included. Against that kind of competition, it was unlikely that any one player would dominate so completely. Ponzi, at 6–4, was the only other contestant to win more than half his games. Crane broke even, Caras won four of ten, and Greenleaf and Rudolph finished with records of 3–7. I also had the four or five longest runs and the only run of one hundred or more. One writer who covered the tournament wrote that I had dealt a devastating blow to the principle that practice makes perfect.

Actually, I was never completely devoted to that principle even when I wasn't working full-time. A lot of the other players felt they had to maintain a regimen of three or four hours of practice a day to remain sharp. But I was never able to work up much interest in practicing. It seemed to me that a player goes stale, loses some of his keenness if he practices too much. You tend to let up when you're playing by yourself, you don't concentrate as completely. There also is the tendency to try shots that you would not ordinarily take in competition. Discipline is very important in pocket billiards, as it is in every sport, but how often will you play yourself safe when you're trying to run a rack in practice? There is a persistent tension when you're playing against an opponent, and you can't duplicate it when you're playing by yourself. The psychological element is missing. In competition, the trick is to keep the pressure on the other guy while remaining immune to it yourself. When you practice too much, you get into the habit of playing pressure-free, you relax too much. I very rarely practiced more than an hour or two at a time, and before a game, running a rack was enough for me. So maybe working ten hours a day at the defense plant was the right recipe. I was fresh and sharp when the tournament began, and when it was over I went right back to work and took up my position at the lathe.

The 1942 tournament would be the last one held for the duration of the war. Some exciting challenge matches would be played over the next few years, with the title changing hands several times, but another tournament was not to be held until the end of 1946 when things had returned to normal.

▲ ▲ ▲

Things had not been "normal" in America for some time. The Depression that had flattened the country in the thirties had never really ended but rather ebbed and drifted into a prewar and then a wartime economy. The years of the war were a time of privation and loss. Essential goods were rationed and hard to come by. Luxuries, for the most part, were memories of times past. Automobiles were no longer being manufactured and those who had old ones could not get gasoline to fuel them. And, most tragically, gold stars were appearing in windows in growing numbers, forlorn tributes to fathers and sons who would not be returning. It was an age of artificial materials and jerry-built wares, a time when citizens learned to make do with commodities they would have shunned in happier days. The world of entertainment flourished, though at a scaled-down pace. Movie houses were filled as a war-weary populace sought relief from the drumbeat of news from the front. The legitimate theater, while offering a limited menu, continued to play to packed houses, and the radio served up a lighter fare as ballast for its grim reports of destruction and death.

Sports, too, sustained its schedule, although its product was a pale image of former years. If the twenties were sport's Golden Age, the early forties were, at best, an Age of Bronze. Professional athletes started falling to the draft as early as 1940 and 1941, but with America's entry into the war there began a steady flow from the playing field to the field of combat. Early on, the way had been cleared for sports to continue to operate as best they could, and the word came from the very top. In his famous Green Light letter, President Roosevelt gave baseball the go-ahead and the other professional sports followed suit. Of course accommodations had to be made. Travel was restricted, and road teams tarried longer in each city before moving on. Spring training camps were pitched closer to home, and teams from wintry climes found themselves working out on frozen tundra or in makeshift indoor arenas.

But the critical resource of sports, the athletes themselves, were in ever-diminishing supply. The talent pool was being drained, and as the years passed there were fewer able bodies to fill the roster spots. A one-armed outfielder played for the St. Louis Browns; the Washington Senators signed a pitcher with an artificial leg. Teenagers too young for the draft made premature big-league debuts, and retired players who were too old to serve retrieved their gloves and made belated comebacks. Football teams had an even smaller stock to draw upon. The game was too physically demanding to be played by any but the fittest, and several franchises were obliged to merge in order to field a full squad.

The solo sports, such as boxing and billiards, with no rosters to fill or extended schedules to adhere to, took their action wherever they could find it. With the champions of most boxing divisions in the service, only a handful of title bouts were held and most of the crowns were placed in storage for the duration. Billiards, however, had an older clientele, and while protracted tournaments of the prewar variety were out of the question, head-to-head challenge matches presented little difficulty. Willie, now the champion, was nearly thirty years old and, at least for a while, owned a deferment. Ponzi and Greenleaf were well beyond draft age and eager for a shot at the title. Having finished second in the 1942 tournament, Ponzi had first dibs.

▲ ▲ ▲

Just four months after winning the championship I lost it again. It was the second straight time I had been unable to defend it successfully. As elusive as my first title had been, I was beginning to think now that winning it might be easier than retaining it. My match with Ponzi was held at Kling & Allen's Recreation in Kansas City. It was a classy room owned by two distinguished former athletes. Bennie Allen was world pocket billiard champion in 1913 and 1914, and Johnny Kling was the starting catcher for the Chicago White Sox from 1900 to 1910. I knew both of them quite well and the atmosphere was congenial and comfortable, but from the very start I was unable to get my game together.

We were set up to play a 1,250-point match—ten blocks of 125 points, two a day for five days beginning on April 13. The scoring was to be continuous, which means that a block did not necessarily end when the 125th ball was pocketed. The player was given the opportunity to run the rest of the rack and leave himself a break shot for the start on the next block. The second block would end when someone reached 250 plus whatever points he could add from the balls remaining on the table. It was, therefore, possible for the player who was trailing to make up lost ground with an extended run over a number of blocks. For example, a player might be behind by fifty balls, say 400–350, but if he goes on a run he can continue shooting until he reaches 500. When there is a lag after each game of 125, he is forced to start over and has less opportunity to close the gap. As the match developed, I needed that opportunity badly.

Ponzi, who was as good as anyone when he was hot, was in absolutely dead stroke that opening day. He won the first block 137–2 with an unfinished run of seventy, then extended his run to ninety-two while taking the second block 119–44. So he held a 210-point lead at the end of the first day and then proceeded to increase it. On the following day I shot some of the worst pool of my life. I missed three setups that should have led to long runs. At one point, Andy miscued and scattered the balls but I was able to run no more than fourteen, and at that point I needed to click off one hundred or more if I was to get back into contention. But it didn't happen. I don't know what it was, but I was just never able to relax, I never developed any real rhythm. At the end of the fourth block Ponzi led 509–143. I succeeded in tightening things up a bit over the next few days, at one point cutting more than two hundred points from his lead with some fairly long runs, but I couldn't catch him. Ponzi won the match, and the title, 1,250–1,050.

No one has ever been able to adequately explain what is commonly referred to as an athlete's slump. But in every sport there are days when a player is simply unable to perform acts that on most days he finds routine. By way of compensation, there are other times, equally beyond explanation, when an athlete can do nothing wrong. He manages to achieve a level, bordering on perfection, that he might never attain again. I think it is fair to say that no athlete is really as good as he is on his best days or as bad as he is on his worst. The critical factor is consistency. A champion must sustain a standard of excellence, and he must learn how to win on days when he is not at his best. Apparently, this was a lesson I had yet to absorb.

After my match with Ponzi, I was given some time off from the plant to go on tour and visit some of the army camps. My itinerary took me south from Saranac Lake, New York, down the East Coast to Florida, through some of the southern states, then back north all the way to Minnesota. It was on this tour that I noticed a resurgence of interest in pocket billiards. The game had reached the peak of its appeal in 1927 and 1928 when Greenleaf was champion and every sport, from baseball and boxing to tennis and golf, was enjoying a period of prosperity. But the early years of the Depression eclipsed interest for a while; then it started to rebound, and in the spring of 1943 it appeared headed for new heights. There were pool tables in all the army camp recreation rooms, and the boys had taken to playing the game during their time off. Participation in a sport invariably stirs interest in watching it played professionally, and the rec rooms were filled at every stop I made. There would be a real boom, I thought, when the war was over, and as it turned out there was, at least for a while. However, I came very close to missing it. An accident at the defense plant nearly ended my career.

A few months after I returned from my tour, the index finger of my left hand got caught in a grinding wheel and I almost lost it completely. Fortunately, I was able to work it loose before the tendons were severed, but the finger was cut all the way around and you can still see the scar. It was too close a call. The left index finger is critical in forming a bridge when you're shooting, and had I lost its use it probably would have ended my days as a professional billiards player. It was a risk I could not afford, and when the finger finally healed I began looking for safer employment. My wife was due to give birth shortly, and we decided to stay put until the child was born. Our daughter, Candace, arrived in November, and a few months later I got a job with the Spicer Manufacturing Corporation in Toledo, Ohio, which was just south of the Michigan border. Spicer made parts for tanks and jeeps, but I was hired as an inspector, which kept me away from the machinery and out of danger.

By March, we were settled in and I was feeling fit enough to challenge Ponzi and try to win back the title. The match was arranged as a duplicate of our first meeting—1,250 points in ten blocks over five days at Kling & Allen's. Ponzi, who had spent the past year making exhibition appearances at commercial rooms and training camps, had defended his crown successfully against Crane three months earlier and could be expected to be a bit sharper than I was. In our first match, I had come on strong at the end but could not over-come the early lead he had established. So I felt it was im-portant this time to keep it close in the opening rounds until I could settle into my stroke, and that's pretty much the way it worked out.

Ponzi and I split the first four blocks, with me nursing a narrow lead of 509–486. On the third day, I broke it open, winning the fifth and sixth blocks by scores of 117 to minus 1 and 131–19, inflating my advantage to more than 250 points. Ponzi won the next two blocks, but my lead was secure. I closed out the match with an unfinished run of eighty-five for a final count of 1,250–924, a margin of victory 126 points greater than the score I had lost by the previous year. This, my third championship, matched the number of titles Ponzi had won, and this time I was determined to take better care of it. As for Old Ponzola, he challenged once more but never managed to win one again.

▲ ▲ ▲

Andy Ponzi, born Andrew D'Allesandro, was cut from the cloth of big cities. He grew up in South Philadelphia, not far from the Mosconi residence, and, nine years Willie's senior, he played the role of big brother to Philadelphia's growing array of pool pros.

Ponzi had learned to shoot pool under his doctor's orders. While a schoolboy, he had mangled his right hand and broken the wrist in a trolley car accident, and his physician recommended light exercise as therapy to restore full movement and strengthen the wrist. Ponzi found billiards not only therapeutic but an enjoyable (and some time later, profitable) pastime as well, and he seized every opportunity to follow his doctor's advice in the gymnasium of a Philadelphia church. Nonetheless, several of the bones never healed completely and, through all his playing days, Ponzi stroked the cue with a loose, freehand swing that became his trademark and lent an additional touch of dash to a style that already oozed with flamboyance. He shot rapid-fire, with the rat-a-tat-tat percussion of an automatic rifle. He shot faster than Willie, faster than anyone, faster perhaps than prudence warranted. His manner of play was consistent with his personality, for Ponzi was an effusive, sometimes volcanic type, impulsive and high-strung, described by one observer as "nervous as a cat with a dozen kittens."

Though not a hustler in the literal sense, Ponzi had an abiding taste for causing other players to part with their money. He moved from room to room with the concentrated intensity of a cat stalking new prey. When he became too well known around his home precincts, he ventured as far north as New York, a city whose vast complexity assured the anonymity he craved to ply his trade. The consistency with which he won and the variety of techniques he employed to siphon cash from other people's pockets to his own prompted his associates to affix the nickname of "Ponzi." The man for whom he was good-naturedly named, Charles (Get Rich Quick) Ponzi, was a notorious Boston swindler whose much-publicized scam, the Ponzi Game, drained millions of dollars from the bank accounts of unsuspecting marks and sent Ponzi into exile in Rio de Janeiro, where he remained until his death in 1949. The nickname stuck, and Andy entered his first few professional tournaments under the name of Ponzi. Once he had achieved a level of prominence, he wanted to use the name D'Allesandro, but the Billiard Association, for reasons not entirely clear, refused to authorize the change.

Ponzi was a name that suited him well, however, and he wore it with distinction. His friends referred to him lovingly as Old Ponzola. He was an affable sort, short and chunky, whose quick movements and stylish grace with a pool cue somehow belied his appearance. He enjoyed a good laugh, at his own expense as well as at others', and could apply the needle deftly. His favorite targets, Ralph Greenleaf being foremost among them, were those he regarded as a bit starchy and perhaps too much taken with their own high purpose.

Ponzi first achieved national notice in 1933 when he lost a challenge match to Greenleaf. Later that same year, he was runner-up to Erwin Rudolph in a ten-man round-robin championship tournament, and in 1934 he snatched the title from Rudolph in a challenge match. He won it again in a six-man league tournament in 1940, and for the third and final time, four years later, against Willie.

"Ponzi was a better player than most people gave him credit for," Willie recalls. "He was a daring shot-maker and he played great short position. But he could be erratic and at times he was his own toughest opponent. He tended to be very fidgety and overly emotional, and sometimes the slightest setback could throw him off his game. But when he was right, he was as tough as they came. Old Ponzola could drop those balls faster than you could count them, and when he was in dead stroke he could run out on you before you got comfortable in your chair.

"He was a Big Mahah in the neighborhood when I was growing up, always strutting around, never at a loss for words, kidding everyone in sight, but always with good cheer. Because of his good nature, people who didn't know him sometimes took him for a clown but not for long, not once he picked up a cue stick and stepped to the table. He could really play, and I learned a lot from him when I was in my teens, watching him play and trying to beat him."

Willie can rarely suppress a smile when he speaks of Ponzi. He had a genuine respect for most of his opponents but he reserved for Ponzi an undisguised affection. Ponzi, in his turn, made no attempt to conceal his admiration for his neighbor and colleague. After ceding the title back to Willie in 1944, Ponzi remarked: "When you play against this fellow you can't afford to make a single mistake; one misplay and you're doomed."

CHAPTER

8

When I returned to Toledo after my match with Ponzi, I had a difficult time getting back into the work routine. Being an inspector was better than working at a machine ten hours a day, but it was not something I looked forward to when I got up in the morning. The work was dull. The fixed routine was stifling, and after two years I was sick and tired of it. "Who needs this?" I thought. "I'd rather be in the army." So I quit the defense job and was immediately reclassified 1-A. The war, at that time, had just begun to turn in our favor. It was the spring of 1944, a few months before the D-Day invasion, and I decided my time would be better served touring the armed service camps and entertaining the troops. I was nearly thirty-one years old and the father of two, and it figured to be a while before I was drafted. So I hit the highway again, making appearances at posts all over the country.

This time, appearing as the world champion, I attracted even larger and more enthusiastic crowds than I had the previous year. I gave exhibitions, offered instruction, and put on displays of trick shots, and the troops loved it. At each stop I accepted the challenge of the best player on the post, and I'd often break open the rack and let him have his shot at me. Over the years you would be amazed at how many people claimed they had played Willie Mosconi when they were in the army. If I had played them all, we would have been engaged in the longest war in history. But I took on as many as time allowed. I performed both day and night, often seven days a week, and including the travel time, was probably putting in more hours than I had in the defense plant. The difference was that I was doing something I enjoyed, something that was more a part of me, and I felt I was making a greater contribution to the war effort than I had before.

At the same time, I was keeping myself in playing shape. I did not feel I was at by best when I played Ponzi. I had blown hot and cold, and I thought I was lucky to beat him. Of course Ponzi wasn't that sharp either. He hadn't been playing in regular competition, and it's tough to stay at the top of your game when you're idle for long periods. You can't do it with practice alone. By the end of the year I felt I was in pretty good stroke, and I would have to be because I was getting ready to play a long challenge match with Ralph Greenleaf.

Ralph, like most of the other players, had also been traveling the country, entertaining the troops. The word was that he had taken hold of himself again and was back in shape. He had won a few exhibitions against some of the other contenders; now he was ready to stage yet another comeback, to take one more shot at the title. We were booked for what would be the longest head-to-head championship match ever played—fifty blocks of 125 points, to be played over the course of four weeks, from January 29 to February 24. We were scheduled to open in Kansas City, then move on to Chicago, Detroit, and finally New York. The original itinerary included a week in Rochester, but that stop had been canceled, and by way of compensation, Ralph and I staged a one-day exhibition there on Thursday, January 25, in Dunham's Academy. We played two 150-point blocks, and I had things pretty much my own way. It was hard to say how well Ralph was playing because he didn't have much of a chance to shoot. I missed only three shots all day and closed out the match in eleven innings.

▲ ▲ ▲

Willie won the exhibition by a score of 300–63. Rarely had a player of Greenleaf's caliber been dismantled so totally and with such dispatch. After playing safe or taking deliberate scratches over the first five innings, Willie erupted with the reckless intensity that was fast becoming his trademark. Covering the match for Rochester's *Democrat Chronicle*, Conrad Ohlson waxed rhapsodic:

> Mosconi, warming up to his stroking as he went along, skyrocketed to a string of 116 uncompleted in the evening. So phenomenal was the Philadelphia master's play that the scorer's card showed but three misses for his whole day's cuing—and one of the three misses was recorded on a perfectly hit break-shot that jumped out of the pocket on a freak twist.
>
> Mosconi had a maximum degree of success at position-playing the cue ball. He rolled it in and out of the variegated maze of object balls as though a string were attached to it.
>
> Perhaps the most incredible part of it was the fact that at one time Mosconi trailed, minus two to Greenleaf's 41, in a contest that was to wind up 300–63, in his favor. In other words, Mosconi accounted for 302 points while Greenleaf was getting

22, hitting such a torrid clip that the riptide of points inundated Greenleaf.

At night, Greenleaf diverted his attention to sideline chatter. Greenleaf had only one chance at the balls, and after that his cue rested against a wall.

Mosconi scored 45, 57, 41 in successive innings in the afternoon. The high string of 57 was brought to an abrupt halt when a ball spun back onto the table after being sent smack-dab into the center of a pocket.

Throughout the day Mosconi played in methodical fashion, stepping about at a brisk pace, taking in the situation at a glance, and frequently stopping to powder his hands and to shake some of the talcum on his cue. He faced twenty-one break shots and made all but one. And that one "miss" was the ball that jumped out.

Only thirty minutes were required by Mosconi at night, as he scored a 148–14 victory after winning 152–49 in the matinee.

▲ ▲ ▲

My one-sided victory in Rochester did not seem to trouble Greenleaf at all. The psychological aspects of this game are important, but the view held by many observers, that a sound drubbing will crack a player's confidence, is vastly overrated, particularly in the case of an experienced professional. Ralph wasted no time in dispelling any such doubts and laying to rest the notion that he was all washed up.

He won the first three blocks of our title match convincingly and in eye-catching style. His effort in the evening session on opening day was a masterpiece of strategy and daring. After running fourteen in the first inning, he took three deliberate scratches to fall to minus four, then, in the next two frames, he ran forty-seven and eighty-two to close out the game. The following day he dazzled the audience by twice making cushion-first shots to keep long runs going and finished with an overall lead of 375–133. But I broke the spell in the fourth block, won the next four to take the lead at 758–709, and stretched my run to seven straight before Ralph stopped me. When we left Kansas City, I had won eight of twelve blocks and led by 221 points, 1,200–979.

In Chicago I continued to stretch it out and even picked up the pace a bit. I won the nineteenth block by a score of 125 to minus 1, and at the end of twenty I had built my lead to 561 points. I had my best game on our final day in the Windy City. After taking two scratches, I ran 127 and out, tying the championship record for longest run set by Greenleaf against Frank Taberski in Detroit in 1929.

Detroit was now Ralph's hometown, but the change of venue did not help him very much. I won four straight, and my lead now was beginning to appear insurmountable. On Tuesday, February 13, I won both blocks and at the same time was notified that the Billiard Association of America officially recognized my record-tying run of 127. But the best news of the day had nothing to do with the playing of billiards. It came from my draft board.

My draft status had been a matter of concern to me for some time. I was prepared to enter the service, but the mechanics of my induction—where and when I would be required to report—had become snarled in the machinery of government and I had been trying to unravel it for several months. I was living in California when the Selective Service System was put into effect and had registered with a draft board in Los Angeles. It didn't matter where I was registered while I was working in a defense plant because my job granted me a deferment. But now, having been reclassified, I was ordered to report for a preinduction physical in Los Angeles on February 16. I, of course, was in Detroit at the time, and in those days a trip from Detroit to California was a journey of some magnitude. To complicate matters further, I had moved my family back East when I quit my job in Toledo, and they were living with my father in Barrington, New Jersey. So I was spread out all over the map. My papers were being transferred from the West Coast to the East, and here I was in the Midwest, three days before I was due to report, hoping they would allow me to take my physical in Detroit.

As it turned out, they did even better than that. Between my afternoon and evening matches, I learned that my papers had been transferred to the draft board in New Jersey, and that if I passed my physical I would be inducted on March 16. That would allow me to finish my match with Greenleaf and give me three weeks to get my affairs in order before I left. It was a relief to know, finally, what the future held, and I celebrated by winning six of the last eight blocks in Detroit and increasing my lead to more than one thousand points before we headed for New York and the last week of competition.

The games in New York were scheduled for the Strand Billiard Academy in Times Square. Ralph and I had played there many times before, and I could not help but be amused when I recalled an exhibition we put on there some years earlier. I had been given a pair of tickets to an evening performance of *Abie's Irish Rose*, which had been a hit Broadway show and at the time was enjoying a sellout run in a revival.

Curtain time was at 8:30 in a nearby theater, and my match with Greenleaf was to start at 8:00. Ralph broke the balls and he never got to take another shot. I ran 125 and out in seventeen minutes, performed a few trick shots, and when the curtain went up I was in my seat riffling through the playbill. That story became a fable in New York. It's been told so many times, and in so many different versions, that I've sometimes wondered whether it really happened. But it did. For days afterward, people were coming up to me, eager to discuss it.

"Do you realize you were averaging seven balls a minute? That's almost one every eight seconds."

"Well," I said, "we had a fast referee too. He racked those balls in a hurry."

One of the things I remember vividly is that Greenleaf was sitting in his chair fuming. It was not the run I was making that bothered him so much as the speed with which I was shooting, as though I were showing him up by not planning my shots more carefully. He did everything he could to slow me down, making remarks, blowing cigarette smoke in my direction, he even tried to trip me a few times as I sped by him. But I just kept moving, picking up momentum. I think I was shooting faster at the end than I had at the start. I just didn't want to miss the show.

However, I might have been thinking too much about that night when play opened in New York, because for only the second time since Ralph opened the match with three straight wins, I lost two blocks in a row. But I got myself straightened out and took nine of the last ten and finished with a winning margin of 1,760 points—5,498–3,738.

When the match was over, I went home to New Jersey and began making arrangements for my induction in the service. I was in fine shape and had no doubt that I would pass my physical. Ralph would continue on his way. He still had some good pool left in him, but there was a fine edge gone from his game. He was in his mid-forties by then, and he had lost some of his stamina and some of his intensity as well.

▲ ▲ ▲

The match with Willie was Greenleaf's last dance on center stage. He played a number of exhibitions over the next four or five years, many of them with Mosconi, but he never again competed in a tournament, never challenged for the title. After twenty-five years on the hustings, he had taken his first steps into the lonely twilight that sooner or later awaits every athlete.

It is a truism of sports that as an athlete advances in years it is his legs and his reflexes that will finally betray him. Yet history suggests that billiard players, whose trust in those assets is minimal, nonetheless find that their careers turn the corner all too soon. Time is a versatile opponent; it subverts an athlete's gifts from many directions. No matter how tame their sport or what their age, few remain at the top of their game for more than fifteen years. Greenleaf won his first championship at the age of nineteen; he passed his crest at thirty-three. Willie was twenty-eight when he gained his first title; he was forty-three when he retired.

The demands of competition exact their price, and they are relentless. An intensity of concentration, an utter devotion to task are the tolls that all athletes pay, and in time their resources wear thin. Finally, with less to draw upon, they are obliged to husband their energies, to be selective in how and when they choose to mine down deep enough to summon a piece of the past. They can still, on occasion, call forth their best efforts, but the road narrows more quickly and at every turn something is left behind.

In his match with Willie, Greenleaf flashed his old brilliance from time to time, but he could not sustain the pace any longer. Of course he was never a man to treat his gifts gently. His lifestyle was legendary, his appetites Ruthian, and his thirst for the sauce beyond one man's quenching. Some who saw him perform in 1945 would later attest that they sensed his end was near.

"He was a shell of what he used to be," one observer noted, "he was half in the bag, I'm telling you it was pitiful."

Willie, too, knew that Greenleaf's best days were now a part of history. The baton had finally been passed, not so much from champion to champion as from one monarch to another, for Mosconi, still a few years from his peak, was beginning to tighten his grip on the crown.

▲ ▲ ▲

The army was as good as its word. I was inducted on March 16 and assigned to Fort Dix, New Jersey, for basic training. The war in Europe was nearly over by then. The siege of Germany was under way and the Allied forces were pushing toward Berlin. I knew I would not see any combat, not at my age with the war winding down, but I was still required to complete a full eight weeks of basic training, and it was no easy matter. I was almost thirty-two years old, and while I was in pretty good shape for my age, my life-style had not prepared me for the rigors of army life. But I got through it all right, then was shipped to North Carolina for eight more weeks of advanced training, and when that was over I was assigned to Special Services, in the entertainment division. I was in charge of the swimming pool, the recreation room, all the facilities that were set up to boost the morale of the troops. Of course by that time morale was already pretty high. The war ended in early August, and although draftees were subject to two years of service, we all knew that for the balance of our terms we would be serving in the peacetime army.

I was also fortunate enough to have a good commanding officer. He liked to play pool, and he granted me leave time occasionally to play some exhibition matches. I was given several promotions along the way and attained the classification of T-5, which in Special Services was the equivalent of corporal. So, despite the early hours and the regimentation, I cannot say that army life treated me too harshly. But just about the time I felt I had made my adjustment, I was told I was eligible for early discharge. It was not under the happiest of circumstances.

One day, I was contacted by the Red Cross and told that my wife, Ann, had moved back to Michigan with our children, deposited them in a foster home, and disappeared. No one knew where she was. The children were apparently being well cared for by an elderly couple who were friends of Ann's, but they were not given any money for the children's support and did not even know how to reach me directly. They got in touch with the Red Cross, and it was through the Red Cross that I learned what had happened. Ann never told me, never called or wrote, and years would pass before any of us ever heard from her again.

I was given a hardship discharge, I picked the kids up in Michigan—I think it was Kalamazoo—and moved them back East. Billy was four years old and Candy had just turned two. My father owned an old, three-story house in Audubon, New

Jersey. Two of my brothers lived on the first floor, and my sister Marie and her family occupied the second and third. There was plenty of room, and we moved in with Marie. She had two sons of her own and didn't mind helping me look after Billy and Candy.

So now, all of a sudden, I was a civilian again, and I was returning to a life far different from the one I had left. I never did find out why Ann took off the way she did, and I have no idea if things would have been any different had I not been in the service. We had been married almost five years, and I suppose my life-style made things somewhat difficult. I was on the road a lot, and even when I was home I often played a match at night and slept late in the morning, so she was alone with the children a good deal of the time. It takes a special kind of person to accommodate to that kind of arrangement, to withstand the stress of raising a family while the father is out earning a living, and I suppose that Ann was not particularly the domestic type under even the best of conditions. She had a taste for the night life and not much of a night life was to be had when you were married to a professional billiard player and had two young children at home.

Given the circumstances, I was not in the best frame of mind when I returned home. I was the world pocket billiards champion, but I was growing sick of the game and weary of the demands it made on those who played it professionally. However, I was also in need of money. It was not as if I had a regular job to return to, where I could begin collecting a salary. All my life I had earned my living at the game of billiards, and now there was no new direction in which I could easily turn. With the war recently ended, no tournaments had been scheduled for the early part of 1946, and I needed a payday and I needed it in a hurry.

At that point, fortune turned in my favor. I was approached by C. P. Binner, the promotion manager of Brunswick. He offered me a contract, similar to the one I had signed with them in the thirties. I would represent the company, help sell their equipment, and play exhibitions under their sponsorship. I don't remember how much I was to be paid, but at the time it was a godsend, and I accepted the offer. I told Binner that I wanted a title match as soon as possible and the longer the tour the better. He was quick to oblige. He set up a cross-country challenge match with Jimmy Caras that, to this day, is the longest one ever played. It began almost immediately and continued, uninterrupted, for two months. So I was back in action now and would remain so for more than a decade. In a sense, my career was starting anew, and what better place to begin than at the top?

CHAPTER

9

The match with Jimmy Caras was all I could have asked for. It would be played across two full months—from February 4 to March 30—which meant I could count on a steady income, and I needed the money to get back on my feet. Also, we would be appearing in ten cities, opening in Philadelphia and proceeding to Wilmington, Delaware; Perth Amboy, New Jersey; New York; Buffalo; Cleveland; Detroit; Kansas City; St. Louis; and finishing up in Chicago. For the first time in many years, I was looking forward to hitting the highway. I had been stuck for more than a year in army camps and it would be refreshing to visit some of the cities I had played in before. Then too, I felt that a change of scenery would do me some good.

The shock of Ann's leaving me and the kids without a good-bye or a word of explanation had just begun to settle in. It hit me hard at first, but there were so many details to attend to—mustering out of the service, gathering up the kids and making arrangements for their care, moving back East from Michigan—that the full force of what had occurred, the feeling of loss and betrayal, did not make itself felt until all the details were attended to and I began to unwind. I had no idea why Ann left so suddenly or where she went, and there was also the uncertainty of if or when she might choose to reappear.

At the start of 1946 I knew I had to reorient myself, to give my life a new structure and, in a sense, start over again. A long match in defense of my title was the ideal prescription. And, if the truth be told, there was no one I would rather have defended against at the time than Jimmy Caras.

I don't intend that as a slight to Caras. Jimmy was a great player and a former champion, but he was basically a shot-maker. Given a choice between taking his chances on an extremely difficult shot and playing safe, you could generally count on him to take the shot, and if he missed it was easy pickings. That style of play fed my strength, opening the possibility of some long runs and making for a fast game that did not strain my patience. In any event, I never had as much trouble with Jimmy as I had with opponents who were more defense-minded.

The format of the contest dictated that we would play eighty-six blocks of 125 points each, lagging for the break after every game as opposed to the more common continuous style of play. Since it was more difficult to make up ground in that type of game, the player who got out in front early would have a decided advantage, and that was exactly what I did.

I won four of the six blocks in Philadelphia and opened a lead of more than one hundred points. Then I took five straight before Caras was able to put a few wins back-to-back, and I was never really headed. By the time we completed our week-long stay in New York, I led by almost seven hundred points, with the match one-third over. In Kansas City, the eighth stop on our tour, I tied a championship record, running 127 balls after taking two scratches, and won 127 to minus 2. My lead at that point was close to twelve hundred points, and with only twenty-four blocks still to be played, there was little likelihood that Jimmy could catch me. He held his own the rest of the way, but when the match ended in Chicago, I held a margin of 1,221 points, 8,729–7,508.

The tour was as much a success for the promoters as it was for me. More than eleven thousand spectators paid to see the matches in the ten cities we appeared in. That may not sound like a lot when compared with a baseball game or a prizefight, but a billiard auditorium holds only a few hundred people, and some of the cities on the tour were historically poor sites for a pool tournament. I never understood why, but St. Louis was an unattractive location, while Kansas City was one of the best; Cleveland was never as good as Buffalo although it had a much larger population. But we drew well even in those cities that were traditionally weak. With the war over, it seemed that people were hungry for sports of all kinds, and with the economy back on track, they were ready to go out and spend some of their postwar dollars.

▲ ▲ ▲

With the end of World War II, spectator sports embarked upon a voyage that spanned two eras. The past was being resurrected, but it was being drawn on a new landscape, bent toward a future that would soon transform the shape of the games people watched. With many of the prewar stars returning from the service and new prospects waiting their turn, attendance records were set in every city that had a professional franchise. Fans who had suffered the loss of players like DiMaggio, Williams, and Feller were eager to renew acquaintance, and those too young to remember were impatient for their first look at what baseball was like when it was played by the very best.

But the quickening of interest was not to be measured simply by increased attendance. Professional sports was spreading its wings, opening new frontiers. A new football league, the All-America Conference, challenged the National Football League with franchises in major cities like New York and Chicago while at the same time opening the gates to the West with teams in San Francisco and Los Angeles. The newly formed Basketball Association of America shifted the center of major-league basketball from small midwestern towns to the hubs of big cities, leading to the creation of the NBA.

A subtle revolution was on the way. Sport's undeclared color barrier, which kept black athletes from playing in the big time, was on its way down. Ailing franchises, some of them more than half a century old, would soon begin moving to virgin outposts. Territories west of the Mississippi were found to be ripe for occupation and easily accessible with the advent of commercial jet travel. Leagues were expanding, welcoming new franchises in cities that had never hosted a big-league team, and no matter what the location or the sport, fans, in numbers never before contemplated, were paying for the privilege of watching.

Billiards, a marginal spectator sport that chiefly attracted the intimately initiate and a handful of connoisseurs, was now extending its appeal to a new clientele, in the main college students studying under the GI Bill who were learning to play the game in their campus rec rooms. The market for pool tables was approaching a peak and, combined with an attractive champion who at age thirty-three was nearing his own peak, the game of pocket billiards, for the time at least, appeared to be at the threshold of a period of glamour and glory unequaled since the Age of Greenleaf in the twenties.

▲ ▲ ▲

The first championship tournament to be held in four years was scheduled for December 1946. But a month before it opened I was booked to defend my title in a challenge match against Irving Crane. It was not common practice for a champion to put his title on the line just before the start of a tournament, but those were unusual times. The billiard business had been rather flat during the years of the war, and everyone felt they had some catching up to do. I, for one, was not about to pass up a payday, and frankly I didn't think I would have much trouble with Crane. He was a good all-around player and an exceptional shot-maker, but I thought that my long match with Caras had served to bring me back close to my prewar form, and I was feeling pretty confident.

The publicists had a grand time promoting the contest because Crane and I were coholders of the high-run exhibition record of 309 balls. Irving had set the mark in Layton, Ohio, in 1939, and I equaled it in October 1945 while I was still in the army. It was ironic that my run ended at precisely 309 when I knew I needed one more for the record, but if there was ever a time when I felt a rack of balls had been spooked, that was it.

I was playing Joe Procita in Perth Amboy, New Jersey, and I knew I was getting close to the record when I pocketed my 300th ball; no one but Crane had ever run 300 before. My 308th shot was the last of the frame, and I had left myself in ideal position for the break, the open ball near the corner pocket, just to the left of the pack. I thought I played the shot perfectly. The object ball dropped in the corner pocket, tying the record, and the cue ball slammed hard into the pack. A number of the balls scattered, as they were supposed to do, but unaccountably, the cue ball burrowed its way into the pack and at first flush I appeared to have left myself safe. I took my time studying the table and saw only two possible shots. Both the fifteen ball and the eight were lined up near the right corner pocket, and either one could drop on a combination shot from inside the pack. I would have to hit both of them, and I calculated that the fifteen, just a shade closer to the pocket, had a better chance of falling. I was wrong, but not by much. The shot went just about as I had planned it, but as the fifteen neared the lip of the pocket, the eight hit the cushion, nudged the fifteen aside, and dropped in the hole. I had, as it turned out, called the wrong ball.

So Crane and I remained tied at 309, and there was a lot of ballyhoo about records falling when we met. But those things tend to happen on their own, without prompting, and there were no astonishing runs in our match. We were scheduled to play thirty blocks continuous, which meant that the match would end when someone reached 3,750 points. We opened in Rochester, New York, which was Crane's home base, and I could tell from the start that three weeks of playing Irving Crane would not be my idea of entertainment. He had a deliberate, colorless style under the best of circumstances, and it was clear that he intended to play a cautious game even for him. He won the first block 125–93, but I put together runs of sixty-seven and fifty-five to take the second 157–77, which gave me a forty-eight-point lead. It was the next day's games that really tried my patience. In the third block, Crane played safety after safety. Unless he had a shot that even his grandmother could make, he played it safe, and I was fuming.

I started trying shots I shouldn't have taken, and after an hour and a quarter of pussyfooting he led 74–23, which gave him an overall lead of 276–273.

At this point, he played safe again, but I thought he had left me something to shoot at. It was a difficult shot; I had to use the stick bridge to reach the cue ball and I missed the shot badly. I was frustrated as hell, and I threw the bridge to the ground and went stomping and muttering back to my chair. My little outburst might have unnerved Crane a bit, because in his next turn he scratched on a break shot, and that was all the encouragement I needed. I ran off fifty-nine balls, then came right back with forty-three more to win the block 125–91.

It took Crane three hours to win the fourth block, but I continued to edge ahead, and after a while he adopted a somewhat more daring approach in an effort to catch up. He didn't. When we left Rochester for Philadelphia I had built a lead of more than 250 points. I continued to stretch it out in Cleveland and finally in Chicago, and ended up winning the match 3,750–2,919. But I had not seen the last of Irving Crane, not by a long shot.

The championship tournament was a brief affair—a round-robin with eight contestants, played over ten days in Philadelphia's Town Hall—and Crane won it. He finished with a record of 6–1, losing only to Jimmy Caras. I placed second, with losses to Crane and Ponzi. It was one of those contests in which I led in all the statistics but the one that counted. I registered the most total points, the best points-per-inning average, the high run of 125, and the best game, two innings. Crane received two thousand dollars in first-prize money, while I earned fifteen hundred dollars for second place and one hundred dollars each for longest run and fewest innings. There was a difference of only three hundred dollars in earnings, but Crane came away with what I wanted, the championship. It was the third time I had lost the title, and I would be looking to get it back as soon as possible. No new tournaments were scheduled, and that was just fine with me; I preferred to play head-to-head, and the longer the match, the better.

Tournaments, especially the short round-robins, always involved a measure of luck. You play each guy once, and if you stumble once or twice you're out of it. You can beat the eventual winner and not even be in contention. What you have to remember is that everyone playing in those tournaments is good, very good; they are all capable of running out at any given time. Even an amateur can beat a top professional on occasion. Billiards is a game, like golf, that is played individually, and someone who is at the top of his game can, on a given night, beat anyone in the world.

What separates talented amateurs from professionals, and journeymen pros from champions, is consistency. The trick is to play at your best, to beat top competition, over an extended period, to be able to play through the rough spots and come back strong. Short tournaments are won by the hottest hand, sometimes with the help of some joker who upsets the champion and puts him out of contention. In a challenge match, the better player will almost always prevail. It's hard to hide the flaws in your game when you're playing one man day after day for several weeks and you need to score two or three thousand points to win it. So I was eager for a head-to-head shot at Crane's title, even though it was never a particular pleasure to deal with Irving daily.

▲ ▲ ▲

Irving Crane was something of a novelty among the elite
pool players of his day. Just a few months younger than
Willie, he was born in 1913 in Livonia, New York, a
small village some twenty-five miles south of Rochester.
Unlike most of his contemporaries, he did not learn to
shoot pool in small rooms snuggled away in the recesses
of big-city streets. He was favored at birth, the son of a
prosperous attorney who provided the boy, at the age of
twelve, with his own pool table to keep him off the streets
and out of Livonia's only pool hall. Irving had more than
his share of natural ability. He had a smooth stroke and
a dead eye and he made his shots with a crisp, clean
precision. Given some home instruction and lots of practice, he was soon being booked by his proud father for
exhibitions in Rochester and other nearby cities.

When he had graduated from high school, his father
sent him off to Hobart College in upstate Geneva, New
York, to prepare him for a career in the law and an
eventual partnership in his father's firm. But one year of
study was all young Crane needed to know that he was
not destined to follow his father's lead. His future, he
felt, was as a professional billiards player. He was good
and he knew it. He thought that one day he might become a champion. The elder Crane pled his case elo-
quently but finally relented. He bought his son a pool
hall and set him up in business, and Irving, in his sedate,
unassuming fashion, began stalking fame on the professional pool circuit.

Crane soon became known as "the gentleman of the
game," a sobriquet that did not displease him. At better

than six feet, he was taller than his colleagues, lean and lank, with a prominent chin, a high forehead, and his hair parted squarely in the middle, giving his face a triangular look and the expression of a man who intends nothing but business. All in all, his aspect and carriage called to mind the image of a country preacher, and it was not long before he acquired the nickname of Deacon.

Crane came onto the professional scene at about the same time Willie did, but they had little else in common. While Willie exhibited a daring, sometimes reckless flair, Crane's was a steady game, precise but unspectacular. Still, he played careful position, his shots were usually letter perfect, and he was the model of consistency, never finishing worse than fourth in a championship tournament.

He first achieved a measure of prominence in 1937, when he tested Greenleaf for his title but lost badly, 1,500–550. Three years later, he finished second to Erwin Rudolph in a twelve-man round-robin. Then he took the title from Rudolph in a challenge match in 1942, a year after Willie had won his first championship. To Crane's misfortune, it put the two men on a collision course they would pursue for more than a decade.

▲ ▲ ▲

It might be something of an exaggeration to call my rematch with Crane a grudge match, but it was certainly more than a friendly competition. It was no secret that Crane was not a favorite of mine. He was bland and overly conservative, and he didn't seem to realize that this was a business and that as a performer you had an obligation to entertain the spectators. They were, after all, paying our fees with their admission

money, and you could sense their restlessness when he went
into his delaying tactics. Of course his slow-downs were intended, in part, to upset his opponent. That kind of games-
manship was not uncommon. Players did whatever they could
to get their opponent riled. They would move slightly to get
in his line of sight when he was shooting or blow a cloud
of cigarette smoke in his direction. But Irving had his own
technique. He had long legs and feet big enough to fill a
rowboat, and when you were shooting anywhere near him he
would cross his legs and dangle those big shiny shoes just
beyond the pocket. But I had the answer to that maneuver.
When I powdered my hands between racks, I often missed
and his shoes and pants legs got a generous sprinkling of
talcum.

Our rematch, in May 1947, was a sixteen-block, 2,000-point
contest divided between Perth Amboy and Chicago. It was
over almost as soon as it had begun. I won the first six blocks
by close to 450 points and never let up. In the end I more
than doubled Crane's score, winning 2,000–918 while taking
fourteen of the sixteen blocks. In the process, I set a championship record by averaging 15.89 points per inning with runs
as high as 139. Irving and I exchanged few pleasantries during
the course of the match; we were both pretty intense.

▲ ▲ ▲

A report in *Time* magazine described the scene this way:

> Mosconi and Crane eyed each other like two men
> trying to flag the same cab on a rainy night. Mos-
> coni, shooting almost too rapidly, made runs up to
> 139. But when he missed he banged the table . . .

sat down and snapped irritably to spectators who stood in the doorway: "Come in or get out."

After eight days of play, when Willie had beaten Crane 2,000 points to 918, a fan who tried to console the defeated champion was told: "I don't need your sympathy or advice."

▲ ▲ ▲

Just before the Crane match I had moved to Kansas City. I had no intention of living there permanently, but it seemed to be a good place to settle for a year or two. Bennie Allen was out there and so was another former player, Walter Franklin, and they set up some exhibition matches for me. For some reason, there was a lot of action in that area and the fees were generally higher than they were in the East. I was still under contract to Brunswick, but I wasn't making the extended tours I made before the war and Allen was a pretty good promoter. He was part owner of Kling & Allen's Recreation and he attracted a lot of the top players and a good clientele. Of course Allen and Franklin were pretty good attractions themselves. Bennie had held the title for a while back in the teens, and Walter was a former professional although he never won a championship. When things were a little slow, we sometimes played some interesting matches among ourselves.

One time I was playing Bennie and he was giving me a sound trimming. I couldn't figure out what was happening. All of his corner shots were falling into the pockets like dead ducks and mine were hanging on the rims. Franklin was laughing so hard that his face turned red. Finally, I saw what the problem was. They had cut the pockets so that the angles were off a bit. If you hit the corner the way you normally would, the ball jawed back and forth but it wouldn't drop. But if you tailored your shot to account for the difference, the ball would get sucked into the pocket as if it were a vacuum. Once I caught on it was child's play. Bennie missed a shot and I ran 125 and out. Then Franklin started ribbing Allen, and I said, "What are you laughing at? Grab a cue, you might not get to shoot either." This went on for two days. Finally, Franklin got to shoot—on the third day.

So for the next year or two I played most of my exhibitions in Kansas City, but we went up to Chicago and St. Louis quite often. Chicago, of course, was a great town for billiards, but St. Louis was the pits. The fees were low, the crowds were sparse, it always seemed like a hick town to me. Things happened in St. Louis that I thought couldn't happen anywhere else. One summer afternoon I was playing one of the locals in a room on the second floor, and the table was set up on a platform and surrounded by rows of seats. It was as hot as it gets in St. Louis, which is as hot as it gets anywhere, and the window was wide open. This guy takes a shot, and he's giving it all kinds of body English, trying to coax the ball into the pocket. I'm watching the ball, which doesn't even come close to falling, and when I turn around the guy is no longer there. He had backed right out the window and fallen into the street. Fortunately, it wasn't much of a drop and he wasn't hurt badly. I waited for him to come back up and said, "Hello, how do you feel?" Then we finished our match.

The past two years had been a busy and sometimes trying time for me. Since coming out of the army, I had moved twice, competed in four championship matches, and played a regular schedule of exhibitions. But in the fall of 1947 I received the proverbial offer I couldn't refuse. I was invited to play in a championship three-cushion billiard match. Jake Schaefer, one of the top carom players in the world, had fallen ill, and the Billiard Congress of America needed a replacement. I suppose they thought it might be interesting to have the pocket billiards champion show what he could do at a different game, and it also gave them a chance to bring me together with Willie Hoppe, who had held the three-cushion title for longer than most people could remember.

Three-cushion, as it is called, is one version of carom billiards, just as straight pool is one of many pocket games. But each was designated by the BCA as the official championship game in all its tournaments. Caroms is played on a slightly larger table—which looks like a pool table without pockets—and with only three balls, a red and two whites. Each of the white balls, one of which is marked with a black dot, is assigned to a player as his personal cue ball for the duration of the contest. To score a point, the shooter must hit the other two balls and at least three cushions with his cue ball. It does not matter in what order the balls and the cushions are struck. So three-cushions is principally a game of English, requiring control of the cue ball and the ability to envision a shot from the position of the three balls on the table.

It is a difficult game for beginners who are not adept at the various uses of English but, contrary to popular belief, it is easier to play caroms than pocket billiards at the championship level because there are fewer balls to control. A number of pockets players—Crane for one, Joe Procita for another—occasionally competed and did fairly well in three-cushion tournaments. But no carom player, not even the immortal Hoppe, was able to play with the best pool-shooters. I represented my pockets brethren fairly well in the 1947 tournament, finishing in a tie for third place and ahead of the number-one challenger to Hoppe's crown. I was pleased enough with my performance to entertain thoughts of going after the three-cushion championship if and when Hoppe ever decided to retire.

For the time being, however, I was quite content to get back to the more familiar table with the holes in it. Later that fall, I took on another challenge from Jimmy Caras—our second long match in less than a year—and I won it by an even wider margin, 4,000–2,334. I had now defended my title in seven head-to-head matches and won six of them. Between March 1946 and November 1947 I had competed for the championship five times. I felt the need for a bit of a break, and I was somewhat relieved to learn that the championship tournament the BCA had scheduled for 1948 would have a new format. They designated the top twelve contenders for my title and set up a national tournament to be held at the Chicago Outdoors Show at the Navy Pier in March, with the winner challenging me for the world championship. The Outdoors Show was an annual event that attracted people from all over the country to see boats, trailers, hunting and resort equipment, and the like, and a specially constructed arena was built on the Navy Pier for the billiard matches. A three-cushion tournament was to be held simultaneously under the same rules, so the customers would have a chance to see both Hoppe and me defend our crowns.

To my delight, Andrew Ponzi won the national tournament in a close finish with Arthur (Babe) Cranfield. The Old Ponzola was not well at the time; he had a serious heart condition, he was down on his luck, and I knew he could use an extra payday. I always had an especially warm feeling for Ponzi. He was an emotional sort of a guy; it was easy to needle him and get his goat, but he always took it in good spirit and he was quite a practical joker himself. We had a lot of good times together, a lot of laughs.

I remember one afternoon in Bensinger's we were having a bite of lunch together, and a fairly good journeyman player by the name of Joe Sebastian came up to us and challenged Ponzi to play some nine-ball at fifty dollars a game. Nine-ball was a short rack game, played mostly by hustlers, that involved as much luck as it did skill. It was played with only the first nine balls; the shooter had to hit the lowest-numbered ball on the table, and whatever dropped stayed down. You didn't have to call a ball or a pocket, just slam away and take your chances, and whoever made the nine ball won the game. Ponzi had no interest in playing nine-ball, but the guy kept at him and wouldn't let him eat his lunch. Sebastian had a backer with him and the two of them wouldn't let up. Finally, Andy, who was never more content than when he was eating, turned to me and said, "Willie, why don't you play this guy and shut him up?"

I won the lag for break and began ripping off rack after rack. At the end of each game, the backer peeled off fifty dollars and dropped it on the table. When I had won thirteen straight, the backer said, "That's it, I quit."

"Quit? How can you quit?" Sebastian said. "You haven't seen me shoot yet."

My affection for Andy did not cause me to ease up when we met for the championship. We played nine blocks of 150 points, and I took them all, winning the match 1,350–643. I had an easier time of it than Hoppe did with his opponent, Ezequiel Navarra, who managed to win three of their nine blocks. The carom tournament illustrated the competitiveness of pockets players at three-cushion billiards, because three pool players—Crane, Procita, and Johnny Irish—finished second, third, and fourth behind Navarra in the elimination tournament.

There were some who said I had never shot better pool than I did in my match with Ponzi. I had quite a few high runs and not very many misses. In fact, I averaged nineteen points per inning, breaking my old record by more than three balls.

When the match was over, I was looking forward to a change of pace, a more relaxed lifestyle. The BCA had no tournaments scheduled for the rest of the year, and at that particular time there didn't seem to be any logical contenders for my crown. I had beaten Caras and Crane twice each in the past two years, and now Ponzi. Greenleaf was permanently retired, and there seemed to be no bright new stars on the horizon. So I decided to put my title on hold for a while and go for another change of scenery.

CHAPTER

I spent much of 1948 touring college campuses around the country. The college scene was not entirely new to me. I had made campus appearances in previous years; I even coached the University of Pennsylvania billiards team one year in the early forties. It was a fellow by the name of Charley Peterson who first got me involved. Charley was a former player, a trick shot artist mostly, and he had told me that Thomas Hueston, who held the title from 1905 to 1909, had paid his way through the University of Michigan by coaching the team and managing a billiard room. I had no intention of studying for a degree, but I found a university to offer a congenial atmosphere; it was free of pressure and the youngsters were an appreciative clientele. However, when I won my first championship I became too immersed in the game to spend much time on campus. But now, with the action a little slow, I became affiliated with the Association of College Unions and traveled from one institution to another, giving instruction and putting on exhibitions.

Charley was still active on the college circuit, and he set up most of my dates. The colleges had become hotbeds of billiard activity after the war. The Big Ten schools in particular had adopted the game with enthusiasm. The Universities of Michigan and Minnesota had championship-quality tables and many of the other schools were having them installed. I sometimes did double duty, performing for Brunswick at the installation of their equipment and perhaps staying on for a day or two to offer instruction. The colleges paid me one hundred dollars a day; I would play the winner of their tournament, perform some trick shots, and do a little coaching if the school had an intercollegiate team.

It was ironic, in a way, that at the same time the professional game was suffering through a slack period, the sport was thriving on college campuses and in privately owned halls and clubs. Brunswick was selling more equipment than it had since the twenties, and the new activity was having a positive effect on the image of the game. The old stereotype of the seedy-looking hustler with a cigarette dangling from the corner of his mouth, lurking in the shadows of a dingy pool hall, was on the way out. The new rooms were bright and cheerful, and the players were often clean-cut college students with books at their side. I had always resented the popular notion that pool players were degenerates with nothing better to do and that pool halls were a breeding ground for crime and corruption. Now, the image of the game was changing and I was delighted to do my part to help it along.

In 1949, for the second straight year, the Billiard Congress of America decided that the championships—both pocket and three-cushion—would be decided at the Chicago Outdoors Show in February. This time, however, they altered the format. Instead of the winner of the twelve-man competition taking on the champion head-to-head, it was determined that the three top finishers would join the title-holder in a double round-robin, with each man playing the other three in two 125-point matches and the best record winning. The reasoning of the promoters was obvious: With more players and more games, there would also be more spectators and more admission fees. It was strictly a dollars-and-cents decision. Either it didn't occur to them or it didn't matter that the champion would be crowned in a less definitive manner. It was much the same thinking that, years later, crammed additional teams into the playoffs of league sports like football, basketball, and hockey in order to increase revenues.

The elimination tournament went according to form, with Caras, Crane, and Ponzi qualifying for the round-robin. Caras was as hot as he had ever been, finishing first by a wide margin. Then he went on to snatch my title with a record of 4–2, while I split my six games and came in second. It was a graphic illustration of why I disliked short championship tournaments. In recent years, I had beaten Caras twice in long matches held over a period of many weeks, and it was never even close. Now, he played six 125-point games in three days, split his two with me, and took the title.

Since I had finished second, I was, according to BCA rules, entitled to a challenge match within six months, and past performances gave me reason to feel confident. But the match never took place. Caras sat on his title and declined every offer to defend it. Finally, he announced his intention to retire, at least for the time being, and the BCA declared the title vacant. I could understand, of course, why Jimmy was reluctant to defend against me, but retiring at the peak of his game seemed a bit extreme. I guess he wanted it in the books that he was champion for a full year. But what kind of champion was he if he was supposed to defend his title and refused to do it?

I had always believed that it was the obligation of a champion to take on all comers, and I never dodged anyone. I felt that if I couldn't beat the rest of the world, then I wasn't a real champion, and if I wasn't a real champion I didn't deserve to hold the title. I always wanted to take on not just the man who finished second but those who finished third and fourth as well. It was the only way to make any money. It was, after all, a business I was in, and I was looking to earn as much as possible. Besides, if you hold yourself aloof and start evading challengers, you sacrifice something. You lose your touch and you risk losing your competitive edge, the mental sharpness that real champions must always maintain. Still, there was nothing I could do now but wait until a tournament was held to fill the vacant title, and that wouldn't happen until the next Outdoors Show a year later. By that time, the conditions under which championship pocket billiards was played had been altered dramatically.

Perhaps the most drastic means of changing the texture of a game is to modify the field on which it's played. Despite more than a century of evolution, the baseball diamond has remained intact; the bases are still ninety feet apart. The football field remains one hundred yards long by fifty-five feet wide. Notwithstanding the incredible growth of basketball players, the baskets continue to be set at ten feet above the court. However, in August of 1949, the BCA shortened the standard pool table from five by ten feet to four and a half by nine. They also widened the corner pockets from five to five and a half inches and the side pockets from four and a half to five. One reason for the change in table size was that manufacturers were producing five-by-tens only for championship play. The proprietors of pool halls had been ordering the smaller tables for years because they could fit more of them into their rooms. But essentially the changes were intended to speed play and generate excitement with the likelihood of longer runs. By way of compensation, the number of points needed to win a game was increased from 125 to 150 for national and world competition. How much of a difference did all of that make? Enough to say that starting in 1950 the game of pocket billiards was transformed; it became a markedly different game.

The pockets on the new tables looked as big as bushel baskets. Not only were they larger, they were closer to the shooter; it looked as though you couldn't miss. It no longer made much sense to play defense. On the one hand the shots were easier to make; on the other, it was more difficult to leave your opponent safe, for he would always be closer to the object ball than he would have been on the larger table. Almost immediately, records began to fall, encouraged both by the enlarged dimensions of the table and by the extended score of each game. It was now possible to run 150 balls or more in a single game, and it wasn't long before such runs were recorded.

The change in table size had another consequence, which went largely unnoticed. It opened championship competition to players from the South. For some reason, the four-and-a-half-by-nines had always been standard in the southern states. That's why no tournaments were ever held in that part of the country. It's also why there never were any championship-caliber players from the South until after 1950. The difference of a foot one way and six inches the other may not sound like a lot, but a player from North Carolina or Georgia would come up North and bend over a five-by-ten and it would look like a football field to him. Switching from the larger table to the smaller one had, of course, the opposite effect, and the difference was apparent in that very first tournament in Chicago.

With the title vacant, all twelve contestants had to compete in the nationals, with the top four qualifying for the round-robin, and right from the start the games were short and the runs were high. I set a new record with a run of 133 against a player by the name of Willis Covington. The next day I defeated Al Coslosky 150–3 in three innings, with a high run of sixty-five. Even with the additional twenty-five points needed for victory, most of the games were decided quickly and were as fast-paced as the promoters could have wanted.

I won the national competition after finishing in a three-way tie for first and appeared to have the world championship in hand until I ran into Irving Crane in my final match. The lanky Crane, who looked like he could span the length of the table with his long arms, made quick work of me, winning 150–14 in four fast frames to set up a playoff. The title match was a tough one. Both Irving and I had been finishing our games in six innings or less, but with the championship at stake, this one stretched itself out. I held a 118–112 lead after seventeen innings, but then Crane played a safety and left a little too much. I ran thirty-two and out and regained the title for the fifth time. It would be quite a while before I relinquished it again.

Willie Hoppe, my counterpart in the world of carom billiards, also needed a playoff to win the three-cushion tournament. I think it was his forty-ninth championship, but Hoppe was past sixty by then and nearing the end of the line. No one had ever dominated a sport more totally than Hoppe had. He had begun playing professionally not long after the turn of the century and was still going strong. In the early days, the championship carom game was called balkline, or 18.1, and it was a very difficult game with comparatively few participants. In balkline, there was a grid of boxes on the table, and you not only had to hit the two object balls, you had to drive them out of the boxes and then back again, and it was a tough and tedious game because you had to be able to control all three balls. In the thirties, three-cushion replaced balkline in championship competition, and Hoppe had to make the adjustment.

The two games required different techniques. In balkline, you used a straight stroke; it was more a game of touch, you needed a feel for the balls. Three-cushion required a sweeping stroke, with more English, and you really had to hit the balls hard. It took some power to make the cue carry across the table and hit three cushions and two object balls. But it didn't take Hoppe long to adapt. I think he finished fourth in his first world tournament, but he won the title the next year and from that time on no one could beat him. It takes a lot to stay at the top of your game for three or four decades, but Hoppe's conditioning and his lifestyle helped.

He always kept himself in excellent shape. He didn't engage in any physical training program; he got enough exercise walking around the table. People don't realize how much walking you do in the course of a billiard tournament. But Hoppe pampered himself. He ate in the finest restaurants, got plenty of rest, and he stayed away from the sauce. You might even say that he lived an ascetic existence. He'd rarely go to a movie because he didn't want to strain his eyes, there were certain foods he wouldn't eat, he turned down most party invitations, he set himself particular hours for sleep. Everything revolved around his billiards. He never married and, so far as I could tell, he didn't have much of a social life. Of course, as a consequence, he was not very much fun to be with. He kept his distance from most people and, although he always behaved like a gentleman, he had a rather sour disposition. I didn't even enjoy having dinner with him on those rare occasions when we dined together. He was a great champion, but he paid the price.

Hoppe began his career as a pockets player but switched to caroms at a very early age. I guess he felt the field was a little thinner in caroms and it would be a quicker trip to the top; it is easier to play caroms at a championship level than it is to play pool. That's not the conventional wisdom, because almost anyone can step up to a pool table and knock a ball in a pocket. But the same player can look at the three balls on a carom table and not have the first idea how to make a shot. Played professionally, however, pool is a much more scientific game. You have five times as many balls to control, you have to be able to look ahead as many as fourteen shots, and perhaps most important, you can never afford a mistake because your opponent can run out at any stage of the game. It takes fifty points to win a three-cushion match, and no one has ever run one out. I don't know what the record is, but a run of fourteen or fifteen is like running a hundred balls in pool.

A professional pool player can pick up the carom game a lot quicker than a carom player can learn to play championship pool. In fact, I once beat Hoppe in a game of three-cushion. I had to get lucky to do it, but that's the nature of the game. You can luck into a shot occasionally because you're aiming to put the ball in a given area. In pockets, you either make the ball or you don't; it requires greater precision. Hoppe was well aware of the distinction. He told an interviewer that although it's tougher to make shots in caroms, it's an easier game in competition because you know that you're likely to get thirty or forty turns at the table. In pockets, he said, you can't afford to miss.

Once, when asked to compare the relative difficulty of the

two games, I remarked, cynically, that I would switch to caroms when my eyes got so weak that I couldn't see the object
ball. I had always resented the public perception that pockets
is a bum's game while carom billiards is a gentleman's pastime.
Over the years, I've run into as many bums who were carom
players as I ever saw in a pool hall. But in truth, when I
reclaimed my title in 1950, I gave some thought to entering
the three-cushion competition. I thought that once Hoppe
retired, with a little more practice and concentration, I might
be able to win that title, too. The reality was that competition
was getting a bit scarce on the pool circuit and aside from the
annual tournament, there were few opportunities for significant matches.

With the pickings slim and no tournament scheduled until
1951, Ralph Greenleaf was being nudged out of retirement.
It had been several years since Ralph had played in earnest.
His drinking problem had become serious enough that the
BCA barred him from competition because he could no longer
be counted on to appear for his dates. But Greenleaf deposited
a thousand-dollar guarantee and surety of appearance, and we
were scheduled to play a twelve-block match at Allinger's
beginning March 20. The match never took place. On March
15, Greenleaf died of a cerebral hemorrhage after being
rushed to the hospital from the St. Francis Hotel in Philadelphia where he and his wife had been living in recent months.
He was only fifty years old, and I think it would be fair to say
that he literally drank himself to death. It was a tragic loss for
the game, and of course I felt it personally as well. I had
known Ralph since I was a young boy and we had spent many
months on the road together and I had learned more about
pocket billiards from him than from anyone else. I suppose
that aside from Ponzi, whom I considered a personal friend,

I felt more warmly toward Ralph than any of the other players of the time.

Greenleaf was largely responsible for putting the game in a national spotlight. He was more than just a great player or a personality; he was, all by himself, an institution. He attracted the attention of crowds in the same way that Babe Ruth did, simply by the force of his nature. He was colorful, he was spectacular, he was theatrical in the way that all great actors are; he basked in the light cast by an appreciative audience. One of his favorite crowd-pleasing routines was to study the table from every angle and raise his arms in despair at the hopelessness of his situation. Then, with a shrug and a flourish, he would execute a shot he had seen from the start and bow graciously to the audience. They loved it and so did he. Although he could be temperamental at times, he was always polite and conducted himself with the style and grace of a John Barrymore striding the boards.

As a matter of fact, Ralph sometimes worked in the theater with his wife, Princess Nai Tai Tai. Her real name was Amelia Ruth, but hardly anyone knew that. She always used her stage name. She was quite an entertainer. In the twenties, she often played the Palace in New York. She would make her entrance wearing a full-length white ermine coat and say, "Hello, out there," in a throaty voice that sounded like Tallulah Bankhead's. When Ralph worked with her, he would come on stage in a tuxedo, his hair slicked back, looking almost as elegant as she did. A pool table was set at center stage with a big black curtain as a backdrop and a dozen mirrors were suspended at various angles above the table. Princess Nai Tai Tai stood to the side of the table and announced, "Ladies and gentlemen, Mr. Greenleaf, the greatest pocket billiard champion of all time, will now perform a series of intricate trick shots—your undivided attention if you please." Then Ralph ripped off the same trick shots he performed on the road, with the mirrors picking up every movement of the balls. It was quite an act, and Ralph was as much at home on the stage of the Palace as he was in a billiard academy. There were not many like him, in any field of endeavor, and something was lost from the game when he departed.

▲ ▲ ▲

With Greenleaf gone, Willie, who had already grown accustomed to the feel of the championship crown, was now being fitted with the mantle of all-time supremacy. Comparisons were being made between the fallen monarch and the one now reigning, who gave every evidence that the world might not yet have seen him at his best. They were measured against each other in every dimension: titles won and lost, margins of victory, length of runs, head-to-head meetings. Sports, after all, was one of those rare lines of work that yielded itself to definition—the verdict each time was rendered in the brickwork precision of numbers. However, the passing of generations had a way of blurring the lines of distinction. Greenleaf had won his first championship when Willie was only six years old, and although they crossed cues many times, Willie's star was in ascendance while Greenleaf's had begun to flicker and fade. In the end, it did not matter very much. If clear definition was the marrow of sports, it was the possibility of conjecture that provided the meat. It was enough to know for certain that pool's greatest champion had been succeeded by one who was worthy of the name, who was just now reaching the crest of his powers, and who carried himself with style and distinction.

Willie had, in the past decade, evolved from the mercurial young flash who won his first title in 1941 to a rather stately gentleman who had grown into his years with an elegant grace. He was thirty-seven years old now. His hair, prematurely gray, seemed to add a touch of sparkle to eyes that shone pleasantly when he was away from a pool table but that reflected the glint of cold gray steel when he was at work. For time had done nothing to blunt the edge of his desire. Achievement and acclaim had not the least bit softened his compulsive need to win each time he lifted his cue. He played each frame of every match with the pulsing intensity of a man who believed that the past was of no account and that success rested always on his next performance.

By 1950, Willie was a national celebrity. He had, in a way, outgrown the sport that bestowed the gift of fame upon him. His face was familiar and his name known to those who had never seen a pool table, who could not tell you how many balls were contained in a rack. National magazines that ordinarily shunned the coverage of sports devoted their pages to chronicling his life and achievements. Though basically a private man with little taste for bright lights or late hours, he was well-acquainted with the glitterati from the worlds of show business, sports, and politics. He had become, all things taken, a part of the fabric of American life. Still, he never quite saw himself as anything more than a guy who had to work hard for a living and who was better than most at the trade he had chosen.

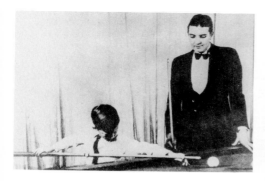

Seven-year-old child prodigy Willie Mosconi takes on world champion Ralph Greenleaf in 1920. *(Courtesy of Charles Ursitti)*

Nine-year-old Willie Mosconi is featured in the pages of the May 27, 1922, issue of the *Police Gazette*. *(Courtesy of Charlie Ursitti)*

Ralph Greenleaf reigned as world pocket billiard champion during much of the 1920s and 30s. *(Courtesy of Willie Mosconi)*

Ruth McGinnis, women's world pocket billiard champion, attracted national attention at age nine when she played young Willie Mosconi for the unofficial juvenile championship. *(Courtesy of Charlie Ursitti)*

Ralph Greenleaf and his wife, Princess Nai Tai Tai, were much a part of the Jazz Age culture during the roaring twenties. (*Courtesy of Charlie Ursitti*)

Willie looks over the lay of the table during the 1935 world championship tournament at the Pennsylvania Hotel in New York City. (*Courtesy of Charlie Ursitti*)

Willie Mosconi in his first championship tournament in 1933 at Chicago's Bensinger's billiard hall. (*Courtesy of Charlie Ursitti*)

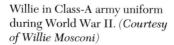

Willie in Class-A army uniform during World War II. (*Courtesy of Willie Mosconi*)

Willie congratulates Bob Hope on his receiving a Sportsmanship Award for his efforts in boosting the morale of the armed forces. (*Courtesy of Willie Mosconi*)

Neither Willie (left) nor his book on pocket billiards appears to be much help to puzzled comedian Jerry Colonna. (*Courtesy of Willie Mosconi*)

Willie (left) and Jimmy Caras prepare to decide the 1949 world championship. (*Courtesy of Charlie Ursitti*)

Onofrio Lauri, a flashy, hot-headed competitor from Brooklyn, gave Willie some tough matches but never won a title. (*Courtesy of Willie Mosconi*)

Willie (right) and Irving Crane before one of their championship matches. *(Courtesy of Willie Mosconi)*

George Kelly, one of the bevy of tournament players from Philadelphia, represented the Four Corners Billiard Parlor in Newark, N.J., in the 1941 championship tournament. *(Courtesy of Willie Mosconi)*

Bennie Allen, referee and former champion, looks on as Andrew Ponzi (left) and Willie Mosconi lag for break in a 1943 title match at Kling & Allen's in Kansas City, Mo. *(Courtesy of Charlie Ursitti)*

Cuing up for the 1946 world tournament. *Left to right:* Bennie Allen, Jimmy Caras, Willie Mosconi, Irving Crane, and Andrew Ponzi. *(Courtesy of Charlie Ursitti)*

Film star Van Johnson (center) gets some pointers from Jimmy Caras (left) and Willie Mosconi. *(Courtesy of Willie Mosconi)*

Willie offers some advice to the Mills Brothers vocal group. *(Courtesy of Willie Mosconi)*

Willie demonstrates one of his trick shots: 16 balls in one shot. *(Courtesy of Willie Mosconi)*

Willie jumps the cue ball from one table to another, making six balls on the second table. *(Courtesy of Willie Mosconi)*

Entertainers Phil Ford (center) and Mimi Hines (right) mug for the camera as Willie prepares to sink a chippie at Chicago's Palmer House Hotel. (*Courtesy of Willie Mosconi*)

Willie looks overmatched as he tries to guard former NBA star George Mikan. (*Courtesy of Willie Mosconi*)

The Mosconi family in the basement of their Haddon Heights, N.J., home in 1956. Candace and Billy are standing, while two-year-old Gloria sits on daddy's lap. (*Courtesy of Willie Mosconi*)

Flora Mosconi, Willie's wife, displays her technique to Willie and their seven-year-old daughter, Gloria. (*Courtesy of Willie Mosconi*)

Willie waits patiently as Howard Cosell has a word with Minnesota Fats before the great shootout between Willie and Minnesota Fats in 1978. (*Courtesy of Charlie Ursitti*)

Cuing up for the legendary stars competition in Las Vegas in 1982. *Left to right:* Babe Cranfield, Joe Balsis, Irving Crane, U. J. Puckett, Joe Russo, Jimmy Moore, Minnesota Fats, and Willie Mosconi. (*Courtesy of Willie Mosconi*)

Willie exchanges greetings with (from left) former hockey star Gordie Howe, Joe DiMaggio, Dave Hanlon, president of Resorts International in Atlantic City, and singer Andy Williams. (*Courtesy of Willie Mosconi*)

Paul Newman, Jackie Gleason, and Willie Mosconi on the set of the classic film *The Hustler*. (*Courtesy of Willie Mosconi*)

Willie is in the chips working as executive host at Ceasars Boardwalk Regency Hotel and Casino in Atlantic City. *(Courtesy of Charlie Ursitti)*

Omar Sharif (left) and Willie look on as Ronee Blakely lines up a shot on the set of *The Baltimore Bullet,* a 1979 film about high-stakes pool hustling. *(Courtesy of Willie Mosconi)*

Willie is in fine form, shooting in the low 80s at a golf tournament in Inverarry, Fla. *(Courtesy of Gloria Dickson)*

Tom Cruise received some helpful tips on the art of pocket billiards for Cruise's 1986 film *The Color of Money,* which was a sequel to *The Hustler. (Courtesy of Willie Mosconi)*

▲ ▲ ▲

The owners of Allinger's decided to honor Greenleaf by holding a match each year on March 15, the anniversary of his death, and awarding the Ralph Greenleaf Memorial Cup to the winner. The holder of the cup would defend it the following year against a top challenger, and anyone who won it three times in a row would gain permanent possession. The first such match was scheduled for March 20, the date on which Ralph and I were to have begun play, with a percentage of the proceeds going to Ralph's widow. Irving Crane was selected as my opponent, and I took six of the first eight blocks and won the match easily. But the world of pocket billiards hardly had time to adjust to the loss of Greenleaf when it suffered another setback.

Just a few days after the Memorial Cup was presented, Andrew Ponzi was stricken with another heart attack, and on April 11 he died in the same hospital in which Ralph had passed away. Even though we all knew how sick Andy was, it was still a terrible shock. For several months he had been aware that his playing days were over, and he was hoping to open a small business of some kind so that he could settle down and take life easy. He was only forty-seven years old, but he had lived a tough life. He was raised in an orphanage since the age of four, then as a teenager his right hand was almost crushed in a trolley car accident, and not long after that he was struck on the head by a rock falling from a building under construction and was injured rather badly. Then, once he turned pro, he spent most of his time on the road, as all of us did, and the steady grind of travel and intense competition takes more out of you than most people imagine.

The last time I played Ponzi was in January, a few months

before his final heart attack. We were in the midst of a ten-block exhibition match at Allinger's when I happened to have one of the best games of my life, while making perhaps the most difficult shot I ever made in competition. Ponzi had scratched on the break and I ran off 112 balls in rapid succession, but on my break shot I left the cue ball frozen against the pack. There seemed to be just two shaky combinations open—the four ball, which just didn't seem to sit exactly right, and the two ball, which, if I made it, could end in a scratch. The thirteen was perched near the far side pocket neatly shielded by the other racked balls. Normally, I would have played safe, but with a big lead and my title not at stake I decided to take a chance on it. I sent the cue ball around the rack, angled it off the far rail and into the thirteen ball, which dropped cleanly in the pocket. The hardest part was visualizing the shot, figuring out just where the ball was going to go. The rest was easy. I picked off the next twelve balls to close out the game 125 to minus 1. Andy shook my hand after the game and kidded me about getting lucky on the thirteen ball. He was a warm, good-natured guy, and I knew I would miss him.

With Greenleaf and Ponzi gone, it was as if an era had ended. The old pros had largely disappeared from the scene, and no one had come along to replace them. Those who were coming into prominence at the time didn't seem to be much better than ordinary. Yet, there was no shortage of people who enjoyed playing the game. The Second World War had produced a great number of new enthusiasts. By some estimates, there were as many as ten million billiard players in the country in the early fifties, but the quality wasn't there. To most of the newcomers, pool was more of a social pastime than a sport to be taken seriously. The number of first-rate billiard halls—places like Bensinger's and Allinger's, where you could watch and learn from the best around—was dwindling. Postwar rents had risen drastically and a lot of the good rooms could no longer afford to stay in business. Some of them closed, others added bowling alleys, bars, and pinball machines and were converted into recreation and entertainment centers. Serious billiard players do not ply their trade amidst the clatter of bowling pins or the intrusive clang of pinball machines. The reality was that pool was on the way to becoming a popular, leisure-time activity, and top professional players are not likely to emerge from such an environment.

Ironically, the economic prosperity of the fifties did not help the game either. Sports like golf and tennis, which in the twenties and thirties were played almost exclusively by the well-to-do, were now accessible to a growing segment of the population. Youngsters who in earlier days might have spent their Saturday mornings shooting pool were now out practicing their ground strokes or learning to drive from the tee. These sports also had become more lucrative for the pros. In the old days, there were only a handful of golfers who made as much money as the leading billiard players. But in the fifties, especially once television got into it, the purses grew and golf became more attractive to professionals.

All in all, the future of billiards did not appear to be very bright. Crane was my only rival of reputation, and a challenge match was arranged for January 1951 as a prelude to the round-robin tournament to be held a month later, for the fourth straight year, at the Navy Pier in Chicago. We played twenty blocks of 150 points, the first ten at Allinger's, the final ten at Kling & Allen's in Kansas City. Irv led the match just briefly. He won the opening block 150–61 and held a 109–20 advantage in the second. But at that point I found my stroke.

I ran 130 and out and from then on I was never headed. With three more runs of over one hundred, I left Philadelphia with a lead of 1,500–1,135 and closed the match with a margin of almost seven hundred points. The victory earned me one thousand dollars, 60 percent of the contestants' share of the gate, and a bye in the tournament.

Surprisingly, Crane did not win the national title in Chicago. It went to a relative newcomer named Joe Canton, from Upstate New York. Irv finished second and the quartet was rounded out by the Canadian champion, George Chenier. It was an easy tournament for me. I won all six of my matches and closed out by defeating Chenier 150–45 and Canton 150–15. Since Crane had finished second, he normally would have been given first crack at the title, but I had just beaten him a month earlier and the promoters didn't think a rematch would be very attractive. By the same token, neither Chenier nor Canton had made a strong showing. So, for the time being at least, there did not appear to be a serious challenger for my title.

With no championship action in sight, Brunswick, which did not welcome the prospect of paying me a monthly stipend to sit at home, booked me, along with some of their other players, on a tour of air force camps all over the world. In those postwar years, the United States still maintained heavily manned bases wherever there had been a theater of war, and we visited most of them. We went to Germany, Austria, North Africa, France, and Japan. I put on exhibitions and played the servicemen, and we had a wonderful time. "Hey, soldier," I would say, "how much money have you got in your pocket?" Then I would spot them balls and offer all kinds of propositions that looked like a sure thing but that they couldn't possibly win, and I showed them what it was like to get hustled. Of course no money ever changed hands; it was just entertainment and they seemed to enjoy it. All told, I was away about three or four months during the spring and summer, and when I returned there was still not much action.

The BCA abandoned the Chicago Outdoors Show and elected to hold the 1952 championship tournament in Boston. I don't know why, because if there was a billiard town in the United States worse than St. Louis, it had to be Boston. Perhaps they thought that bringing the world's top players to a city that hadn't seen much championship pool would generate some excitement. Whatever the reasoning, the tournament was set for early April, but in March I decided to attend to a piece of business on my own.

There was a pool hustler of some repute in Washington, D.C., who went by the name of Rags Fitzpatrick. He was part of a subculture that received more attention than it was worth and, so far as I am concerned, soiled the reputation of pocket billiards. To the public, they were heralded as colorful characters who could work wonders on a pool table, but the most colorful thing about them was the names they were known by—Cornbread Red, Boston Shorty, Tuscaloosa Squirrel, and of course New York Fats, who later became Chicago Fats, and still later Minnesota Fats. They didn't adopt their aliases without reason. They preferred anonymity because they made their living hustling people they knew they could beat, taking money from unsuspecting marks who had no chance of winning. Then they used to go around crowing that they could beat any of the tournament players because the pros played for fun while the hustlers played for money. It was a twisted piece of logic to contend that people whose livelihood depended on their ability to defeat other professionals in a structured competition were only playing for fun, but that was about all you could expect from a hustler. The truth was that there wasn't one of them who, on his best day, could have beaten any of the top tournament players, which is why they rarely chose to compete.

Rags, however, decided to take the plunge and entered the elimination tournaments in 1952. He managed to win the sectional but lost a playoff to Babe Cranfield in the eastern regionals. He was so encouraged by his performance that he started blowing off steam about how good he was and about how he could "beat Mosconi any time, any place." The word spread pretty quickly, and I took him on in a ten-block match and won nine of the ten. I hated losing even the one block, but I must confess that Rags played a pretty fair game. As a matter of fact, he got himself invited to compete in the nine-man round-robin in Boston, filling out a field that included Crane, Canton, Chenier, and a number of other new faces, most prominently "Cowboy" Jimmy Moore, from Albuquerque, New Mexico, who remained a leading contender for years without ever winning the title.

I waltzed through that tournament with little trouble. I set a low-game record of two innings while beating Chenier 150–2 and won my first eight games to clinch the championship before losing my last match to Crane. For the third straight year, Crane finished second, and you could see that it was beginning to get to him. Since winning the title in 1946, he had finished second to me in three tournaments and lost all three of the challenge matches between us. I think there were times when he might have preferred to finish third or fourth rather than be runner-up again. Always the bridesmaid and never the bride is a condition that no athlete can endure without a measure of grief.

▲ ▲ ▲

Crane, of course, was painfully aware of his circumstances, and he was not without insight into the nature of the problem. In an interview after his second-place finish in 1952, he put his finger to the pulse.

"I've sat down many times and tried to figure it out," he said. "There's not a thing he [Mosconi] can do on the table that I can't do. It must be psychological. You know, when he gets you down, that's when he tramples on you. You get so you're afraid to leave him any sort of a shot, and you start to play him instead of playing the balls on the table. I have to fight against that. And I know I'm too soft. I find that unconsciously, when I have a guy beaten I begin to let up on him a little. From now on I'm going to be like he is. When I've got him down, I'll kick him. You've got to have that blood lust."

But Crane didn't quite have it, and it is a trait not easily developed in one's fourth decade. Few athletes had the "blood lust" that had been part of Willie's nature since his youth. His instincts had been honed on the hard rock of necessity. Many athletes hated to lose; Willie, from the very start, knew that defeat was a luxury he could not afford.

"I had to win," he said. "I had to support my family. Times were tough, my father was sick, my mother wasn't feeling well, and I was the only one who could bring home the money. Those circumstances toughened you. Most of your greatest boxers came from poor backgrounds, didn't they? When you have to win to eat, you learn to play the game a little differently, and you can't turn it off. If I had my own grandmother at the table, I'd beat her 150–0 if I possibly could."

Crane never had to win to eat. There was no one who questioned his competitive desire. He had an athlete's pride and all the skills, but he had never played a game of pool in which the stake was greater than his collateral. So he could never quite muster the frenetic urgency that Willie brought to the table. For Willie, the prospect of losing unleashed the demons of his deepest dread. Ralph Greenleaf was renowned for being most dangerous when he was behind. To Willie, the score never mattered. He played always with a quickened intensity that was just the other side of despair. Any opponent, at any stage of a game, was deemed a threat he could not abide. He often said that he had learned to hate any man he was playing, but it was not the man he hated, it was the specter of defeat that the man embodied, the haunting recollection of his youth that bread might yet be snatched from his table.

CHAPTER

In 1953, San Francisco was chosen as the site of the world tournament for the first time in almost fifty years. It was a beautiful city with its steep hills and quaint architecture set against a backdrop of mountains and ocean, and I arrived there in precisely the right mood to enjoy it, for accompanying me was my newly acquired bride, Flora. We had gotten married a month earlier, on February 11, and cut short our Florida honeymoon to drive leisurely across the country to San Francisco. After my first rather unhappy experience at wedlock, I had determined that if I ever married again I would choose more wisely and that it would be for keeps. Now, more than forty years later, I can say with conviction that I made good on that pledge.

I had been introduced to Flora by a cousin of mine about a year and a half earlier and we navigated our way through a courtship that was constantly interrupted by my trips across the country. However, Flora managed to overcome that obstacle, and she found a way to catch me even as I was on the run. Her maiden name was Marchini, and I always suspected that the reason she married me was that the change of her name would not require too great an adjustment.

▲ ▲ ▲

"The minute we met I knew we were going to get married," says Flora Mosconi. "I remember coming home and saying to my brother, 'I'm going to marry Willie Mosconi. Did you ever hear of him?' My brother said, 'Sure, I didn't know you knew him.' I said, 'I just met him tonight.' My brother got hysterical laughing. He said, 'You just met him, how do you know he wants to marry you?' 'I just know,' I said.

"I was in my mid-twenties at the time, living at home with my parents, and I worked for the telephone company in Philadelphia. Willie's cousin worked there too; we got to be pretty friendly and she set up a double date. She told me her cousin was Willie Mosconi, but I had never heard of him. I don't think I had ever seen a pool table at that time. We went to dinner and a movie, and I just knew we were going to get married. He was handsome and very gracious and well-mannered, and I could tell that he took to me too. I felt that he probably had never met anyone like me before. I was what I suppose you would call an old-fashioned type of girl, still living at home and family-oriented. Traveling from town to town the way he did, I figured he was accustomed to meeting a different kind of woman, with more expensive tastes and a leaning toward the night life. I was never that way and neither was Willie. Even with all his travel, he was basically a stay-at-home type. He had two young children and he was interested in someone who would make a good wife and a good mother.

"My instincts turned out to be right. On our second date, Willie asked me if I was seeing anybody else, and

I told him I wasn't. 'Well,' he said, 'I want you to be my girl.'

" 'Wait a minute,' I said, 'how do you mean that? I can't go traveling with you.'

" 'No, no,' he said. 'I don't mean that. I just don't want you to go out with anyone else.'

" 'Well,' I said, 'what are your intentions?'

" 'My intentions are honorable' he said.

"I said, 'Okay, as long as I know that.'

"So that was it. It was an unusual courtship, what with Willie being on the road so much, but we went out quite often when he was home. We went to the movies and ball games, and occasionally to the fights, which I never cared for very much. But during all that time, I never got to see him play until we went to San Francisco. Even then, he told me I would bring him luck but he didn't want me to be a spectator. He said it would make him nervous. I finally got to watch him in his last game, against Jimmy Moore, because by then he had clinched the championship."

▲ ▲ ▲

The San Francisco tournament, which was played in the Downtown Bowl, was a nine-man round-robin, and I pitched a shutout, winning all eight of my games. Caras came out of his so-called retirement to compete for the first time in four years, and Crane was there, and so was a relative newcomer to championship play by the name of Luther Lassiter. Lassiter, who came from Elizabeth City, North Carolina, was one of those players from the South who moved up when the smaller tables came into vogue. He was basically a nine-ball player, but he could shoot a respectable game of straight pool, and I had played him quite often when my exhibition tours took me to North Carolina. He was a nice guy, soft-spoken, a real southern-gentleman type. Everyone called him Wimpy, after the character from the Popeye comic strip, because he seemed to eat nothing but hamburgers. In all the years I knew him, I don't think I ever saw him sit down to a regular meal. He became a dominant player in the sixties, after I had retired, but in 1953 he wasn't quite ready for that kind of competition.

It was against Lassiter that I clinched the championship. I ran seventy-nine balls off the break, but then Wimpy stepped to the table and reeled off a long run of his own. He made thirty-three straight but then missed position on a break shot and had to use the hand bridge to try a shot in the far corner pocket. The ball wobbled there and hung, the cue ball scattered the rack, and I ran seventy-one and out in a matter of minutes. I equaled my best-game record of two innings, won my fourth straight tournament and my eleventh title, putting me just two behind Ralph Greenleaf. There were some who said I was now shooting better than I ever had before. One writer described my finishing run as having the "aspects of a blizzard" because of the speed with which I made my shots. The following day, with Flora watching, I mopped up against Jimmy Moore to finish the tournament undefeated.

When the tournament ended, we headed back home, and I was booked to play a series of exhibition matches with Caras and Crane in Washington, Philadelphia, and New York. However, we barely had time to settle into our home in Haverford, Pennsylvania, a suburb of Philadelphia, when we became enmeshed in a domestic hassle. Out of nowhere, it seemed, my ex-wife surfaced and demanded shared custody of the children. We had hardly heard from her in the past eight years, and she had shown little interest in the kids, but when she heard I had remarried she decided she wanted to be a mother again. Billy was nearly twelve at the time and Candace was nine, and they didn't even know who their mother was. For the past eight years they had been living with my sister and now they were with Flora and me, and we were all looking forward to establishing a more normal family situation. Flora and the kids got along well together. Unlike Ann, she was a maternal type of woman, and you could tell from the start that she would be a wonderful mother. Ann, who was still living in Michigan, asked for the right to take them with her occasionally and to obtain a greater degree of custody over time. It was the last thing they needed, I thought, to have their lives fragmented just when they were acquiring some real stability. I refused her request, she sued for custody, and we embarked upon a court fight that lasted three months. It was finally settled when the judge asked the children whom they preferred to live with. They said they wanted to live with me, and the judge granted their wish and denied Ann any custodial rights at all.

▲ ▲ ▲

Bill Mosconi, now a development officer at Drew University, in Madison, New Jersey, recalls the scene vividly.

"The judge called Candy and me into his chambers and said, 'If you had a choice to live with either your mother or your father, which would you choose?'

"I said, 'Wow, I don't even know who that lady is. I don't think I ever saw her before. I don't want to leave my father.'

"The judge then asked me if my father had told me to say anything, and I told him he hadn't. In all those years, my father never said an unkind word about my natural mother. He very rarely mentioned her at all. The judge said that at that point our testimony was all he needed, and he awarded custody to my father.

"My natural mother had based her claim on the fact that my father was away so much of the time, but I didn't understand what all the fuss was about. I guess you adjust to those things, because it never seemed to me that my childhood was anything but normal. I had been living with my aunt and cousins, and we were a close family. And of course when my father came home it was wonderful. Once we got past his inspection—he always checked to see that every inch of our bodies was scrubbed clean— we had a great time with him. He always brought home big boxes of toys and goodies and spent a lot of time with us when he was home. In the meantime, I played with the other kids in the neighborhood and was well taken care of. Then, when he married Flora, it was even better. She adopted us legally and was as loving a mother as anyone could ask for.

"It was just around this time that I became aware of what my father was doing when he was away. I didn't know he was a pool player, and I certainly had no idea that he was world champion. He never boasted about it and was very unassuming with respect to his accomplishments. Even when I had learned a little about it, he always tried to play down its importance. He took me to watch him play only once or twice at Allinger's, but I began to follow his career on my own. When he was playing in a tournament I used to get up early in the morning and run out and get the paper to see how he had done. I remember doing that even when he was playing in Philadelphia because he would get home after

I was asleep and then he slept late in the morning and I couldn't wait until he got up to find out the results.

"I sometimes asked him why he didn't teach me anything about pool. He said, 'Because that's the last thing in the world I'd want you to do. I wouldn't want you to live this kind of life, on the road all the time, having to deal with that kind of pressure. I want you to get an education and associate with a better class of people. I don't want you hanging around pool halls and betting on the games.' He hated gambling and always discouraged it. I think he even convinced himself that when he was young and supported his family by playing for money he was not really gambling. The way he looked at it was that instead of a sponsor putting up the purse, he and his opponent put up the purse between them. He never felt that he was gambling when he bet on himself.

"There was a great deal of irony in his attitude toward the game he played. He had a fierce pride in his ability and was utterly devoted to excellence, yet he always seemed to feel that what he did was not all that important. It was a business like any other and he worked hard at it to support his family in the best way possible. It is curious to think that someone who was better than anyone else at what he did would have preferred to be doing something else. What are the chances that he might have excelled in the same way at another line of work?"

▲ ▲ ▲

My legal entanglements did not interfere with my schedule or affect my game very much. After the San Francisco tournament, I took a few weeks off, then hit the highway again, playing a round of exhibitions in the Midwest. On April 22, I broke the straight-run record of 309 that I shared with Irving Crane, running 322 during an exhibition in Platteville, Wisconsin. I don't remember the name of the guy I was playing, but I can still picture him, a fairly tall, heavyset fellow with a ruddy complexion. I was conscious of the old mark as I approached it, but the table was wide open and I knew I would have no trouble exceeding 309. The new record did not last long, however.

In November, on Friday the thirteenth, I ran 365 while playing Nixon Jones in Wilmington, North Carolina. I knew Nixon fairly well. He was the owner of the establishment, and I had played there quite often when I was in that part of the country. What was most interesting about that game was that I made the run off my own break. I called the one ball, at the front of the triangle, in the left side pocket. It's a shot that can be made maybe one time in three, but you can never take a chance on it in a tournament. What you do is hit the cue ball high and drive it into the right side of the one ball. If you hit the cue ball in the center, it will force the object ball forward; if you hit it high, with force-follow, the one will carom and bounce back toward the left side. On this occasion, the ball dropped in the pocket and I went on from there, without missing, for more than an hour and a half. It's a long time to stay on your feet, concentrating, walking around the table without taking a break. People often don't realize how great a part fatigue can play in a long game of pool. It's a physically, as well as mentally, stressful occupation. In the months ahead, however, I would be given ample time to gather my resources.

For the first time in more than a decade, the Billiard Congress of America sanctioned no championship matches in 1954. No tournament had been scheduled and no challenge match was deemed sufficiently attractive to invite public notice. So the BCA chose to call a one-year hiatus and see if a new challenger might emerge. It was a decision that did not sit well with a number of players and promoters.

Early that year, Crane, along with Marty Ross, the manager of Allinger's, decided it would be a good idea to run their own championship competition, with or without the blessings of the BCA. They scheduled an eleven-day tournament, to begin on March 15, with nine players competing. Of course I was expected to take part, as the defending champion, but when I learned that the tournament was not sanctioned by the BCA I turned down the invitation. So did Joe Procita, who had finished second in the 1953 competition. The BCA, after all, was the sport's governing body, and it seemed to me that without its sanction the tournament was a maverick affair with no official standing. I told that to Ross and Crane, but they saw things differently. Crane, who was the chief representative of the Better Billiard Players of America, the equivalent of a players' organization before the days of athletes' unions, had queried the BCA the previous fall about its plans to hold a tournament. Shortly, he received a response from John Canelli, the secretary-treasurer, explaining that the decision to forgo the tournament was a financial one, based on an insufficient flow of funds. Crane was not satisfied with the explanation and elected to stage his own competition among seven players—himself, Joe Canton, Erwin Rudolph, Jimmy Moore, Luther Lassiter, Mike Eufemia, and a newcomer who went by the name of Snooks Perlstein.

Crane and Ross must have understood that they did not have much of a championship event without the champion competing because they tried several times to coax me to enter, but my position was straightforward: It did not make

sense—either professionally or financially—for me to compete unless the BCA sponsored the tournament. For where
was the purse to come from? Ordinarily, the Congress put up
about $40,000 in tournament prize money. The defending
champion would be assured at least $1,000 just for taking part.
In their maverick tournament, each player was putting up
$150 of his own money to ensure his appearance. Then, after
the first $1,050 in admission fees was collected, each contes-
tant would receive $150 toward his expenses, with the winner
getting 25 percent of whatever was left over from the gate
receipts. If the gate wasn't large enough, you could end up
playing for nothing. Did that make sense? I was the defending
champion, I was earning more than $20,000 a year represent-
ing Brunswick. Why would I enter an unofficial tournament
that might not even cover my expenses?

Ross was particularly irate at my refusal to play. "What if
the BCA doesn't hold a tournament for twenty years," he said,
"does that mean that Mosconi remains the champion without
playing?"

That remark brought things to a boil. Ross made it sound
as if I were trying to protect my title by remaining idle, and
he knew well enough that I never ducked a contender. I
responded that his tournament didn't count for a row of lopsided eight balls. "It was the equivalent," I said, "of two
stumblebums getting together and challenging [Rocky] Marciano for the world's heavyweight boxing championship. When
Marciano pays no attention to them they go out in the back
alley and fight it out. Then the winner says he's champion."

Just to make sure they got the point, I issued a challenge
to the entire field. I offered to play them one at a time,
in succession, fifteen hundred points each, for twenty-five
hundred dollars a man, with all receipts going to charity. But

there were no takers. They were content to go ahead with their little tournament and crown their own champion. That was just the beginning of the hostilities. Before they were over, the matter would be before a judge in U.S. District Court.

The tournament went ahead as scheduled, but I didn't stay around to see the results. I was playing some exhibitions in the Midwest, and in one night I captured more headlines than the seven "title contenders" did in a week and a half. On March 19, in Springfield, Ohio, I ran 526 balls, a record that still stands. I was playing a two-hundred-point match against an amateur by the name of Earl Bruney in the East High Billiard Club. He made three balls off the break, then I ran two hundred and just kept going. The run took two hours and ten minutes, which means that over that span I averaged four balls a minute. I finally missed a difficult cut shot, but by that time I was weary; it was almost a relief to have it come to an end. There were about three hundred people in the audience, and one of them was an attorney who prepared an affidavit attesting to the validity of my claim to a new record. A few days later, the BCA gave it its stamp of approval.

I don't know what the long run was in the Philadelphia tournament, but Luther Lassiter came away the winner, with Crane and Jimmy Moore tied for second. The BCA promptly issued a statement to the effect that the Philadelphia tournament was not a championship event and that "Mosconi will not be read out of his title." I offered the press my own statement, saying, "I have defended my title more times than any living player, and I'll put it on the table anytime the BCA asks me to." By this time, however, Crane had apparently placed himself beyond the jurisdiction of the Congress. He responded by announcing his intention to challenge Lassiter for the world championship. At that point, I made a few comments of my own, repeating my original challenge and offering a personal one to Crane.

"Lassiter is of no consequence," I said. "I've beaten him repeatedly, once seven times straight in his hometown. Crane was the man behind the tournament. He got it up to further his own ambition and then couldn't win it. I am the recognized world champion and there can be no new champion without first reckoning with me. If Mr. Crane doubts it, let him put up five thousand dollars and I'll match it. Then we'll play twenty-five hundred points on a winner-take-all basis for the title, anytime, anywhere; he can name it. As for the others, I'll take them all on, one at a time, for fifteen hundred dollars, winner take all. What do they say to that?"

Crane, of course, had already been rebuffed by the BLA in his attempts to arrange a tournament. "It appeared to me, therefore," Crane said, "that the BCA was not interested in professional tournaments. So in December I made several trips to New York and Philadelphia trying to organize the players. I listed the top fifteen with Mosconi at the top of the list, and I felt the list offered the most in drawing power, ability, appearance, and so forth. We decided to hold the championship at Allinger's in Philadelphia, which has been one of the best sites for more than fifty years. Marty Ross, who runs the place with his sons, welcomed the event. In January, Mosconi was contacted but refused to play on grounds it was not sanctioned by the Billiard Congress. As the start of the tourney neared in March, Ross telephoned Mosconi in Georgia, but again he refused to play. . . . We wound up with several of the better players. Lassiter won the title, with Jimmy Moore and myself tied for second place. Moore came all the way from New Mexico to compete. We asked the

Billiard Congress, prior to the tournament, to sanction it. They refused—giving us no good reason. . . . So far as Mosconi playing Procita [for the title] is concerned, well, Mosconi could play Procita ninety times and never lose a match. Don't get me wrong. I'm not belittling Mosconi's ability. The man is a helluva player. Frankly, if it weren't for him, I'd have won more championships."

As for my challenge, he responded: "He challenged me once before to a five-thousand-dollar bet. That is ridiculous. I'll play him for five hundred dollars, but not five thousand. I simply haven't got that kind of money. But he can meet me right now—I'm ready—at fifteen hundred points, for five hundred dollars, and we'll split the take 60–40."

It was an empty challenge, because Crane was already booked to play Lassiter for his so-called title on February 21 at Allinger's. The time and place were carefully chosen, for on that same day I was scheduled to defend the BCA title against Procita at Earl Newby's, just five blocks away on Chestnut Street. On the same day the matches were to begin, I filed a $200,000 suit with the U.S. District Court requesting that it order Lassiter and Crane to "cease and desist" from calling themselves champions and to enjoin Allinger's from billing the match between the two as a "world champion pocket billiards match." The suit asked actual damages of $50,000 and punitive damages of $150,000 on the grounds that the defendants "have conspired to deceive the public through rumors and statements that the plaintiff constantly refuses to accept challenges."

Meanwhile, when the Crane-Lassiter match moved from Philadelphia to Crane's home turf in Rochester, Procita and I moved with them to Keogh's Academy, which was not far from where they were playing. I wanted to fight fire with fire and give Crane a dose of his own medicine. I put on a real show up there. I won the opening block 150–7 in two innings and ran 150 and out in the second. Someone calculated that during one string of one hundred balls I rolled the cue a total of only 375 feet, just over three feet a shot. I also cut the pie a little. Borrowing a crowd-pleasing gesture from Ralph Greenleaf, I would place my finger on the spot where I expected the cue ball to come to rest after a shot and then put the ball within an inch of where I had pointed. The spectators loved it. I won the match easily, and to no one's surprise, Crane had little trouble with Lassiter.

While in Rochester, I extended another invitation to Crane in the local press. "I would like to post a certified check for one thousand dollars to challenge Mr. Crane," I said. "So far all he has put up is conversation. I want to embarrass and taunt him into accepting this challenge. I am willing to leave all the arrangements in Crane's hands. If he can get a suitable spot here in Rochester, it will be fine. Let's have done with all this talk and get down to action."

About three weeks after it was filed, Crane and Lassiter responded to my suit. They contended that the agreements that players signed with the BCA before entering a tournament stipulated that the championship was good for one year or until the next tournament was held, whichever came first. Therefore, since I had won the title in March 1953, it would become vacant a year later if not defended. Of course even if that were so, their own tournament was held in February, not March of 1954.

In any event, the matter would soon become moot, because Peter Tyrrell, the general manager of the Philadelphia Arena, proposed a four-man, double round-robin, sanctioned by the Congress, to be held on six nights beginning April 16. In addition to Crane and myself, the field was to include Erwin Rudolph and Jimmy Caras. By some bizarre twist of logic, Caras, who had competed only once in the past five years, and lost, had also laid claim to the title. His reasoning was that he had won the crown on a five by ten foot table and never defended it on such a table because the four-and-a-half-by-nines were put into use the following year. How that would make him a defending champion on the smaller table was beyond my powers of deduction. Caras had voluntarily retired after winning the title in 1949. He came out of retirement in 1953, participated in the championships that year, and in doing so he acknowledged, it seemed to me, that the championship was decided on whatever size table was used. His claim made little sense, but it made for good publicity to stage a tournament in which three of the four participants claimed to be champion. Tyrrell was enthusiastic about the prospects. "I believe championships in all sports should be decided on the playing field," he said, "and I believe the four should get together and settle the title." His enthusiasm, it might be noted, was not dampened by the fact that the Arena could seat as many as four thousand spectators within viewing distance of the table.

The publicity no doubt had the desired effect because attendance was good and interest seemed to be heightened, at least for the time, by the controversy over who owned the title. As fate would have it, Crane and I each completed our schedules with records of 5–1, necessitating a playoff. I don't remember ever wanting to win a single game of billiards as much as I wanted that one, but it wasn't to be. Right from the start, the game developed a rhythm that was not to my liking. We each played safety after safety. It's hard to believe, but at the end of twenty-one innings, I led by a score of minus 1 to minus 5.

That's a little like having a 3–2 score at halftime of a basketball game. The pace of a game and who sets it can be critical to the outcome, and here I allowed Crane to set the tempo. I probably should have taken a chance at breaking the game open but, uncharacteristically, I let Crane's caution seep into my own style. He had had a number of long runs in the tournament, and I suppose I was wary of leaving too much of an opening.

In the twenty-second inning, Crane broke only the second rack of the match and ran three balls. I followed with a cluster of twenty-seven before scratching. Then Crane got hot and ran twenty-eight, fourteen, and twelve in consecutive innings. Five frames later, he put together a string of fifty-five to take a 104–40 lead. I had one more chance, but I scratched after clicking off forty-eight balls, and Crane closed out with an unfinished run of forty-six. The final score was 150–87. It was a bitter defeat for me, but there was nothing I could do except shake his hand and wait until the fall when I would get a chance to meet him in an extended challenge match.

My loss of the title was leavened that month by the birth of a daughter, Gloria, who arrived just a few days before the tournament opened. Billy was twelve at the time and Candy was nine, and with a newborn baby, Flora and I presided over a cheerful, bustling household. I stayed home for a while, to help out and enjoy the children, before hitting the highway again. I played my usual round of exhibitions in the usual places, but my mind was mostly on my rematch with Crane. I wanted the title back and, with each passing month, my taste for revenge grew sharper.

CHAPTER

Although I had lost two tournaments to Crane, I had defeated him in each of our other meetings, four times in tournaments and by wide margins in three head-to-head title matches. In fact, since losing my first challenge match to Ponzi in 1943, I had won nine in row, so I had reason to feel confident about my showdown with Crane. The format would be fairly standard: ten blocks of 150 points; play continuing until a player reaches a plateau that is a multiple of 150; first man to get fifteen hundred points wins. The match was to be played over five days at Allinger's, two blocks a day—one in the afternoon and one in the evening. When we opened, on Monday, November 28, Crane and I shook hands, but neither of us was smiling. Crane would have no cause to smile for the rest of the week.

I won the first two blocks by a total of 300–186, but I was just getting warmed up. On Tuesday afternoon, I ran 150 and out in the fourth inning; that night I chalked up another four-inning victory, this time by a score of 150–15. At the end of the first two days I had amassed a lead of four hundred points. Crane made use of the continuous play rule to make up some ground in the fifth block, winning it 235–150. But I stretched my lead in the evening session, with a 150 to minus 1 victory and led the match by 900–434. On Thursday I won both blocks

by a total of 300–157 and swept again on the final day, 300–85.
The final score was 1,500–676. I had more than doubled
Crane's total while winning nine of the ten blocks.

The victory was as satisfying as any of my career. Pyschologi-
cally, I needed not only to win but to win decisively, for now
I felt that the issue of who was champion was finally settled.
Crane, I thought, would not be looking for a rematch anytime
soon, and I settled back to enjoy the holidays with my family.
It was a period of relative ease and contemplation for me. I
felt I had reached something of a plateau in my career. Since
1941 I had held the title in twelve of the past fourteen years
and either won or defended it successfully sixteen times. I
was forty-two years old now, the fifties were half over, and
the future did not look exceptionally bright for the trade I had
chosen.

▲ ▲ ▲

The decade of the fifties was, in its own quiet way, a
hinge in time. It was a transitional decade, coming as it
did after ten years of Depression, five years of war, and
a brief period of recovery, and serving as an intermission
before the wild, helter-skelter bullrush of the sixties. It
was in the fifties that the landscape of America shifted
more dramatically and with longer-lasting effect than at
any time since the Industrial Revolution when an agrar-
ian society packed its bags and headed for the thumping
drumbeat of big-city streets. Now, with automobile en-
gines humming, the gray, concrete canyons of the cities
were left behind in an odyssey to the suburbs—sprawling
patches of green lawns, shopping malls, drive-in the-
aters, and highways that cut like scars across the face of
towns and villages that, ten years earlier, could not be

found on a map. It was a quiet time, to all appearances. College campuses were occupied by what became known as the Silent Generation. A devotion to bedrock values brought with it what looked like a new stability. The country needed a rest, and to the casual eye, it seemed to be getting one. But America, without really knowing it, was sleepwalking through a revolution.

Everything changed in the fifties: the way we traveled, the way we shopped, the way we washed our clothes and cooked our food, the way we entertained ourselves. Television had come to the marketplace and with its advent, nothing stayed the same. Sports underwent a particularly radical transformation. All the big-league sta-diums and arenas were located in the maws of the cities. Few were within easy access of highways and virtually none had facilities for parking. Thus, with games often available at the twist of a dial, attendance at ball parks began to slip. Only New York and Chicago were still able to support more than one major-league franchise.

The games people played also took on a new texture. Postwar prosperity had spread the nation's wealth across a greater swath of the population than at any time in its history. Throughout the suburbs, new country clubs were being built to accommodate the new arrivals, and each was complete with a manicured golf course and freshly laid tennis courts. Once the preserve of a select cadre of the socially elite, sports such as tennis and golf were now becoming the property of the social climbers. Unlike billiards, they were played outdoors on sunlit afternoons, in an atmosphere that glistened with the aura of success and achievement. Young businessmen on the rise closed their deals during leisurely rounds of customer-golf. Not many such deals were likely to be sealed in a billiard hall.

The game of billiards, to the extent that it was still played, had become something of a social pastime. Tables were often sprinkled through sprightly decorated recreation halls that also offered bowling and Ping-Pong. The game had begun to lose the hard edge that had given it a life and color of its own since the early part of the century. Pool, like boxing, was a sport that seemed to produce its best during hard times. Now, amidst the economic boom of the fifties, it appeared to be on a slow track headed for oblivion, and its undisputed champion was of a mind to begin weighing his options.

▲ ▲ ▲

Immediately after regaining the title I offered to take on all prospective contenders regardless of their ranking. Then, I said, I would like to challenge Harold Worst for the three-cushion championship he inherited when Willie Hoppe retired. The first to accept my offer was Jimmy Caras. Jimmy, who was forty-six years old at the time, was selling bowling and billiard equipment in the Philadelphia area. He had a wife and three children to support, and the days when Brunswick maintained a large stable of players who toured the country giving exhibitions were long gone. So we scheduled a rather lengthy match, beginning at the end of January and continuing through most of February, forty-two blocks to be played in Philadelphia, Washington, Milwaukee, Rockford, Illinois, and Chicago, finishing up in Detroit.

It was not much of a contest. Caras had been playing infrequently since coming out of retirement, and he was not in his best stroke. I took an early lead in Philadelphia and continued to pull away. I swept all ten blocks in Chicago while outscoring Jimmy 1,500–577. I also established two new records, running 151 balls in the second inning of one block and averaging 21.1 balls an inning for the ten-block series. By the time we got to Detroit, the outcome was academic. I closed out the match with more than a two-to-one margin, 6,300–3,007. It was a milestone for me. Winning the championship for the thirteenth year equaled Ralph Greenleaf's achievement. Only Alfredo De Oro, who won his first title in 1887, exceeded that number, but De Oro had played almost his entire career under single-rack rules, before 14.1 continuous became the official championship game. So Greenleaf and I now shared what might be called the modern-day record.

Still, I had no intention of hiding my prize from the competition. No sooner had I defeated Caras than I agreed to put the title on the line against Jimmy Moore in an eighteen-hundred-point, twelve-game contest starting March 15 in his home town of Albuquerque. Moore did not fare any better than Caras had. I again more than doubled his score, winning 1,800–879. The two matches—a total of forty-four blocks in less than two months—served as a tuneup for an eight-man tournament to be held in April in Kinston, North Carolina. The Kinston tournament would be a memorable one, even historic, in several respects; it would mark the end of an era.

The tournament was a double round-robin, with each contestant meeting every other player twice. In addition to myself, the field was made up of Crane, Moore, Luther Lassiter, Rags Fitzpatrick, Mike Eufemia, Rudolph, and a new arrival to championship play, Richard Riggie. I opened with wins over Rudolph and Riggie, then blanked Eufemia 150–0. Lassiter gave me a bit of a tussle in my fourth match, but I won it 150–141. I followed that with successive victories over

Moore, Crane, and Lassiter to close out the first round of games undefeated. Beginning the second round, I easily toppled Rudolph and Riggie again but once more had my hands full with Lassiter. I held a commanding lead of 146–72 when Luther got hot and reeled off seventy-three in a row before missing a difficult shot. I pocketed the last four balls for my tenth straight win.

The next day, I had an easier time of it, beating Eufemia 150 to minus 1. That assured me of at least a tie for the title, and I clinched it in my next match, against Eufemia. My thirteenth straight win, a decisive 150–52 decision over Crane, established a record for consecutive victories in tournament play. I needed one more to finish with a perfect slate, and I got it in grand style, running 150 and out in the first inning against Jimmy Moore. The first-inning freeze-out was another new record, as was my perfect slate of 14–0. Those records, along with the others I held, were certain to stand for quite a while because, as circumstance had it, there would be no further championship billiard activity for the next seven years.

I had become, in a way, the victim of my own success. Every available contender had taken part in the Kinston tournament and none of them had mounted a serious challenge. Crane finished second at 10–4 and Moore was 8–6. Lassiter was the only one who came close to beating me and he finished with a record of 6–8. The BCA did not come right out and say it was suspending future tournaments but it wasn't scheduling any either, and there were other signs indicating that activity had ground to a halt. The owners of rooms that promoted championship matches expressed no interest in booking a new one. There seemed to be no pairing attractive enough to ensure a profitable gate. I had beaten the current field repeatedly in recent years, and there was no young sensation on the way up. Professional competition was clearly in a period of eclipse, and while I still was making a reasonably good living playing exhibitions for Brunswick, I began looking in other directions.

In the spring of 1956 I bought a pool hall, the Superior Billiard Parlor, which was located at Broad and Rockland in Philadelphia. It was a good-size establishment, with seventeen tables, and I thought it would be a sound investment. I hired someone to run it for me when I was out of town and spent a good deal of time there when I was home. I was still giving about three hundred exhibitions a year and logging about twenty thousand miles of travel, but I was beginning to wear down a bit, and owning my own establishment gave me some additional income and a place to hang my hat when my schedule tapered off a bit.

In truth, I did not mind having a break in championship play. Travel was physically wearing, but it did not take the emotional or psychological toll that playing professionally did. The strain of competing in a tournament or a challenge match could drain you dry, and it was the same no matter who my opponent was; my concentration was total. Someone could be doing a dance on another table, and if it was not in my line of sight I wouldn't notice. Once I started shooting I forgot that the other guy even existed. I felt as though the entire world consisted of just myself and the balls and the table. You pay a price for that kind of concentration, and the mornings and evenings before a match weren't very relaxing either. I felt the tension from the beginning of play to the end. I smoked too many cigarettes and when I wasn't smoking I was working over a wad of spearmint gum. I don't know if it was the pressure that turned my hair gray while I was still in my thirties, but it probably helped.

▲ ▲ ▲

Bill Mosconi recalls what it was like at home when his father was engaged in competition.

"Oh, man, I'll tell you," he says. "I remember it clearly because when he was involved in a tournament you didn't even blink. He was on a different schedule; he got home late, he slept late, and when he got up he hardly spoke at all. He came down in his pajamas and his robe and walked through the house, into the kitchen to have his coffee, and win or lose, he didn't say a word. He might have spoken to my mother on occasion, but my sister and I just got out of the way; we didn't go anywhere near him. And if we had spoken to him I'm not sure he would have heard us; that's how intense he was. He wanted to win so badly that he shut everything else out.

"One of my uncles once told me a story of an incident between him and Irving Crane that took place during a tournament in Allinger's. My father apparently had things well in hand, and he and my uncle were having a bite to eat in a diner before that evening's match. Crane was in contention for second place, and he stopped by my father's booth and said something like, 'Well, Willie, you have things pretty much wrapped up, you can relax tonight.' My uncle said it seemed plain to him that Crane was joking, but my father didn't take it that way.

" 'Your father just stared at him,' my uncle told me. 'He didn't respond but just locked eyes with him until Crane turned and left. You could tell that Crane knew he had misspoken but was too embarrassed to explain. That night your father mopped him up. He was shooting like he was on a holy mission and for him, in a way, it was. When the match was over, he walked up to Crane and said, "Don't you ever imply that I don't have to play my best," and then he walked right by him.' "

▲ ▲ ▲

Sometime after the Kinston tournament I was interviewed by a newspaper reporter who wanted to know who I might defend against next since no future tournament was scheduled.

"I don't know," I told him. "I'm a bit weary right now. I'm not tired of the game; I'm tired of the competition. I may appear to be rather calm when I'm playing, but I'm not. Sometimes I think I'd like to quit and give nothing but exhibitions. What do you think of that idea?"

CHAPTER

Two days after Christmas in 1956 I was sitting in my billiard room polishing a ball when I heard a great roaring in my ears. It sounded like a freight train was running through my head. Then everything started whirling around, I felt all my muscles stiffen, and I keeled over onto the floor. I knew something serious was happening to me, but I didn't know what. I couldn't speak, couldn't move, couldn't do anything. But I never lost consciousness. I was aware that people were rushing around, I could hear their voices, but everything seemed to be happening at a distance from me, very far away. The next thing I knew, I was being rushed to Mount Sinai Hospital in an ambulance. I didn't know what hit me, but I was scared as hell.

It turned out that I had had a stroke. A blood vessel had popped in the front of my brain. It was described to me later as an aneurism, a sudden surge of blood to the brain that caused a vessel to burst. As strokes go, however, it was a minor one because it occurred in the front of the brain, in a location that was not life-threatening. I was up and about in a few days, but I was partially paralyzed on my left side, my speech was slurred, and when I walked I felt like I was falling to the left. It was a frightening situation. I was only forty-three years old, in the prime of life, and I didn't know what the future held for me.

I remained in the hospital for about two weeks, then was sent home and told to remain in bed. I was in a state of emotional upheaval that passed through several stages. When the initial fear abated, I began feeling sorry for myself, and with that I experienced a loss of confidence. I had always been a pretty cocky guy; I felt I could do whatever I set my mind to, that I could lick any opponent who crossed my path. But now I felt overmatched, helpless, and that feeling was more disturbing to me than my physical handicaps. But after a few weeks in bed I could sense the old feeling of defiance begin to stir in me again. I read biographies of people like Lou Gehrig and Babe Ruth, who knew they were sick and dying and had the courage to face it. I knew that my condition was better than theirs had been, that I had a chance to recover completely, and I decided to stop feeling sorry for myself and do something about it. I remember thinking, "This is ridiculous. I'm not going to lie here and watch myself rot. I'm going to get the hell out of bed and beat this thing. One way or the other, I'm going to get it all back." And that was that. My recovery began with my determination to recover, and I went at it with the same commitment I brought to the billiard table.

After spending two weeks in the hospital and another six lying around at home, it felt good to get moving again. I was told that walking was the best therapy for me, and although my equilibrium was off a bit, I walked every day until I was weary. I also began squeezing rubber balls to get the strength back in my hands. I carried them everywhere I went and worked them hard anytime my hands were free. I was a heavy coffee drinker, but I cut it out entirely because the doctors said the caffeine was not good for my condition. I gave up my three-pack-a-day cigarette habit. I had always gotten plenty of sleep—eight to ten hours a day—so that was no problem. After a week or two of exercising, I started working out on the pool table. In a way, that was the most trying part of my recuperation. My stroke was off; I didn't have the same smooth delivery I had had since I was a kid. I missed easy shots. I couldn't control the cue ball with any kind of precision. That was the toughest part of it. I could still visualize the table the way I used to. I could see the sequence of shots and I knew where the cue ball should come to rest, but I wasn't able to execute it. My body was not able to do what my brain told it to do, what it had always done as a matter of reflex. It shakes your confidence when you can no longer perform simple acts that had come so naturally to you. It was as if I had to learn what I once knew all over again. But as I continued to work out, I could see the improvement, and the better I shot, the more my confidence returned. Soon, I began to feel that I could get back pretty close to where I was before I was stricken.

Still, the psychological impact of the stroke persisted. It preyed on my mind from time to time. It had happened suddenly and without any warning. You never really learn what causes something like that so you begin to speculate, hoping that you might be able to prevent a subsequent occurrence. At one time or another, I blamed everything I could think of. On the morning of the stroke I had attended the funeral of an employee who worked for me in my billiard hall and I thought that might have upset me. It was a big responsibility to run a business—there were people who depended on you for their living—and that worried me on occasion. And of course there was no way to measure the accumulated effect of all the years of competition, the pressure of feeling the need to win, the stress of travel, the irregular hours. I would sometimes lose as much as eight pounds during the course of a long tournament. Billiards may be a great tranquilizer for the harried executive, but for the tournament player it can be real torture. It's a war of nerves. The biggest strain is just sitting there, helpless, while the other man is making a run. Some players are bleeders; they feel the pressure but never show it, never even twitch a facial muscle. Jimmy Caras was that way. Others, like myself, squirm and mutter. The tension makes us restless and there is nothing we can do to relieve it. It wears on you; it takes its toll.

▲ ▲ ▲

"He was a nervous wreck during a tournament," Flora Mosconi recalls. "Even before the tournament began, there was pressure, anxiety. The coffeepot would be on all day long, and he drank one cup after another, smoking cigarettes along with it. He was as jumpy as a cat. I don't know how he ever managed to calm his nerves when he played. Once he got to the table, he was cool as can be. Everyone marveled at how he never got rattled, always seemed to be in control. But when he wasn't playing he was like a time bomb waiting to explode. Of course it was a shock when he had the stroke, but looking back it seemed almost inevitable.

"I remember that when the call came I was holding Gloria in my arms. She was two years old then. One of the employees at the billiard hall told me that Willie had collapsed and was rushed to Mount Sinai. I brought Gloria to a neighbor's house and drove to the hospital. When I saw him it was really frightening. His tongue was hanging out, he couldn't speak, he couldn't move his left arm. It was horrifying to see him that way. But the doctors assured me his condition was only temporary. They said he would regain his speech and that all other body movements could return to normal, but he would have to work at it.

"At first it was difficult. He was under doctors' orders to rest as much as possible, and he spent a good deal of his time at home brooding on his condition, wondering whether he would ever be able to play again, worrying about his billiard hall, which was being run by his employees. But after a few weeks he began to bounce back and the rate of his recovery was amazing. He went at it with the same intensity that he had when he played pool. It was like his illness was an opponent he had to defeat. He walked for hours at a time, he exercised his hands, he began going into his billiard hall in the afternoon, not just to look after the business, but to practice. He spent more hours practicing at the table than he did when he was preparing for a tournament. Then one day, no more than three months after the stroke, he announced he was ready to resume activities and that he was going to Detroit for an exhibition match. His doctors advised against it, but once Willie made up his mind there was nothing to stop him."

Bill Mosconi, a teenager at the time, recollects the fierce determination with which his father endeavored to heal himself.

"I remember being told by my mother that he would never be able to play professional pool again. But my father thrived on such challenges. You tell him he can't do something, his first reaction is that he's going to do it. So he drove himself really hard. It seemed that every second of every day he was doing something to get himself back in shape. But it was not easy to be with him. If he was intense under ordinary circumstances, now he was ten times more so. He was not able to drive the car, so my mother had to drive him everywhere, and that was a harrowing experience for all of us. He'd be sitting there and yelling, 'Watch out for this, watch out for that,' shouting at other drivers, giving constant instructions to my mother. He could not bear the feeling of dependence. But it was his need to regain control, the same traits of character and temperament that made him such a relentless competitor, that helped him to recover so completely and so quickly. He could never tolerate the idea of losing, not at pool, not at anything else, and it didn't matter who his opponent was or what the occasion.

"I remember an incident that occurred on the day of my sister Candy's wedding, many years after he had retired from competition. The ceremony was in the morning with a lunchtime reception, and after that, some of the relatives were invited back to my parents' house. A lot of my uncles and cousins were there, and some of us went down to the basement where my father has a table. I teamed up with a cousin who was around my age, and my father took an older cousin of his as a partner to play a game of eight-ball. My father played one-handed with his left hand to even things up a bit. At one point, he tried to make a combination shot on the eight ball and he missed and I ran out the game. He was fuming. At first, everyone thought he was joking, but he wasn't; he was really angry, not at me but at himself for having missed a shot he thought he should have made that cost him the game. I was dumbfounded that he could get that upset over losing a game under those

circumstances. But that's the way he was; he couldn't
help himself. He just could not abide losing, and he
could never understand why everyone didn't feel the
same way.

"I was going to St. Joseph's College in Philadelphia
in 1961 when there was a nationwide basketball betting
scandal. Players in colleges all over the country were found
to have accepted bribes from gamblers for shaving points,
which is manipulating the scores of the games so that their
teams either lost or did not win by too big a margin. St.
Joe's, which had a nationally ranked team at the time, was
involved in the scandal. Three of their players had taken
bribes to hold down the scores. I knew the guys and I was
really disillusioned and disgusted. I spoke with my father
about it after school one day, and he was absolutely incred-
ulous; he couldn't believe it could happen.

" 'I don't understand how an athlete can do something
like that,' he said, 'even if it's just shaving points. It
doesn't seem possible to me that they would not do their
best, try to win by as much as they could. If you're not
giving it your top effort every second of the game, then
you're not being true to yourself, you shouldn't be out
there. I can't think of anything, any sum of money, even
if I was hungry, that would cause me to play less than
my best. How can an athlete intentionally lose a game,
or even take a chance on losing? It's something I just
can't understand.'

"And he meant it. He spoke about it again and again.
He simply could not comprehend any athlete not being
appalled at the prospect of losing, as though it ran
counter to nature. I think most great athletes feel the
same way. Their desire to win is so intense it's as though

they move into another plane of existence. That was certainly true of my father.

"His recuperation proceeded more rapidly than anyone had expected; even the doctors were surprised. But he was not nearly back to normal when he decided to keep an exhibition date in Detroit. I can remember him discussing it with my mother. She was distressed and emphatic. 'You're not going to Detroit,' she said. 'I'm going,' he said. He went."

▲ ▲ ▲

The exhibition in Detroit had been booked for months, long before I had the stroke. I don't remember the terms of the agreement or who I was playing, but I know it was a weekend appearance at the Detroit Recreation, which was probably the largest billiard room in the country. I knew the owners well and I knew that my appearance was important to them. In all the years I had been playing professionally I had never failed to honor a commitment. But there were also personal reasons that prompted me to make the trip. One was that I needed the money. It was not like I was on a company payroll and collecting sick pay or benefits when I was out of work. If I didn't work, I didn't get paid. I was drawing some income from my billiard room, but it was not nearly enough to pay the bills, and I was growing concerned. I had seen what had happened when my father was too sick to work, and that must have been in the back of my mind. What would I do for a living if I was not able to play anymore?

There was also the psychological reality that I had to contend with. I could see that my condition was improving, that I was able to do things at the table that I couldn't do five or six weeks earlier, but I was still getting dizzy spells on occasion and my concentration was off; I would tire quickly and could not plan as far ahead as I used to. So I wanted to prove to myself that I could still play. If I couldn't, then that would be the end of it; I would have to find something else to do. But I had to find out, and I was too impatient to wait very long. We spoke to my doctor about it, and he gave his approval, if a bit reluctantly. He gave me the name of a neurologist in Detroit and told me to call him if I had any problems.

As it turned out, things went as well as could be expected. I could feel my head spinning when the plane took off, but other than that I was fine. I can't say I put on a great exhibition, but I didn't embarrass myself either, and most important, I did what I felt had to be done. I certainly was in no shape for championship competition, but I played well enough to assure myself that I could win my share of games, draw a crowd, and make a living. So I considered the trip a success, and when I returned home I was able to relax without worrying about whether I would ever be able to play again.

I played very little during the balance of 1957. I worked out in my billiard hall and gradually resumed a regular schedule there, and I also used some of my spare time to revise a book I had put together ten years earlier with Harry Grove, who had been head of the Brunswick company's public relations department at the time. The book, a pocket-size paperback, was called *Willie Mosconi on Pocket Billiards*, and it offered instruction on the techniques of every aspect of the game. It took us a few months to add a few touches and make some changes in the first edition, and it helped occupy my time while I was home.

By 1958, I felt I was nearly back to normal, and I started playing again but kept as close to home as possible. When I was at the top of my game, I was as good as I ever was, but I didn't have the endurance needed to play long matches and I still could not concentrate intently for extended periods. Nonetheless, in April I was able to muster enough of my old skill to win an unofficial invitational tournament played at Allinger's and my own Superior Academy in Philadelphia. Although the title was not at stake, it was no pushover field I defeated. Among the other contestants were Crane, Lassiter, Jimmy Moore, and Dan Tozer, all championship tournament players. The purse was not especially large, so the victory did more for my confidence than for my bank account, but that was fine with me.

In 1959 I hit the highway again, but on a much-reduced schedule. The reduction was due, in part, to my desire to go easy on myself, but circumstances beyond my control also were responsible. There was simply less demand for the product. Interest in the game of billiards continued to decline throughout the fifties, and by the end of the decade it had reached the lowest point in its history. Production of billiard tables was down to about two thousand units a year from its high of fifty thousand in 1913, the year I was born. In the mid-twenties there were more than forty thousand pool rooms in the United States, four thousand in New York City alone. Now, there were only about ten thousand throughout the country and little more than five hundred in New York. The Billiard Congress of America had declined to schedule a tournament for the second year in a row and none was yet planned for the sixties. The future of the sport—at both amateur and professional levels—looked dim indeed. But help was right around the corner, and it came from a totally unexpected source. It began, oddly enough, with the making of a movie. The movie was called *The Hustler*, and it triggered a revival of interest in the game that could never have been anticipated. A renaissance of significant dimension was on the way.

CHAPTER

14

My involvement in *The Hustler* began with a phone call from an old army buddy whom I had not heard from in almost fifteen years. He was the Pulitzer Prize–winning musical composer Frank Loesser, who wrote the scores for *Guys and Dolls*, *The Most Happy Fella*, and other Broadway shows. Loesser and I were bunk mates in the service, purely by chance, because the army does everything alphabetically and "M" follows "L." We got to be pretty friendly. We were a couple of goldbricks, and we had some good times together, but we hadn't been in touch with each other since the war ended. He called me up out of the blue one day and told me that Robert Rossen, the movie director, was working on a film about a pool hustler. He briefed me on the plot and asked if I could recommend someone to play the part of Minnesota Fats. I immediately suggested Jackie Gleason, who was an old friend of mine. He seemed like a natural; he was big enough and fat enough, he was a great entertainer, and he knew his way around a pool table. As a matter of fact, it was over a pool table that I first met Jackie, and he was the only guy that I ever really hustled.

We were brought together by Toots Shor, who owned and operated a popular restaurant and saloon in the Theater District during the forties and fifties, which was a gathering place

for the Broadway night crowd. It attracted a full range of show
business people, professional athletes, journalists, politicians,
and an assortment of the types of characters made famous by
Damon Runyon. Toots, of course, was as much a character as
any of them, cut from the stereotype of the amiable Irish
saloonkeeper. He seemed to be on a first-name basis with
everyone who walked into the place, and no one, regardless
of stature or position, was immune to his crusty, good-natured
wit. At one time or another, he addressed everyone as a
"crumbbum" but if, for whatever reason, he really didn't like
you, he would make it abundantly clear that you were not
welcome in his place.

I had known Toots for quite some time. He was originally
from South Philadelphia, where he worked as a bartender and
bouncer, and my whole family knew him. My cousin Charlie,
the dancer who later became a Broadway ticket broker, was
especially friendly with him. So I was acquainted with Toots
before he got to New York, but it was after he opened his
restaurant and I started playing professionally that we really
got to be friendly. Toots and Gleason were long-time drinking
buddies and Toots had taken good care of Jackie before he
became a television star. He was often broke when he was
trying to make a name for himself in show business, and Toots
would stake him to dinner and lend him some money when
he needed it. But Toots was a practical joker and Jackie, for
all his street-wise bluster, was an easy target. Toots could
never resist the opportunity to put one over on him, and it
was through just such an impulse that Gleason and I first met.

Jackie fancied himself an accomplished pool player, and
he was not above hustling the unsuspecting clientele that
frequented Toots's place for twenty or thirty bucks a game.
Actually, he was not as good as he thought he was—he could

run forty or fifty balls on occasion—but he was good enough to beat all the suckers who hung around the saloon. And Jackie, never known for his modesty, was not above boasting about how he could beat any man in the house. Toots decided to teach him a lesson in humility, and he brought me in on the scheme.

We met at the restaurant, and Toots introduced me as a cloak-and-suit guy by the name of Shulman, a rich dress manufacturer from Philadelphia who liked to play an occasional game of pool for money.

"Ohhh," said Jackie, "a piece of Philadelphia cheeeese, eh?"

He was wearing a smile as broad as his face, and you could almost see him licking his chops. This was back in the early forties, and although Gleason no doubt had heard of Willie Mosconi, he didn't connect the name with the face and was more than willing to play this guy Shulman for some of his dress company's profits. We went over to one of the nearby billiard halls and Toots suggested that we play a one-hundred-point game for fifty dollars. I played just well enough to win, but erratically. I would miss an easy shot, then make a difficult bank shot or combination that appeared to owe more to luck than to skill. At other times I would pass up an easy shot, as though I didn't see it, call a ball that had no chance of going, and "accidentally" leave him safe. I won the game by something like 100–70, and Gleason was perplexed and frustrated.

"Where did you find this guy?" he asked Toots. "He must have been born with a horseshoe in his mouth." Then he turned to me. "Shulman," he said, "how about playing another one for one hundred dollars? You must have used up a year's worth of luck in that game."

"Sure," I said, "let's play one more."

Jackie played safe on the break, but he left a little too much. This time I didn't hesitate. I clicked off seventy balls right-handed, then ran the last thirty left-handed, and there was Gleason with that "homminuh, homminuh, homminuh" look on his face. Toot was laughing so hard that he couldn't stand up straight.

"Jackie," he said, "say hello to Willie Mosconi."

"Willie Mosconi!" Gleason said. He called Toots a few choice names, then let loose with one of those full-bellied laughs of his that almost shook the place. "Willie Mosconi!" he roared again. We shook hands, he put his arm around me, and we became close friends when I assured him that he could keep his 150 bucks.

Toots enjoyed the prank more than either of us. He ribbed Jackie for weeks about how he allowed himself to get hustled, and finally I decided to show Toots that he was not hustle-proof either. He was not as good a player as Jackie, but he could handle a cue stick and I offered him a proposition that he didn't think he could lose. I bet him four steak dinners that I could make one hundred balls before he could make a single shot in a side pocket. We went over to the Lambs Club, and Jackie tagged along, acting as Toots's second and freely offering advice. I ran ninety-five, then left him safe with one ball open at the bottom of the table, nowhere near a side pocket. After consulting with Jackie, Toots used that ball as part of a three-ball combination, and we all watched in astonishment as it banged around the table and finally dropped into a side pocket. It was a one-in-a-million shot, and I often reminded Toots that he was responsible for the worst defeat of my career. As for the four steak dinners, I told him that making a crazy shot like that was reward enough, and out of gratitude he ought to feed me free for the rest of my life. Of course Jackie took full credit for masterminding the play and offered to help eat the steak dinners no matter who paid for them.

By 1960, when *The Hustler* was being cast, Jackie was an acknowledged star, known chiefly as a funny man and most particularly as Ralph Kramden in *The Honeymooners* television series. But I had seen him in a few dramatic roles, and I felt he would be perfect as Minnesota Fats. Rossen took my suggestion, giving Gleason the part, but he ignored my recommendation for the lead in the movie, the role of Fast Eddie Felson, a small-time hustler whose dream it was to defeat the legendary Fats. I offered the name of Frank Sinatra, who I knew had shot some pool from time to time, but Rossen followed his own instincts and selected Paul Newman for the part. He also hired me as technical adviser, at a fee of ten thousand dollars, and my first job was to show Newman which end of a cue stick you hold and which you use to hit the ball, for he had never shot a game of pool in his life.

I had never met Paul Newman, although I had known his father for many years. He owned a sporting goods store in Cleveland, and I once played an exhibition at his place to demonstrate the equipment. Paul was away at college at the time, so when we first met it was as colleagues in the film industry. Basically, it was my job to make him look like a player, and I had to start from scratch: how to chalk a cue, how to crouch behind it and line up a shot, how to bank the seven ball in the side pocket without looking like a plumber.

Our first problem was finding a place where we could work without interruption. A public pool hall was out of the question, because once the word got out that Paul Newman was there, we would have attracted crowds from all over the neighborhood. I took him to the Lambs Club, but in no time at all he was surrounded by actors looking for work. Then I remembered an old friend of mine, Dr. Roland DeMarco, who was president of Finch College, an exclusive girls' finishing school on East Fifty-seventh Street in Manhattan. I had known him since his student days when he used to hustle pool to pay for his tuition. His home was on the college campus, and he had a pool table in the basement, and he said he would be delighted to have us. So that became our classroom. We knew there would be chaos if the girls ever discovered that Paul was there, so we arranged for him to enter through a back door to the basement. He drove up on a motorcycle, wearing sunglasses, every afternoon at about two o'clock, and we would practice for two or three hours.

It was his mannerisms we were most concerned with. Movie cameras can work wonders, and I would be able to make the shots, if necessary, with the cameras shifting from Paul's eyes to my hands. But we had to teach him to look like a pool player, to acquire the movements and attitudes of someone who was at home in that environment, and Paul made it easy. He is a great actor and a consummate professional, and it was a pleasure to work with him. He was entirely without pretense; he listened carefully, did whatever I asked him to do, and in a matter of a few weeks he looked as though he had been playing all his life. Once he got the movements down, we began working on the shots. Paul was the type of actor who really wanted to feel the part he was playing. If he portrayed a boxer, as he did in the Rocky Graziano movie, he learned how to box, and if he was going to play the part of a pool hustler, he wanted to learn to shoot pool. He even had a table installed in his Manhattan apartment so he could practice on his own. I began by teaching him the simplest shots. I lined up the cue ball and an object ball and said, "Paul, you're going to have to make that thing, it's a straight shot." Then I'd set up a more difficult shot. I was amazed at how fast he picked it up. After about four months of regular practice, he was making some really tough ones—bank shots, combinations, even some of the trick shots. All in all, he had become a pretty fair pool-shooter. By the time we started filming, you would never have guessed that he was new to the game. Of course I set up the shots and told him what to do, but he made almost all of them himself. I had to execute only the most complex maneuvers, like rail-first banks and massé shots, which would literally have taken years to learn. It was absolutely remarkable how quickly and easily Paul learned the nuances of the game.

▲ ▲ ▲

Newman, though doubtless a quick study, does not hesitate to credit Willie for his rapid conversion from a neophyte into a player of some skill.

"Willie was a great teacher," he says. "He was patient, generous, savvy, a complete professional. I thought he might be put off when he learned he had to start from scratch with me, but he wasn't. He just began at the beginning and proceeded from there. He taught me how to make a bridge, how to stroke, everything. It's ironic that I had never learned to play pool because I had worked my way through Kenyon College, in Gambier, Ohio, racking balls at fifty cents an hour. But it was just a way of earning money; I never developed an interest in the game and I had never heard of Willie Mosconi until we met. But he taught me all the essentials, and when we started shooting he was as helpful on the set as he was in our private sessions.

"The picture was filmed entirely in New York, and most of the pool sequences were shot in McGirr's or

Ames. Willie would set up the shots and Jackie and I would shoot them. Gleason was a really good player and needed far less help than I did. I just followed Willie's instructions as best I could, and I ended up making most of the shots myself but not necessarily on the first try. Movies are a wonderful thing; you can miss a shot ninety-three times, and if you make it on the ninety-fourth, that's the take. No one gets to see all the times you flubbed it, and you end up looking pretty good. Willie set up the shots as many times as was necessary, he explained what I had done wrong and told me how to correct it.

"It was a great community set and of course Gleason was fun to work with. I never got to be anywhere near the player he was—a run of twelve or fifteen balls was really good for me—but we played nine-ball from time to time and tried to hustle each other. One afternoon we played five games for a buck a game and I beat him three of the five. Then we played one more for the big money—I think it was fifty bucks—and he won it. The next day I paid him off with fifty dollars' worth of pennies. So we had our laughs, but there wasn't too much of that kind of by-play. Sets tend to assume the disposition of the film being made, and *The Hustler* was not a very light picture. But we all worked well together and Willie was very much a part of the scene."

▲ ▲ ▲

My duties as technical adviser extended beyond setting up the shots and seeing that they were made properly. I was responsible for creating an authentic environment, orchestrating the movements and attitudes of the people who were watching the game. You couldn't have a bunch of guys in shirts and ties in the background. We needed some pool-hall types, and we would often select them from among those who happened to be on premises. The director would pick them out and set the scene and say, "Is this right, Willie?" I would make certain that the scene looked realistic. I worked a little with George C. Scott too. He was the money man in the movie; he bankrolled Fats and, at one point, Fast Eddie, and I advised him on some of the mannerisms of that type of character. Scott is a magnificent actor and he didn't need much help from me, but I would position him in the spot in which he would be sitting and tell him how the money would be handled and when the payment would be made. I had a bit part in the movie myself, but you had to watch closely to find me. I held the stake at the start of the game and then disappeared into the background.

In between takes, I had a grand time needling Gleason and hustling him in games of nine-ball. He'd be chalking his cue stick, getting ready to shoot, and I would swipe the nine ball from the table and put it in my pocket. He was so busy bragging about how he was going to beat me that he didn't even notice it was missing. Then, when he turned his head, I would put it back on the table to form a perfect combination with the two or the three and just like that the game was over. Jackie was always a great guy to be around, and although our workdays were long and reshooting the takes sometimes got to be tedious, I was, in a way, sorry to see it end.

All the pool sequences were shot in about six weeks and that concluded my initiation into the world of film-making. It was a great experience for me, and my family enjoyed it as much as I did. I stayed at the St. Moritz Hotel in New York throughout the filming, and Flora and Gloria used to join me on weekends and occasionally during the week. Flora was thrilled to be on the set and rubbing elbows with big-time movie stars. But I think Gloria got the biggest kick out of it. She was only about six years old at the time, but she was taken up in the excitement of it. She was a sprightly, gregarious kid; she loved the attention and got plenty of it.

▲ ▲ ▲

"I remember going up to New York on the weekends and staying at this big hotel," says Gloria Dickson, now the mother of three youngsters, who resides a short distance from her parents' house, in Haddonfield, New Jersey. "Of course I liked it best when we went there on weekdays, and I did my homework in the hotel suite. I felt like Eloise except that the St. Moritz was better than the Plaza. I had no idea who Paul Newman or Jackie Gleason were at that time, but I knew that a movie was being made and I was fascinated just being on the set. Everyone was really nice to me, but Paul Newman was especially nice. Jackie Gleason, surprisingly, tended to be somewhat aloof and reserved with everyone but my father, but Paul was just wonderful. He had children about my age, so I guess he was used to having kids around and amusing them. He would play pantomime games with me, winding an imaginary string around his finger, then stuffing it in his ear and pulling it out the other side. It was great fun.

"I also got to stay up way past my bedtime. The shootings often ran late and it was sometimes nine or ten o'clock before we went to dinner, usually at Toots Shor's. That was almost as much fun as being on the set. There were always lots of people around us; everyone seemed to know Dad, and they kept coming up to him and he introduced us. But now and then I wandered around on my own, and on a few occasions I got to introduce Dad to some well-known customers.

"One time, I was walking around the restaurant when this nice gentleman reached out to me and said, 'What a sweet little girl. What are you doing here all by yourself so late at night?' I told him I was with my mother and father, and he asked me to sit down at his table. He was with some other people, and they were all making a fuss over me, and finally I asked him if I could bring my father over. So I told Dad that I wanted to introduce him to my new friend, Dick, and he was astonished when he found I was chatting casually with Richard Nixon, who was then vice-president of the United States.

"Another time, I went off to the powder room, because I used to like to talk to the attendants there. When my mother noticed I was away longer than usual, she went looking for me and found me at a corner table under the arm of Frank Sinatra. He was telling me about his daughter Tina, who was a little older than I was, and he was as sweet and friendly as can be. When he found out I was Willie Mosconi's daughter he invited Dad over to the table. They had met briefly some years earlier, but after becoming reacquainted Sinatra would call the house from time to time.

"I once answered the phone when he called, and he said, 'Hello, this is Frank Sinatra, is your father home?' I told him Dad was out of town but that my mother was at a neighbor's house right around the corner. 'Would you get her for me?' he asked. My Italian grandmother, my mother's mother, was staying with me at the time, and I handed her the phone and told her who it was. 'Frankie Sinatra,' she said, 'is this really Frankie Sinatra?' And then they started speaking to each other in Italian. He was wonderful. My grandmother didn't stop talking about her conversation with Frank Sinatra for the next ten years.

"When *The Hustler* finally opened, in 1961, my parents took me to the premiere, and what a thrill that was! There were huge crowds of glamorous-looking people emerging from limousines and moving into the theater. They seemed to be coming from every direction and I didn't know where to look first. Then, when I saw the movie, I couldn't understand where all these other scenes came from. Everything I had seen took place in a pool hall, and now there were all these other people in new settings and I was completely mystified. I was too young to fully understand the plot of the movie; I was just looking for Dad and the scenes that I recognized from being on the set. But I've seen the movie many times since, and I think it's an exceptionally fine film. It isn't just about pool and hustling; there is a lot of psychology in it, and it is also a good, if tragic, love story."

The Hustler, based on a small jewel of a novel by Walter Tevis, was more than either a pool film or a love story. At its heart was the fine old American theme of the Grand Quest, one man's obsession with the need to conquer a foe of mythological proportions. The film's protagonist, Fast Eddie Felson, is driven by the admirable though often destructive impulse to climb the highest mountain, to defeat the fabled Minnesota Fats in a game of straight pool. But simply outscoring his opponent is not enough;

it is Eddie's need to get the Fat Man to cry uncle, to concede, as he finally does at the end of the movie, "I quit, Eddie, I can't beat you."

Felson is a scruffy but endearing pool hustler out of Oakland, California, crude, unfinished, perhaps lacking in character, as he is told by Fats's manager, Bert (George C. Scott), but he has a dream and the soul of a poet. In a moving scene with the film's romantic interest (Piper Laurie), he rhapsodizes over the beauty of the game he plays so well.

"It's a great feeling, boy, it's a real great feeling when you're right and you know you're right. Like all of a sudden I got oil in my arm. The pool cue's part of me, you know, the pool cue's got nerves; it's a piece of wood, it's got nerves in it. You feel the roll of those balls . . . you don't have to look, you just know. You make shots that nobody's ever made before. And you play the game the way nobody's ever played it before."

Eddie has all the skills, the desire, the subtle touch of genius that transcends normal limits, but he lacks the discipline, the polish, the quiet assurance of Minnesota Fats. In their first encounter, Eddie beats Fats from dusk to dawn, but flushed with victory and giddy from booze, he begins to gloat and gets sloppy at the table. He has already taken the ten thousand dollars it was his aim to win, but it isn't the money he's after. "I want *him*," Eddie tells his partner, who urges him to take the money and savor his victory. "The pool game is over when Fats says it's over. Is it over, Fats?" Gleason looks to his financial backer, and Scott nods. "Stay with this kid," he says, "he's a loser." And indeed, Eddie proceeds to do nothing but lose until both his winnings and his stake have evaporated.

The balance of the film, love story and all, centers on Eddie's quest, what has now developed into an obsession, to build a bankroll large enough to challenge the Fat Man again. The specter of Minnesota Fats haunts his sleep, floats at the fringes of his every desire. He is Ahab in search of Moby Dick, Santiago hooked to his big fish in *The Old Man and the Sea*. His instincts are tuned to the playing of a single chord, each of his movements calibrated to inch him closer to his quarry. Inevitably, along the way, things break, people get hurt, they die.

Finally, in the melodramatic finish, Eddie hooks his man. He has been toughened now, given new balance by the twists and turns his life has taken, he has developed discipline and "character," and his focus is as clean and sharp as his resolve. Fats breaks and plays safe. Eddie chalks his cue and looks over the table. "How should I play that one, Bert?" he asks. "Play it safe? That's the way you always told me to play it—safe, play the percentage. Well, here we go, fast and loose." There follows the first of a series of spectacular shots, rack after rack, game after game, until Fats says he's had enough. The mountain has been scaled, and Eddie walks out with his encased pool cue tucked under his arm.

The Hustler, a huge success, was nominated for an Academy Award. So were its four stars—Newman, Gleason, Scott, and Laurie—and its director and scriptwriter, Robert Rossen. But it was their collective misfortune that year to run into a movie classic, *West Side Story*, which made a virtual sweep of the Oscars. Nonetheless, the film left its mark. It spurred a renewal of interest in the game of pool that no one fully anticipated.

▲ ▲ ▲

The speed with which the game bounced back after the release of the movie was truly astonishing. In the twenties there were about 22 million people playing billiards in one form or another. By the late fifties, it was estimated that the number had dropped to about 3 million. In 1962, just one year after *The Hustler* opened, the figure jumped to about 17 million. But the participants, for the most part, were different from those who had played the game in the early days, and the rooms they frequented bore little resemblance to the old, grimy pool halls with the dim lights and shaded windows.

Some 450 colleges installed an average of ten tables each. The recent popularity of bowling also helped. It had become perhaps the fastest-growing participant sport in the fifties, and now many of the old bowling establishments were moving out of the basement into large, air-conditioned spaces, and the proprietors began putting in billiard tables as an added attraction. The new billiard centers also took on a new look. They were bright and cheerful and inviting, and they appealed to a new clientele. Women took up the game in record numbers, and it was not unusual to see whole families gathered around a pool table. People began discovering that billiards required a kind of skill and imagination that were lacking in other games and pastimes. They could get a special satisfaction from mastering something that was intricate and demanding, as well as relaxing, if they didn't take it too seriously.

The people at Brunswick responded to the game's new look by sprucing up their equipment a bit. After some discussion, they took my suggestion and replaced the traditional green cloth with colors like beige, blue, gold, and tangerine. The tables also were remodeled and streamlined. They were outfitted with rotating numerals built into the frame of the table as a score-keeping mechanism, replacing the old button score-markers strung on overhead wires that had to be flicked from one side to the other with the end of the cue stick. The whole package seemed to fit well together, because by the middle of 1962 orders for new tables were coming in so fast that Brunswick fell six months behind in filling them. Things were looking so good, in fact, that for the first time in seven years the Billiard Congress of America scheduled a championship tournament for the spring of 1963.

CHAPTER

By 1963 I was fully recovered from my stroke, but I nonetheless declined an invitation to compete in the championship tournament. I was nearly fifty years old then, and I felt I had had enough. There was nothing left to prove to anyone; I had beaten them all in my time, and now my time was up and it remained for the younger players to carry the game forward. Luther Lassiter, who won the title I had vacated, was emerging as a dominant figure, and there was Jimmy Moore, who finished second, and Babe Cranfield, and Cisero Murphy, the first black player of championship caliber. Also, Irving Crane was still active. He was the only player from the old days—from as far back as the thirties—who was still in competition.

Although we were products of the same era, Crane and I had always felt differently about the game. He was truly in love with it; he enjoyed playing and would have continued to play regardless of the circumstances. For me, it was chiefly a business. I had great respect for the sport and was grateful for the opportunities it gave me, but I was always conscious of the fact that this was what I did for a living. From the time I was a teenager, billiards had provided me with my livelihood, and I was never able to think of it as a pastime. I rarely played just for the fun of it.

By the mid-sixties, my schedule was as cluttered as it had

ever been. I was back on the highway for the better part of ten
months a year, visiting college campuses, giving exhibitions,
demonstrating new equipment for Brunswick at the opening
of new rooms, usually in conjunction with bowling alleys. I
had, I suppose, become something of a goodwill ambassador,
traveling the country and preaching the gospel of billiards. I
was still a pretty fair attraction. There is something about
being a retired champion that stirs the imagination and invites
the interest of two generations. Those who saw you play
twenty years ago are eager to relive a part of their past, and
those who were too young to see you when you were in your
heyday are looking for a sign of confirmation that you were as
good as everyone said you were.

One of the biggest crowds that ever turned out for an exhibition match with nothing at stake came to see me play a benefit
with Onofrio Lauri at Julian's, on Fourteenth Street in Manhattan, in 1965. Lauri, a sixty-five-year-old veteran out of
Ovington's Billiards in Brooklyn, was in failing health and
unable to pay his medical bills. I don't recall what his condition
was—he was certainly still able to play a fair stick of pool—
but he needed costly medication, and retired pool players
don't have pension plans to draw upon.

Of course I can hardly take credit for having been the sole
attraction that night. Lauri was a show all by himself. He was
a fiery little Italian guy with a head as smooth and as bright
as a cue ball and, as I saw on more than one occasion, at least
as hard as a wrecking ball, for during the course of a match,
Lauri often used his head in more ways than one. While other
guys might show their frustration by tossing their cue sticks
or pounding the table when they missed an easy shot or blew
a close game, that was not nearly dramatic enough for Lauri.
He would lower his head and ram it into a wall, and you could

hear the thud all over the room. It would have knocked most people unconscious, but not him. He was given to all sorts of histrionics. Once, when we were playing at the Navy Pier in Chicago, he misplayed a shot that cost him a game and, still carrying his cue, he tried to throw himself off the dock and into Lake Michigan. I helped to restrain him, and he finally settled for breaking his cue stick over his head.

Lauri was one of the great characters of the game and a pretty good player, and he probably would have fared a lot better if he had been able to keep his tantrums under control. He had been playing since the twenties but never finished higher than fourth in a championship tournament; he just couldn't seem to break through. But he was not an easy opponent. You wouldn't want him to be the guy standing between you and a championship. He was a sensational shot-maker, and if he got on a roll he could run a game out on you quicker than you could count the balls. I had my own way of dealing with him. It didn't take much to get his goat, and once you got him going he would blow sky-high. One of my favorite ploys was to swipe the chalk from the table before he got up to shoot. "Where's the chalk," he would scream. "Who the hell took the chalk?" He would get so upset that he'd often miscue even after he chalked up. I couldn't keep from laughing whenever I played him. He was a real nut, but a lovable nut, and when he needed help I wanted to do whatever I could.

The owners of Julian's offered the room without charge, and all gate receipts were to be turned over to Lauri. The hall was filled beyond capacity. More than one thousand spectators packed in so tight that on occasion they had to be asked to move back to make room for us to shoot. It was that way for three days. We played two blocks of 150 points each day. The first game was a close one. I won it 150–137, with a high run of eighty-three. Lauri put together a cluster of seventy-seven, so you could say that the customers got their money's worth. But I stepped up the pace after that, winning five of the six blocks, the last one by a margin of 148 balls. There were times, when I was making a long run, that I thought Lauri was going to explode, but he managed to control himself. After the match, some of the spectators gathered around us, and Lauri put his arm around me and said, "When you play with this guy you get punch-drunk."

I was in fine form during my match with Lauri, the best I had been in since the stroke, and I guess I got to wondering whether I could still reach back far enough to hold my own in championship competition. I passed up the BCA tournament in March of 1966 for the fourth year in a row, but I paused to consider the offer when I was asked to compete in a twenty-thousand-dollar Invitational Pocket Billiards Championship to be held in April in Burbank, California. The tournament was scheduled to run for three weeks, so I knew it would be a grind, but some part of me wanted to take the plunge. I had a gnawing ambition to show people I was still the champion. I'd been a fighter all my life, and I was thinking, "This is my game, I ought to take a shot at it." But my mind wasn't finally made up until the sponsors guaranteed me ten thousand dollars—win or lose—to take part in the tournament. It was exactly ten years since I last took part in formal competition, and although the BCA title was not at stake, the promoters publicized the tournament as featuring the comeback of Willie Mosconi.

They had a pretty full field—eighteen players in a round-robin—with the list headed by the reigning champion, Joe (the Meatman) Balsis, who got his nickname because he worked as a butcher in Minersville, Pennsylvania. My old rival Crane was among the number, as were Lauri, Jimmy Moore, and Harold Worst, the three-cushion specialist. But most of the field was made up of relative newcomers, some of them sporting colorful nicknames, which seemed to have become the vogue: William (Weenie Beanie) Staton, a hustler from Alexandria, Virginia; Jack Breit, from Houston, who was known as the Red Raider; Eddie (the Bear) Taylor; Cisero Murphy and Johnny Ervolino from Brooklyn; Mike Eufemia; and a future champion and television star by the name of Steve Mizerak.

The site of the tournament, wistfully called Burbank's House of Champions, was as far removed from Allinger's or McGirr's as California is from the East Coast. It was a converted supermarket and hardly what might be called a classy-looking room. The floor was covered with drab carpeting, and garish, bright blue bleachers had been installed to seat the spectators. Sheets of green plastic, used to shield the ceiling lights, swayed and rippled overhead, and the lookout booth once used by the supermarket manager was still clearly visible. To compound the dismal atmosphere, a gaudy blonde, wearing black velvet pants and sneakers, paraded up and down the aisles selling beer to the customers. But the cheap decor did not discourage the crowds. Day after day and night after night, for three weeks, they filled the bleachers, spilled over into the aisles, and stood in the rear. If the newspapers were to be believed, a good many of them had come to see whether I had anything left.

I always tried to give the fans a good show, and in my opening appearance, against a player by the name of Harold Baker, I ran ninety-two off the break and won the match easily. I went on to win my first seven games, all by wide margins, before stumbling against Cisero Murphy. My record of 7–1, at about the halfway point, tied me for the lead with Joe Balsis. But the Meatman lost the next day while I was defeating Jack Breit, and I took a one-game lead. I maintained my margin for the next five days, boosting my record to 13–1 against Harold Worst with a tournament-high run of 126. With three games to go, Crane, who was in third place, tripped me up, and I fell back into a tie with Balsis. On the next-to-last day of the tournament, I defeated Jimmy Moore, but Balsis demolished Crane 150 to minus 4, with a run of 137. So we were tied at 14–2 going into the final day, and Burbank was close enough to Hollywood for the schedule to match me with Balsis with the championship at stake. I suppose a true Hollywood script would have had the old veteran coming from behind to win it, but reality reversed our roles. I took an 87–73 lead, but Balsis ripped off sixty-three balls and then ran out with a cluster of fourteen.

All in all, while I had fared pretty well, something seemed to be missing from my game. I'm not sure what it was or whether it was discernible to the viewer, but I was able to sense its absence. After ten years, you're just not the same player you were, and I don't think you can ever get it all back again. It's tough as you get older. It's harder to maintain your intensity, your concentration slips a bit, your desire flattens out. You still want to win, but it just doesn't seem as important as it once did. You get the feeling that you have done it before, done it again and again, and you just can't reach that far back anymore. When the tournament was over I was tired as hell, really exhausted—physically, emotionally, psychologically. I had been going through packs of Rolaids the same way I used to go through packs of cigarettes, trying to settle my stomach, ease my nerves. When the tournament was over, I knew that was the end of it for me, that I would never play in actual competition again. And I think I would have felt the same even if I had won it.

▲ ▲ ▲

Now, at age fifty-three, his hair a lustrous gray, his frame padded with a few extra pounds, his courtly manner and easy grace untouched by the years, Willie Mosconi slipped quietly into permanent retirement. During his twenty-four years on the professional circuit, he had written his name beside virtually every record in the books, some of which remain after more than three decades. Perhaps more significantly, he had become a sports legend in the literal sense of the term. His story would be told, repeated, and passed on by those who had never seen him play, his name recognized by many who did not know the striped balls from the solids or caroms from pockets, who could not offer the name of another professional pool player, past or present. Willie had scaled that height which, in any field of endeavor, is attained by only the very few: His name had become synonymous with his calling.

There was only one other player whose credentials warranted comparison with Willie's, and that was Ralph Greenleaf. Charles J. Ursitti, a pocket billiards historian and occasional promoter, compiled some figures designed to suggest which had the more compelling claim to the title of The Greatest: Greenleaf held the title for thirteen years, Mosconi for fifteen. In tournament play, Greenleaf had put together a game record of 192–77, for a winning percentage of 71.4; Mosconi's record was 307–94, 76.6 percent. Greenleaf won nine of ten challenge matches, Mosconi twelve of thirteen. In head-to head competition, Mosconi won four of their six contests in championship play. As for records, Greenleaf's high run in a 125-point game was 126 and his best game, two innings; Mosconi's highs were 127 and one inning. Greenleaf's high exhibition run was 276 to Mosconi's 309 on a five by ten table. Greenleaf never played on the smaller table, on which Willie owns all the standards— high tournament run of 150 in one inning and high exhibition run of 526.

The numbers appear to favor Willie, but numbers alone are rarely conclusive. Times change, conditions vary, speculation remains the heart of spectator sports.

▲ ▲ ▲

Right from the start, I was comfortable with my decision to retire from championship play, and I never had cause to regret it. I continued to be as active as ever, and I earned as much money as I needed without the stress of competition. Exhibitions were easier and the money was guaranteed. I could get one thousand dollars plus expenses for an exhibition. In a tournament, you could win three or four thousand dollars, but you had to come in first or second to make it worthwhile, and tournaments took longer to play, sometimes several weeks. Hour for hour, exhibitions paid better, but the critical factor was escaping the tension. If I needed any prompting, the Burbank tournament reminded me of the strain that accompanied that kind of competition, and I knew I was better off without it. Besides, the popularity of the game had begun to slip again, and much of the grandeur was already gone.

In 1971, just ten years after *The Hustler* breathed new life into the sport, Allinger's, a Philadelphia landmark, closed its

doors after sixty-six years of operation. All of the equipment—
the tables, cue sticks, racks, balls, bridges, even the high-
backed benches used by the spectators—was sold at auction.
It had been one of the classiest, most respected rooms in the
country, and old man Sol Allinger kept it that way from the
day it opened in 1905. He threw out the gamblers, the hustlers, anyone who made noise. He wouldn't even tolerate
swearing. There were special racks where you could keep
your favorite cue stick. Girls were hired to brush the tables
after each game. Every top player in the country played there
at one time or another. But Allinger's wasn't the first quality
room to close and it wouldn't be the last. Ames Billiard Parlor,
on the West Side of Manhattan, where part of *The Hustler*
was filmed, had closed in 1966; Bensinger's in Chicago and
the Detroit Recreation would soon follow. It was truly the end
of an era. The only vestige of *The Hustler* revival that remained now was a real-life hustler by the name of Rudolf
Wanderone, who called himself Minnesota Fats and, so far as
I am concerned, brought no glory to the image of the game.

Wanderone was a self-proclaimed hustler from New York
who was originally known as New York Fats or Broadway Fats,
because in the thirties and forties he used to hang around the
pool halls in the Broadway area hustling anyone with a few
bucks in his pocket who couldn't play the game too well.
Hustlers don't have to be very talented; they just have to
know that they're better than the guy they're playing and
be good enough actors to keep the games close. I had met
Wanderone only once, I think it was in 1949. He came into
Frankie Mason's room in Philadelphia one night, and no one
knew who he was. He was just the guy who carried the cue
case for another hustler, who went by the name of Baby Face
Whitlow. But Fats was looking for some action of his own. He

started mouthing off about how good he was, and finally Mason said to me, "Willie, why don't you play this guy and shut him up?" Fats didn't want to shoot straight pool; it required too much skill for him. His specialty was a gimmick game called one-pocket, in which each player is required to make all his shots in one predesignated pocket. So we played one-pocket, and I beat him five straight times for fifty bucks a game, and I had to lend him train fare to get back to New York.

Some years later, he moved to Illinois, and since the only thing constant about him was his girth, he started calling himself Chicago Fats. He never beat anyone of note, he never played in a tournament, and no one took him seriously. He was just another one of dozens of pool hustlers around the country who made their living off unsuspecting marks. He was, in a word, a con-man, but he was as good a con-man as I've ever known. He had a gift of gab, a quick wit, he knew all the angles when money was at stake, and he recognized an opportunity when one presented itself and knew how to capitalize on it. And the best opportunity of his life came right at him when *The Hustler* was released. Here, in the movie, was a character who hustled pool as he did, who was built like him, even looked a little like him, and who shared at least half his name. Wanderone had probably never set foot in Minnesota at that time, but he claimed that he was the real Minnesota Fats and that the movie was based on his life. It did not slow him down for an instant when Walter Tevis, the author of the book on which the movie was based, said he had never heard of Rudolf Wanderone or any of his aliases.

"I'm annoyed," Tevis said in an interview in *Billiard Digest*, "when people ask me when I met Minnesota Fats. I feel as though I were Walt Disney being asked when he met Donald Duck, you know? It's something I made up."

But Fats, by this time, had a wider audience than Tevis did. I think people wanted to believe that there really was such a character, that the movie was actually a slice of life rather than a work of fiction, and Fats made the most of it. He sold himself to the public as Minnesota Fats, got himself booked on a number of television shows, and displayed his modest gifts on *Wide World of Sports*. He became noteworthy enough that in 1966 he published his autobiography, *The Bank Shot and Other Great Robberies*, which he wrote with a newspaper writer by the name of Tom Fox. The book was further proof that Fats had trouble distinguishing fact from fiction. He claimed, among other things, that back in the thirties he had beaten me so often that my father interceded and asked him not to play me for money anymore. It was one of a number of lies he had written about me, and I filed suit in common pleas court asking $450,000 in damages. Unfortunately, nothing ever came of the suit. I soon discovered that damages are extremely difficult to prove to a court's satisfaction and that in the long run, the only one who was likely to profit from legal action was my attorney. So I dropped the suit, but that only seemed to encourage Fats, who continued to relate phony stories about how beating me would be like taking candy from a baby. "Mosconi is a great tournament player," he said at one point, "but he can't play for the cash. Willie wouldn't bet ten cents that four big dogs could beat one little dog."

Well, I had played for some cash in my time, and I decided to call Fats's hand and see if he was bluffing. I challenged him to play one game of pool, two thousand points, for twenty thousand dollars, and I offered to spot him 250 points. "If twenty thousand dollars isn't enough to interest him," I added, "let him name a figure and I'll meet it, winner take all." The challenge was carried under big headlines in the newspapers, it was repeated on Tom Brookshire's television show, and to make it official I sent Fats a registered letter, advising him that Dan Murphy, the manager of the Sheraton Hotel in Philadelphia, offered the use of the hotel's grand ballroom, which could accommodate about four thousand spectators, from May 22 through the 25th. When I received no response, I offered to increase the spot to five hundred balls; I also agreed to broaden the competition to include his game of one-pocket, nine-ball, rotation, and three-cushion billiards.

"Just let me get him to the table," I said. "I'll play him every game in the book. I'll play him for any amount. That character can shoot off his mouth, but he can't shoot pool. Let him show us how much skill he has. He claims he can beat anybody when the cash is on the line. Well, he can't beat me, and I'm going to show the public once and for all that he is a third-rate character who can't shoot pool. I'm going to put him on the spot. I would like to see television cover this to let the people see what the game of pool is all about. People like this fat person would have you believe pool is played only by sneaky little hoodlums who take your money with a pool cue because they are not man enough to use a gun. I've spent my life playing pool and I won't have this little man disgrace the game. But I predict that he won't show up. He is finished as a pool showboat and he knows it. The table will be there, I'll be there, and the cash will be there. If he doesn't show, that will let the public know just how good he is."

As time passed and we heard nothing from Fats, I upped the ante to one hundred thousand dollars. Joe Magistrelli, a local businessman who owned a big hardware company, put up the one hundred thousand dollars, in cash. Murphy placed a newspaper ad for the Sheraton reading: "MINNESOTA FATS challenged by MOSCONI—'Show Up or Shut Up.' " It announced that tickets would be sold at ten and twenty-five dollars if Fats showed. If he didn't, I would play some local celebrities and put on an exhibition of trick shots, with tickets selling for five dollars. I appeared each of the four nights, and my hundred thousand in cash was kept in the Sheraton safe. But Fats never showed, and I never heard from him. He had a variety of reasons for failing to accept the challenge. First, he said he had never received the registered letter. Then, he said he was busy that week playing in a hustlers' tournament in Johnson City, Illinois. Anyway, that's the story he gave to the newspapers. My response was simple and direct: "He's full of baloney," I said. "Hustler is just another word for thief, and Minnesota Fats is just another name for phony. That's what his real name is—Wanderphony."

So the big challenge match didn't come off, not then anyway. But it was waiting for us down the road. As in the Gunfight at the OK Corral, a showdown between us had become inevitable. It would be a few years in the making, but when it came it would be played before a national audience on network television.

In a curious leap from the ridiculous to the sublime—from an aborted confrontation with a posturing clown to a series of intricate matches with a distinguished British gentleman—I accepted an offer to play a cross-country, mixed competition match with Rex Williams, the world's professional snooker champion. The invitation came from the Smirnoff Beverage and Import Company, which was seeking to promote a new product, Black Velvet Canadian Whisky, and was billing the contest as the $20,000 Black Velvet Challenge. The idea was for Williams and me to alternate games—three games of snooker and one of pool—with the winner to be determined on the basis of a complicated point system that I think only the promoters comprehended. All I understood about it was that the winner would receive fifteen thousand dollars and the loser five thousand dollars, and that was good enough for me.

Snooker, which is the national pocket billiards game in Great Britain, is a rather complex form of our own game, mixing some of the elements of straight pool and rotation. It is played on a six by twelve foot table, which looks as big as a football field, but what makes it particularly difficult to adjust to is that the balls and the pockets are smaller and the edges of the pockets are rounded instead of angled so that all shots have to be made dead center. It is like playing on a table with six side pockets. The game is played with a cue ball and twenty-one balls of various colors—fifteen red ones that count for one point each each and six balls numbered from two to seven. The red balls are set in a triangular rack, much the same as in pool, and the others are placed in designated spots around the table. The shooter is required to make a red ball before he can pocket a numbered ball, calling the shot as he would in pool. When the red ones are made, they remain off the table; the numbered balls are respotted until all the red ones are gone. Then, they must be shot in numerical sequence, as in a game of rotation. When only the black ball, the seven, is left on the table, the first score or penalty ends the game, and the highest point total wins. If the score is tied, the black ball is spotted again.

I was familiar with the rules of the game, but I had had very little experience playing it. McGirr's was one of the few rooms that had snooker tables, and I worked out there for about two months, trying to acquaint myself with the nuances of play. One thing was immediately clear: Once the red balls were off the table, snooker was basically a game of defense. Since the numbered balls had to be made in order, the idea was to leave your opponent without "see"—that is, in a position where the object ball is shielded from the cue ball. In such a case, he was said to be left "snookered."

The match was scheduled to be played over seventeen days in six cities, opening in New York and then moving to Fort Lauderdale, Los Angeles, San Francisco, and Denver, winding up in Chicago. The match was first class in every respect. In New York, we played at the historic India House on Hanover Square, and attendance was by invitation only. Rex Williams, who at age forty was twenty years my junior, was as elegant and dignified as the surroundings. We each wore formal attire, with vests and French cuffs, and the crowd, which was dressed in black tie for the evening session, was as serenely reserved as an opening-night audience at the Met. Except for polite but earnest applause at the end of each game, the match was played in total silence.

I won the coin toss giving me the option of selecting which game we opened with, and in keeping with the tone of the occasion, I said, "We'll play snooker first." Williams, who had held his title uninterrupted for the past seven years, was as good as advertised. His shots were crisp and true, and he played excellent position on the numbered balls. He beat me 85–35 in the first game, but I was watching him closely and picking up some pointers. In the second game, I took the lead for a while, and after I made a good run, Williams smiled and said, "Willie, this is supposed to by *my* game." It was a completely different atmosphere from a pool tournament. He congratulated me when I made a good shot, and I did likewise. Williams rallied to win the second game, but I was beginning to get the knack of it, and I won the third one 89–37. When we switched to pool, it was no contest. I won it 150–8 with a high run of fifty-seven and took an eleven-point lead, 21½–10½, under the tournament scoring system.

As we moved from city to city, I continued to stretch my advantage. I think it was easier for me to adjust to his game than it was for him to adapt to mine. In snooker, you never have more than six numbered balls on the table, so he had difficulty playing position for the long runs that are required in straight pool, where you might be planning ahead for as many as twelve or thirteen shots. By the end of the tour, I had won all six games of pocket billiards and seven of the eighteen snooker matches, which gave me a winning margin of 179–66½.

Williams, ever the gracious gentleman, sent Flora and me a beautiful set of crystal when he returned to England, with a note saying how much he enjoyed our contest. We reciprocated with an appropriate gift, and that concluded my brief venture into the English world of snooker. For the next few years I contented myself with giving some exhibitions, playing celebrity golf in the Florida sun, and taking life easier than I ever had before. I was, after all, in my sixties now, nearing retirement age for most people. Little did I suspect that as I approached my sixty-fifth birthday, a whole new career was about to open up for me. With the inadvertent help of Minnesota Fats, I was about to become a television personality.

CHAPTER

16

Six years after my initial challenge, Minnesota Fats and I finally crossed cues. The showdown came about following an unusual succession of events and a spontaneous confrontation that took place before network television cameras. Fats was preparing to play another self-proclaimed pool hustler, Bruce Christopher, for a segment of ABC-TV's *Wide World of Sports*. Howard Cosell was going to call the match, while I served as color commentator and analyst. The show was being taped on October 22, 1977, to be aired later that year. During the introductions, one of the cameras broke down, and while it was being repaired Fats, never the shy one, entertained the audience. He was bragging about all the tournament players and former champions he had beaten, and when he lumped me in with the others I called him on it. We went at it hot and heavy until Cosell and a few of the others restored order and we got on with the filming. But I guess the seed was planted. A few months later I received a phone call from Bill Cayton, of Big Fights, Inc., one of the leading promoters of boxing matches, offering me the opportunity to play Minnesota Fats on a future segment of the same television program. He was enthusiastic about the prospects of such a match, and his enthusiasm extended to offering me a performance fee as well as a shot at the winner's share of the prize money. All in all, it amounted to one of those proverbial offers that could not be refused. The match was set for February 14, Valentine's Day, 1978. Here, I thought, was the rare opportunity to play executioner in a latter-day version of the St. Valentine's Day Massacre.

▲ ▲ ▲

Charlie Ursitti, who helped initiate the bizarre chain of circumstances that led to the shootout, recalls how it unfolded:

"I was working as production manager for a printing company in New York when Bruce Christopher walked in on a June day in 1977 and asked me to print some posters for him. One of them read, 'Pool Player Beats Maharajah for $70,000,' and he went on to tell me how he went to India and played the Maharajah on a gold pool table and won a small fortune. He also told me a lot of other stories, some true, others not so true. He was an engaging guy, somewhere around my age, and we started to pal-out together. One night he told me that Minnesota Fats had phoned to say he was coming to town for a fund-raiser in Fort Lee, New Jersey. Bruce and I went to watch him perform, and perform is exactly the word for it. He played a little pool, but mostly he entertained the audience with a line of patter that had them laughing hard and long. 'I've been playing this game since Moby Dick was a guppie,' he would say. 'I played the kaiser when he was on the lam in Switzerland.' 'I went to Hong Kong and played Happy the Chinaman and he ain't smiled since.' He sounded a little like W. C. Fields and was almost as funny. People had paid one hundred dollars a plate to see him and no one was asking for a refund. Ever on the alert for a money-making idea, I offered Christopher a proposition.

" 'Bruce,' I said, 'you're billing yourself as the greatest contemporary pool hustler. Fats is the legendary hustler of years past. What do you think we can cook up with that set of ingredients?'

"After a few false starts, I got in touch with Big Fights and sat down to discuss the possibilities with Jimmy Jacobs. He and Bill Cayton liked the idea, and they sold the match to ABC. With the taping coming up in just a few weeks, I told Bruce he had better start working out and I offered to serve as his opponent. We started to play, and I found I was holding my own. Now I was a fairly decent pool-room player but certainly not of the caliber to challenge Minnesota Fats. I said, 'Bruce, let it all out, don't hold back.' He said, 'I'm not holding back.' I said, 'You're having trouble beating me, how do you expect to beat Minnesota Fats?' So I knew right then that I had gotten involved in something of a fiasco.

"The match was scheduled for the Starlight Roof of the Waldorf-Astoria before a live audience, and everyone involved in the production showed up in a tuxedo except for Fats, who was wearing a pair of baggy pants and a pullover shirt. He had his reasons. 'Putting a tuxedo on a pool player,' he explained, 'is like putting a scoop of ice cream on a hot dog.' He obviously was in good form, and as the night wore on it would serve all of us well. I was acting as rules judge, and I introduced Cosell, who was about to introduce Willie when one of the cameras broke down. Those attending had paid as much as one hundred dollars a seat to see the match, so we asked Fats to entertain them while the camera was being repaired.

He tossed off a few one-liners and then started taking questions from the spectators.

" 'You ever beat Ralph Greenleaf?' someone asked.

" 'I played Greenleaf a hundred nights in a row and I beat him a hundred nights in a row,' Fats said.

"He went on that way for a while, explaining how he never lost a cash match in his life, and finally someone thought to ask: 'Did you ever beat Willie Mosconi?'

"Fats never answered directly. He hesitated a few seconds and then he said, 'I played 'em all, and I beat 'em all.'

"With that, Willie bolted from his chair and practically ran at Fats. His face was red and you could see the veins bulging in his neck. 'You beat *me?*' he said. 'You never beat *me!* I played you once in Philadelphia and I had to give you train fare to get out of town.'

"They stood there nose-to-nose until we stepped in and separated them. You could sense the excitement in the crowd. Cosell, Jacobs, and I looked at one another and I think we all had the same idea. When play finally began, Fats completely destroyed Christopher; the match was so dull and the production so poor that the program never aired. Bruce, for his part, proved that he was a better hustler than he was a pool player. But in a larger sense, he served me well, for the Mosconi–Minnesota Fats match was now a fait accompli, and that would produce enough money for all of us to make out pretty well. It was, after all, a storybook confrontation. You could not imagine two men more unlike in background, style, disposition, and temperament, and they had, in the bargain, been involved in a feud of more than ten years' duration."

▲ ▲ ▲

Rudolf Walter Wanderone, Jr., was born in the Washington Heights section of Upper Manhattan on January 19, 1913, the same year Willie Mosconi was born. They both took up the game of pool at the age of six. They had little else in common. From the very start, Fats was taken by the prospect of the easy score. When he was seven years old, to hear him tell it, he hustled another youngster out of a bag of gumdrops and sent him home crying. By the age of ten, he says, he was playing for "cash."

"I've been haunting poolrooms from here to Zanzibar for almost forty-five years," he writes in his 1966 autobiography. "I've played every game in the book and some fantastic propositions you wouldn't imagine. I whacked out every top player in the game, including all those fun players who dress up in tuxedos and play in those big tournaments for trophies and $4 in prizes. The only trouble with those fun players is that they wouldn't bet fat meat is greasy if they had to put up their own cash. They wouldn't play for a grape if they owned a vineyard. But I've beaten them all."

In Fats's lexicon, "fun" players are the tournament professionals, while "cash" players are those who back themselves with their own money, who are willing to play for "the cheese." It is a distinction he makes at every opportunity, and he is untroubled by the fact that virtually every fun player started out playing for cash, some, like Willie, earning their living that way before turning professional. But to seek verification in the Tales of Minnesota Fats is to miss the point entirely.

If the stories he tells do not always conform to reality, it is not because he is a liar but because he is indifferent to the truth, unwilling to allow it to distort the image that his story imparts. Fats is, at bottom, a storyteller. He leans heavily on imagination to embellish the bare threads of the actual. It remains for the listener to sift the one from the other or to ignore the distinction and simply take each story as one would a fairy tale by Grimm, with the payoff being a laugh instead of a moral. For Fats owes his celebrity more to his wit and his gift for invention than to his prowess at the table. He is an entertainer who uses pool as his backdrop in much the same way that Victor Borge, gifted though he is, often uses his piano as a prop for his comedy routines.

Early on, Fats affected a style of delivery that calls to mind the soft, derisive drawl of W. C. Fields. "I'm going to play that fun player, Willie Moscooohnee. Well, Willie, when are we going to play for the cheeeese?" Though he built a large part of his celebrity by scoffing at the high sense of purpose Mosconi brought to his calling, in his rare serious moments, Fats was quick to acknowledge Willie's proficiency with the cue stick. "That kreeetrue could really lay it down," he would say, in his own inimitable fashion.

"I always liked him," says Flora Mosconi. "Face-to-face, he's really a nice person, very kind and very witty. I think most of his bragging and boasting was part of a show business routine that he used to get recognition for himself. You can't help but laugh when you listen to him, he's really very funny, but Willie was never amused. What bothered Willie was that billiards was his life's work and he took it very seriously. He felt it was a prestigious game and he devoted himself to improving its image, and Minnesota Fats made a joke of it. He just used it to promote himself. To Willie, Fats was destroying what Willie had tried all his life to build."

If, as Alexander Pope said, language is the clothing in which thought is dressed, it is perhaps equally true that clothing expresses an attitude that requires no words. The manner in which Willie and Fats dressed for work testified to how each man viewed his occupation. For even his most casual exhibitions, Willie always wore a sports coat; an evening tournament match dictated the wearing of a tuxedo. Fats sneered at such formality.

"A tuxedo?" he said. "I was driving Duesenbergs in 1933 when so many millionaires were jumping out of windows you could walk down the street and catch them in nets, and I never wore a tuxedo. I've played everywhere on earth—twice. I played the shah of Iran when there wasn't any Iran; it was Persia then, and I didn't wear a tux."

When they arrived at the Waldorf for their Valentine's Day tryst, billed by ABC as "The Match of the Century for the All-Time Heavyweight Championship of Pool," Willie was wearing a sports coat and shirt with an open collar. Fats, dressed in a leisure suit and a pullover shirt, removed his jacket when play was about to begin. Jimmy Jacobs asked Willie to do likewise. Willie balked. "I always play in a coat," he said. But not when a television network is calling the shots. "Willie," Jacobs implored, "please take off your jacket for the television show." Grudgingly, Willie complied, and the audience, mindful of Willie's taste for propriety, applauded cheerfully.

▲▲▲

I had practiced intensively, every day, for several weeks before the match. It was not particularly difficult to find my stroke. Although I hadn't been playing regularly for the past few years, the mechanics come back to you quickly. The body has a memory of its own and it retains what it knows in the same way that the mind does. But I was attuned to the strategies and pace of straight pool—150 points to a game—which could be played over the course of an hour or more. Television had no interest in covering such a match, and Fats had even less interest in playing one. We were scheduled to play short-rack games—eight-ball, nine-ball, and rotation. Each of these games involved a measure of luck, since the shooter did not have to call each shot. Anything that fell on the break counted, and a player could sometimes fire into a cluster of balls and take his chances. Nine-ball, in fact, could sometimes be won on the break without another ball being made. These were all trick games that required the mastering of a particular technique rather than the overall proficiency that was needed in straight pool. They were like the spinoff basketball games that kids often play in the schoolyard—"around the world" or "h-o-r-s-e." They require a certain amount of skill, but you just have to be a shooter or a trick-shot artist to win them; you don't need the medley of skills it takes to be a quality basketball player.

So I worked hard at perfecting the techniques required for those games. I approached this match as seriously as I had a challenge match for the title. After all that had passed between us, I did not want to lose any kind of pool game to Minnesota Fats, certainly not in public and with millions of people watching on television. And besides, there was a healthy chunk of prize money at stake, for the winner was to receive ten times as much as the loser—fifteen thousand dollars to fifteen hundred dollars.

Hollywood could not have designed a set more fitting for the occasion than the Starlight Roof of the Waldorf. It was an elegant, luxurious room with eleven chandeliers of ornate crystal hanging from a twenty-four-foot ceiling, and it fairly glistened with old-world chic. The price of admission ranged from one hundred dollars for "golden ringside" seats to ten dollars for the back of the room. But the elaborate setting had little effect on Fats. There was a large audience in front of him and TV cameras grinding away, and that was all the encouragement he needed.

As Howard Cosell started to make the introductions, Fats took it upon himself to summon from the bleachers someone he described as the pool champion of New Jersey and ask him to take a bow.

"All the good pool players live in Joisey," Fats announced. "There's a slew of 'em in the Palisades. You need a bow and arrow to get an even break over there."

"Shut up, Fats, I'm about to go on," Cosell said.

But Fats kept on going without missing a beat.

"Folks, this is just another demonstration of Fats's taciturnity," Howard said. "Fats, you speak with total clarity and absolute irrelevance."

Fats grinned.

"What do we need with Willie, Howard," he said. "We got the show going, you and me. You talk Harvard and I talk Bowery."

"In that case," said Cosell, "you should have said, 'You and I.'"

After Cosell introduced me as "the incomparable, yes, the legendary fifteen-time world champion," Fats chose to make the case for himself.

"How come I got all the cash?" he said. "Six brand-new Cadillacs in the driveway. Every time a bird flies overhead I get another one. I let dogs and cats sit in presidential limousines."

Through all this banter, I just sat back and waited for the games to begin. We were to play nine-ball first, then eight-ball, then rotation, each in a best-of-nine series. Fats had already given his performance, with his mouth, and when we started to play, I gave mine with the cue stick, winning in straight sets, 5–3, 5–2, 5–2. When the match was over, Fats and I each demonstrated some trick shots. Fats missed his closing shot three times in a row. I made mine on the second try, and Fats, unfazed by defeat and irrepressible, announced, "I taught him that one, and he used it to break all the bootleggers in South Philly."

The show was aired on *Wide World of Sports* on February 26 and attracted that show's second-largest viewing audience of the year, exceeded only by the Muhammad Ali–Leon Spinks heavyweight title fight. It was the kind of success that television networks could not ignore. A rematch, billed as The Great Pool Shootout, was booked for the following year at Caesars Palace in Las Vegas. This time, in addition to nine-ball, we played one-pocket, which was Fats's speciality, and my own game of straight pool. Since it took longer to play one-pocket and straight pool, each set was best two of three, but it did not change the outcome. I beat Fats 2–1 in one-pocket and shut him out in the other two. He put on his usual comic performance, relating how he beat this one and that, then proceeded to lose with unruffled good humor.

We were, in a sense, becoming a two-man, television road show. I didn't mind because the money was good, we traveled first class, and there was little pressure on me. We would play each other, in some form of competition, each of the next five years on various television networks. But in 1979, I interrupted my budding TV career to go to Hollywood and make a pool movie called *The Baltimore Bullet*. Now in my mid-sixties, it seemed I was becoming a show biz personality. It wasn't a bad way to make a living.

CHAPTER

It had been almost twenty years between movies, and I was clearly becoming typecast. Whenever a film on pool was being made, my phone rang. This time the call came from John Brascia, the producer. I had known John for many years, and he called to offer me a small part in the movie. My career appeared to be on the rise because this was a talking part. I was to play the role of the expert television commentator at a shootout between a pool hustler named Nick Casey (the Baltimore Bullet), played by James Coburn, and a renowned gambler known as the Deacon, played by Omar Sharif. My services as technical adviser would not be needed since the film also featured ten professional players, including Steve Mizerak, Allen Hopkins, Mike Sigel, and Irving Crane.

The story line owed something to *The Hustler* because it centered around the Bullet's film-long quest for a showdown with the Deacon, who had once beaten him for a large sum of money. But beyond that, the moods of the two movies were entirely different. *The Hustler*, filmed in black and white, was a somber film in the genre of such classics as *On the Water-front* and *Body and Soul*. *The Baltimore Bullet* had a light side to it. It was an action comedy, with Nick and his partner, Billie Joe Robbins (Bruce Boxleitner), getting themselves into and out of all sorts of trouble as they tried to build a stake with which to challenge the Deacon. It got a bit corny at times, but it was an entertaining movie with lots of good pool, and I enjoyed working on it.

I spent three weeks in Hollywood filming the scenes I was involved in, and they were three very long weeks. Flo and Gloria went with me, and they worked almost as hard as I did. Flora wangled them parts as extras, and they discovered that being a movie star wasn't all play.

▲ ▲ ▲

"As soon as we got there, I asked Johnny Brascia if Gloria and I could be in the movie," Flora Mosconi recalls. But he said no, you have to be in the union. I said, 'You don't have to pay us, we'll pay you; I always wanted to be in a movie.' He still said no, but the next day the director came up to us and said we could be extras. The other extras, who were real actors, kept saying, 'How long have you been working in movies? I've never seen you before.' I told them, 'We work out of New York.'

"We put in long hours, but it was great. Gloria and I loved meeting all the movie stars, and they were all as nice as can be. Omar Sharif was just as he appears on the screen. He had smooth, continental manners, and when he looked in your eyes you would melt. But it was really hard work. We were up at five o'clock every morning and went right out to the set, and we didn't get home until six or seven in the evening. You also had to wear the same clothes every day and fix your hair the same way because it could take several days to film a scene that might run three minutes in the movie. When our parts were completed, Gloria and I were each given one hundred dollars for our efforts, but it was well worth it. We had a wonderful time.

"Our last night there, a Saturday night, we were all going out to dinner together. They wanted to go to a fancy Italian restaurant in Westwood, but there were twenty-two of us and we had trouble getting a reservation. James Coburn called and they told him they were all booked up. I said, 'Let me talk to him.' So I got on the phone and spoke to the owner in Italian, and finally he said, 'Okay, signora, we'll squeeze you in.' "

▲ ▲ ▲

After putting in twelve-hour days and playing the same scene over and over again, it was a relief to come back home and return to the television circuit. In the early eighties, pool was becoming a major attraction on TV. CBS began competing with ABC for the rights to some shows, and then ESPN, the sports cable network, got into the act and eventually cornered the market. The tournaments were held in the casino-hotels in Atlantic City and Las Vegas. They drew huge crowds and the taped broadcasts held their own in the ratings. Fats and I were always involved, but the producers varied the formats in order to sustain interest.

In 1981, ESPN introduced a series called The Legendary Stars of Pocket Billiards, which sometimes featured team play as well as individual competition. The most noteworthy of these tournaments was held in 1982 at Harrah's Marina Casino in Atlantic City. It was an eight-man, double-elimination tournament that, in addition to Fats and me, also included Irving Crane, Luther Lassiter, Joe Balsis, Babe Cranfield, Jimmy Moore, and U. J. Puckett, a colorful cowboy hustler from Texas, who was seventy-two years old and still on the move. With five former world champions participating, it was as close to tournament competition as I had come in almost twenty years. But the atmosphere was loose and convivial; it was hard to be serious when Fats was around. We got started fairly early in the morning, an hour not suited to Fats's style of living.

"Hitler couldn't get me up this early if I was in the German army," he announced. He came up to me as I was removing my cue stick from its carrying case and said, "Hey, Mosconi, what you got in there, four rifles? I fought in the Russian-European War and didn't need no outfit like that." Then he went into his routine, which by now I knew almost as well as he did. "I'm the one who started the CIA," he said. "I had spies in every pool room from here to Zanzibar. I heard Cannonball was down in Austin, so I head down to Texas. This man was there," he said, pointing to Puckett, "he'll tell you what I done." "Yeah, Fatty," Puckett said, "you turned ol' Cannonball into a BB." During the introductions, Allen Hopkins, who was doing the color commentary for ESPN, tried to silence Fats. "You can't stand being quiet, can you?" he chided. "Quiet's for suckers," Fats said. "You want quiet, go to a library."

The format of the tournament was double elimination, with the winners' bracket playing the losers' in the final. Each match consisted of a best four-of-seven series of seven-ball, another of nine-ball, and a best-of-three eight-ball set in the event of a tie. As the luck of the draw would have it, my first opponent was Fats, and I won four straight after dropping the first two games of seven-ball, then took four of five at nine-ball. I went undefeated through the rest of the tournament, finishing up with a double shutout of Jimmy Moore to win first-place prize money of ten thousand dollars.

I won the tournament again in each of the next two years, and to my surprise, I found myself growing fond of Fats. How could I not like him? Every time he opened his mouth I made money, and his mouth was always open. In 1983, we were playing at Caesars Boardwalk Regency in Atlantic City, and he came marching in and announced, "I've been playing in Atlantic City since the turn of the century. I was here when there wasn't any beach." I sat there quietly, took some cotton out of my pocket and stuffed it in my ears. Then I beat the daylights out of him and pocketed the check. I was hoping he would never shut up. I was seventy years old, semiretired, and I was making more money than I ever had in my life. In addition to my TV earnings, I was then serving as head of the Billiard Pro Advisory staff for Ajay/Ebonite, a division of the Fuqua Sporting Goods company, and all told I was making over six figures and enjoying every minute of it.

The Legendary Stars competition was discontinued after 1984, but by that time I was as well known in Atlantic City as I was in Philadelphia, and I accepted a position as an executive host at Caesars. I worked Thursday through Sunday, from six in the evening till two in the morning, entertaining high rollers. I sometimes worked with Bob Pelligrini, who was a linebacker for the Philadelphia Eagles in the fifties and sixties. We would greet special guests, have dinner with them, attend parties given by management. But when they started gambling, I got out of there. I wanted no part of it. It was nothing for some of them to lose as much as five hundred thousand dollars at a sitting, and you never knew how they were going to react. I also handed out business cards and promoted the hotel at fund-raisers and charities around the country. It was a nothing kind of a job, and it was dull as hell. I stayed in a suite at the hotel, and Flora came down on weekends. She enjoyed it, but I found it tedious, just hanging around, talking to people I didn't know, not doing anything that seemed particularly useful to me. I stayed at Caesars for a while, then moved to Harrah's, and finally, in 1986, I quit. I wasn't used to working regular eight-hour days and having someone tell me what I was supposed to be doing every minute I was there. I had worked for bosses only a few times in my life, and it was never a situation I enjoyed. So I decided to get out of there and take life easy.

Since then, I've remained active but no more so than I choose to be. I'm under contract to an equipment manufacturer in California called World of Leisure, and I give about a dozen exhibitions a year in various parts of the country. It's gratifying to know that I'm still somewhat in demand and that people still remember. Hardly a day goes by that I don't get three or four requests for autographs, and many of them come from people who were not yet born when I was playing professionally.

But aside from the exhibitions, I'm mostly a homebody now. When the weather permits, I shoot some golf, in the low to mid-eighties on a good day. I used to be able to get down into the mid-seventies on occasion, and I have the hardware to prove it. I won trophies at the Inverrary Classic in 1974 and 1978, and I won the IVB Gold Classic Pro-Am in 1974. But you lose a little when you don't play regularly, and the years take something away as well. It's the same with pool. I can still run a few racks, and I've performed the trick shots so often that I can make them in my sleep, but you have to play regularly to remain sharp, and I rarely play at all now. I practice for an hour or two before an exhibition, but the pool table in the basement serves mostly as a place for Flora to store the laundry when she takes it out of the dryer. It's a four and a half by nine table, the only one I ever owned, and I didn't get it until the early fifties, about ten years after I won my first title. Until then, I had always practiced in public rooms. That comes as a surprise to most people, and it was because that bit of information was so unexpected that I received my table in the first place.

I had been invited to appear on a popular, prime-time television show called *I've Got a Secret.* The show was hosted by Garry Moore, and it featured a regular panel of celebrities who tried to guess the secret of a guest personality. My secret was that although I had been world champion for many years and worked for the country's leading manufacturer of billiard equipment, I did not own my own table. I suppose that Brunswick was a bit embarrassed by the secret becoming public, and a few days later the table was delivered to my home.

It's seen a lot of use over the past forty years, but now the cover comes off mainly when my youngest grandson comes to visit. He makes a beeline for the basement and starts pushing the balls around the table the same as I did when I was his age. People say that maybe he'll follow in his grandfather's footsteps, but I would prefer that he find an easier way to make a living. Professional billiards has its rewards, but it's a tough life.

I've reflected on it a great deal in recent years. Quite often, when I'm scheduled to play an exhibition, reporters for the local papers interview me and, naturally enough, they are more interested in my past than my present. Invariably, one of the first questions I'm asked is who I regard as the greatest pocket billiards player of all time. I never answer the question. It's not for me to say who was the best; it's up to the public to decide. I would rather people remember that I always played it clean, that I respected my opponents and never tried to humiliate or embarrass anyone, that I tried to elevate the game and bring it some dignity. That would be the highest tribute.

▲ ▲ ▲

In the basement of the Mosconi home in Haddon Heights, New Jersey, the present pays its homage to the past. Amidst the random scatter of odds and ends, the room has the aura of an impromptu museum. The walls are adorned with photographs, plaques, certificates, drawings. Trophies stand like timeless sentries on shelves near the foot of the staircase. Each memento has its root in decades past, most dating from the forties and fifties, a time when Willie held dominion over the world of pocket billiards with a sovereignty that few contested.

Across the room, beneath bright fluorescent lights, those days of quiet glory seem to shake themselves awake again. The table, his private field of battle, is draped in a colorless plastic cover. Nearby, an arsenal of cue sticks waits in its rack. Willie, dressed in soft beige slacks and a green pullover shirt, steers his guest in the direction of the table. He moves with the sure, practiced ease of a man who is about to start down a road he has traveled many times before. When he reaches the table, he peels back a corner of the cover and motions for you to do the same at the other end. At Willie's direction, the cover is removed and folded carefully, reverently, with the same respect for detail that a combat veteran might show when laying away a flag that has flown in battle. The table is smooth, spotless, with the cared-for look of finely brushed suede. Willie racks a set of cue balls, eyes it for symmetry. Then, from a soft leather case, he removes the two parts of a hand-crafted, custom-made cue stick. He screws them together, handling the stick like a concert violinist tuning his Stradivarius.

"Wanna see me run a rack?" he asks.

He flicks the nose ball from the front of the pack, lets it roll to a stop. He spots the cue ball quickly, then drives the loose ball into the corner pocket. The cue ball follows its own course. It veers right and hurtles into the pack. The balls burst open in a kaleidoscope of whirling colors.

As you watch, the lights seem to flicker and fade. With a certain weightlessness, you feel half a century melt away and the present roll back upon the past. Glittering chandeliers light the room from high ceilings. Drapes the color of royalty shield the windows, banish the blinking night lights of a city growing dark. The bleachers, banked in steeply ascending tiers, are filled but shrouded in stillness. At center stage, on a wooden platform atop the carpeted floors, a youthful Willie Mosconi, resplendent in black tie and French cuffs, is working his magic. He is moving briskly, with a dancer's grace. You can hear his heels tapping out a staccato beat as he scurries from one end of the table to the other. Each time there is a brief pause followed by a sharp clicking sound and the hum of a ball rolling down the return chute. "Three ball," he says, "fourteen ball . . . six ball." The pace, already rapid, seems to quicken as he moves. The balls are flashing into the pockets with a suddenness that startles the eye. Rack after rack dissolves, is replaced by a fresh one.

The lone figure, a virtuoso playing his own music to a rhythm only he can hear, continues to move about the table, almost trotting now. He is on the way to his next destination before the cue ball comes to rest. The cue stick appears to have a life of its own, as if it is tugging the arm forward. "Four ball, thirteen ball, two ball . . ." until you hear the referee call, "Game, Mosconi."

Now, Willie Mosconi, his face ruddy and full, lined with the trials of nearly eight decades, his thinning white hair combed straight back, his gray eyes as bright and as clear as fine crystal, is chalking his cue stick. He surveys the balls scattered across the table, then leans in. With a sniper's concentration, he sights down the barrel of his cue. He strokes twice, fires.

CAREER HIGHLIGHTS

Championships

1941 . . . . . cross-country tournament
1942 . . . . . tournament, Detroit
1944 . . . . . challenge match vs. Andrew Ponzi, Kansas City
1945 . . . . . challenge match vs. Ralph Greenleaf, two cities
1946 . . . . . challenge match vs. Jimmy Caras, cross-country
1946 . . . . . challenge match vs. Irving Crane, cross-country
1947 . . . . . challenge match vs. Irving Crane, two cities
1947 . . . . . challenge match vs. Jimmy Caras, three cities
1948 . . . . . challenge match vs. Andrew Ponzi, Chicago
1950 . . . . . tournament, Chicago
1951 . . . . . challenge match vs. Irving Crane, Philadelphia
1951 . . . . . tournament, Chicago
1952 . . . . . tournament, Boston
1953 . . . . . tournament, San Francisco
1955 . . . . . challenge match vs. Joe Procita, three cities
1955 . . . . . challenge match vs. Irving Crane, Philadelphia
1956 . . . . . challenge match vs. Jimmy Caras, six cities
1956 . . . . . challenge match vs. Jimmy Moore, Albuquerque
1956 . . . . . tournament, Kinston, North Carolina

Records

High run (exhibition)—526, Springfield, Illinois, 1954

Best game—run of 150 in one inning, vs. Jimmy Moore, Kinston, North Carolina, 1956

Best grand average, world tournament—averaged 18.34 balls per inning, Chicago, 1950

INDEX

ABC-TV, 226, 230, 236
Abie's Irish Rose (play), 113–114
Adams, John Quincy, 14
Air force camp tours, 152–153
Ajay/Ebonite (Fuqua Sporting
    Goods company), 238
Alcohol, 51–52, 53, 54, 116, 145
Ali, Muhammad, 233
All-American Conference, 123
Allen, Bennie, 15, 68, 101, 131,
    132
Allinger, Sol, 216
Allinger's Billiard Parlor
    (Philadelphia), 13, 31–32, 36,
    63, 67, 71, 76, 80, 145, 149,
    150, 151, 162, 165, 168, 169,
    173, 180, 191, 215–216
Ames Billiard Parlor (New York),
    216
Angelo, Joe, 8
Association of College Unions, 137
Astaire, Adele, 4
Astaire, Fred, 4
Attendance records, 122, 171

Baker, Harold, 212
Balkline, 142–143
Balsis, Joe, 211–212, 213, 236

Baltimore Bullet, The (movie),
    233, 234–235
Banks Business College, 18
Bank Shot and Other Great
    Robberies, The (Minnesota
    Fats), 218
Bank shots, 198
Barrett Junior High School, 18
Barrymore, John, 146
Baseball, 3, 12, 16, 17, 19, 20–21,
    49, 83, 87, 100, 122, 140, 175
Basketball, 41, 123, 139, 172, 188,
    231
Battles, Don, 17
Bensinger's Recreational
    Amphitheater (Chicago), 13,
    42–44, 135, 151, 216
Berra, Yogi, 78
Better Billiard Players of America,
    165
Better Billiards Program, 45–46,
    47–61
Big Fights, Inc., 224, 226
Billiard Association of America, 33,
    34, 44, 45, 90, 106, 112
Billiard Congress of America, 33,
    133, 136, 138, 139, 140, 145,
    153, 164–170, 178, 191, 207,
    211, 212

Billiard Digest, 217
Binner, C. P., 119
Black athletes, 123, 208
Black Velvet Canadian Whiskey, 220
Booking agents, 55–57, 60–61
Bowling, 176, 206, 209
Boxing, 1, 2, 4, 16, 17, 100, 155, 176, 197, 224, 233
Boxleitner, Bruce, 234
Brascia, John, 234, 235
Break ball, 50, 74, 88
Breit, Jack, 212, 213
Bribes, 188
Bridge, 2
Brookshire, Tom, 219
Brown, Eddie, 34
Bruney, Earl, 167
Brunswick-Balke-Collender, 14–15, 44–46, 47–61, 73, 76, 119, 131, 138, 152, 166, 176, 179, 190, 206–207, 209, 240
Burbank's House of Champions, 212

Cable television, 236–238
Caesars Boardwalk Regency (Atlantic City), 238–239
Caesars Palace (Las Vegas), 233
Canelli, John, 165
Canton, Joe, 152, 154, 165
Caras, Frankie, 17
Caras, Jimmy, 23, 24, 34, 43, 44, 45, 62, 63–72, 76, 78–80, 82, 83, 87, 91, 92, 94–97, 119, 120–122, 126, 134, 136, 139, 159–160, 171, 176–177, 185
Carom billiards, 133–134, 135–136, 138, 142–145, 176, 212, 219
Cayton, Bill, 224, 226

CBS-TV, 236
Chalk, 210
Champion players, 8–10, 23–24, 33, 42–55, 67–70, 76–92, 94–98, 127, 138, 139, 150, 208, 209. *See also specific players*
Chenier, George, 152, 154
Chess, 9
Chicago Outdoors Show, 134, 138, 140, 151, 153, 210
Chicago White Sox, 101
Christopher, Bruce, 224, 225–227
Church, Arthur, 37
Cigarettes, 183, 185
Coburn, James, 234–236
Coffee, 183, 185
College circuit, 137–138, 188, 206, 209
Commercial jet travel, 123
Concentration, 88–89, 98, 115, 179
  loss of, 66, 68, 75, 97, 190, 213
Consistency, 102–103, 129
Continuous pool, 40–41, 173, 177
Cortelyou, James T., 10–11
Cosell, Howard, 224, 226, 227, 232
Coslosky, Al, 142
Country clubs, 175
Covington, Willis, 142
Crane, Irving, 68, 69, 76, 91–92, 94–97, 104, 124–136, 139, 142, 149–151, 154–156, 159–160, 164–174, 177–181, 191, 208, 212, 213, 234, 236
Cranfield, Babe, 134, 154, 208, 236
Cue ball, 2, 40–42, 49, 87, 88, 97, 110, 125, 133, 150, 160, 164, 184, 221, 222, 241, 242
Cue stick, 2, 42, 87, 209, 210, 216, 242, 243

D'Allesandro, Andrew. *See* Ponzi, Andrew
Dancing, 4–5, 73
Dean, Dizzy, 21
Defense, 88, 121, 141, 222
Delaying tactics, 129–130
DeMarco, Roland, 197
Democratic Chronicle, 110
Dempsey, Jack, 12, 21
De Oro, Alfredo, 8, 15, 40, 177
Depression, 18, 20–21, 37, 56, 62, 73, 90, 99, 103
Detroit Recreation, 189, 216
Diamond, Legs, 26
Dickson, Gloria Mosconi, 185, 200–201, 235
Diehl, Joe, 68
DiMaggio, Joe, 83, 86, 122
Dion, Cyrille, 15
Divisional competitions, 33, 34, 36
Double elimination, 237
Downtown Bowl (San Francisco), 159
Doyle's Academy (New York), 80
Drew University, 161
Dunham's Academy (Rochester, New York), 109–110
Durocher, Leo, 21

East High Billiard Club, 167
Eight-ball, 231–233, 237
English, 2, 133, 143
Erickson, Frank, 56
Ervolino, Johnny, 212
ESPN, 236–238
Eufemia, Mike, 165, 177–178, 212

Fans, 90, 122–123, 129–130, 146, 171, 210, 211, 212
Fatigue, 164

Fats, Chicago, 217
Fats, Minnesota (Rudolf Wanderone), 42, 153, 196, 200, 203–205, 216–220, 223, 224–233, 236–238
Finch College, 197
Fitzpatrick, Rags, 153–154, 177
Florida, 56, 103, 222
Football, 12, 17, 97, 100, 123, 139, 238
Formats and rules, championship, 33–34, 39–42, 70, 134, 138–142, 164–168
Fort Dix (New Jersey), 116
Four Corners Academy (Newark), 80
14.1 continuous pool, 41, 177
Fox, Tom, 218
Fox Billiard Academy (Philadelphia), 26, 27, 34
France, 152
origins of pool in, 13–14
Franklin, Walter, 131–132
French Revolution, 14
Fuqua Sporting Goods company, 238

Gambling, 14, 163, 188, 216, 238
Gehrig, Lou, 17, 183
GI Bill, 123
Gilchrist, Tom, 10
Gleason, Jackie, 192, 193–196, 199, 200, 201, 204, 205
Golf, 87, 89, 127, 151, 175, 239
Goodman, Izzie, 34
Grange, Red, 12, 21
Graziano, Rocky, 197
Great Pool Shootout, The, 233
Greenleaf, Ralph, 8, 9, 12–13, 15, 21, 23, 31, 32, 35, 38, 42–46, 47–56, 63, 68–69, 70, 74–75,

Greenleaf, Ralph (*cont.*)
  79, 83, 84, 85, 86, 90–92,
  94–97, 101, 103, 106,
  109–116, 129, 136, 145–150,
  156, 160, 170, 177, 214–215,
  227
Greenleaf Memorial Cup, 149
Grove, Harry, 190

Hallman, Harry, 27
Hamilton, Alexander, 14
Harrah's (Atlantic City), 236, 239
Hockey, 139
Hollywood, 73, 213, 233–235
Honeymooners, The (TV show), 196
Hopkins, Allen, 234, 237
Hoppe, Willie, 45, 55, 133–134,
  142–145, 176
Horseracing, 12, 56
Hotels, 57–58
Hueston, Thomas, 15, 137
Hustler, The (movie), 42, 191,
  192–206, 215, 216, 217, 234
Hustlers, 23–26, 29–31, 35–36,
  138, 153–154, 195, 197,
  216–220, 224–235

India House (New York), 222
Intercity League tournament,
  76–92
Inverrary Classic, 239
Invitational Pocket Billiards
  Championship, 211–215
Irish, Johnny, 79–80, 136
IVB Gold Classic Pro-Am, 239
I've Got a Secret (TV show), 240

Jacobs, Jimmy, 226, 227, 230
James, Jesse, 26

Jefferson, Thomas, 14
Johnson, Walter, 12
Jones, Bobby, 12
Jones, Nixon, 164
Julian's Academy (New York), 76,
  80, 209–211
Juvenile players, 8–10

Kelly, George, 34, 38, 39, 43, 44,
  62, 63, 80, 81–82, 84, 91
Kenyon College (Gambier, Ohio),
  198
Keogh, Jerome, 41
Keogh's Academy (Rochester, New
  York), 169–170
Killer instinct, 60–61, 155–156
Kinston tournament, 177–178, 181
Kling, Johnny, 101
Kling & Allen's Recreation (Kansas
  City), 101, 104, 131, 151
Knight, Samuel F., 15

Ladies' billiard champions, 10
Lambs Club (New York), 195, 196
Laney, Al, 64
Lassiter, Luther, 159–160, 165,
  167–170, 177–178, 191, 208,
  236
Lauri, Onofrio, 37, 76, 80, 82, 83,
  84, 91, 209–212
Laurie, Piper, 204, 205
Layton, Ohio, 124
Legendary Stars of Pocket
  Billiards, The, 236–238
Little Leagues, 16
Livingston, Sylvester, 55–57,
  60–61, 74, 81
Local players, 58–59
Loesser, Frank, 192
Longo, Phil, 22–23, 67

Louis, Joe, 86
Louis XI, King of France, 14
Louis XIV, King of France, 14
Luck, 127, 144, 231

McGinnis, Ruth, 10, 11
McGirr, Bob, 77, 78
McGirr's Academy (New York), 13,
 77, 78, 83, 198, 221
McGoorty, Dan, *McGoorty: A
 Billiard Hustler's Life*, 53–54
Mack, Connie, 17
Magistrelli, Joe, 219
Man o' War, 12
Mantle, Mickey, 87
Martin, Pepper, 21
Mason, Frankie, 22, 23, 26, 27,
 71, 216, 217
Massé shots, 198
Mingaud, Captain, 14
Mizerak, Steve, 212, 234
Moore, Jimmy, 154, 160, 165, 167,
 168, 177–178, 191, 208, 212,
 213, 236, 237
Mosconi, Ann Harrison, 93–94,
 104, 113, 117–118, 120, 157,
 160–163
Mosconi, Candace, 104, 117–118,
 120, 158, 160–163, 187
Mosconi, Flora Marchini,
 157–159, 160–163, 172, 180,
 185–189, 200–201, 223, 229,
 235–236, 238, 239
Mosconi, Joseph William, 1–10,
 18, 22, 29, 31, 32, 39, 113,
 117–118, 189, 218
Mosconi, William, Jr., 93–94,
 117–118, 120, 158, 160–163,
 180, 186–189
Mosconi, Willie:
 on air force camp tours, 152–153

and *The Baltimore Bullet*
 (movie), 233, 234–235
vs. BCA, 164–170
beginnings in billiards, 2–15, 22
Brunswick contract of, 44–46,
 47–61, 73, 119, 131, 138, 152,
 166, 179, 209, 240
and Jimmy Caras, 63–64, 68,
 69–72, 78–80, 82, 83, 87,
 94–97, 119, 120–122, 134,
 136, 139, 159–160, 171,
 176–177
career highlights of, 244–245
as a celebrity, 86–92, 148,
 224–233
childhood of, 1–18, 155–156
on college circuit, 137–138, 209
"comeback" of, 209–214
and Irving Crane, 91–92, 94–97,
 124–136, 142, 149–151,
 154–156, 159–160, 164–174,
 177–181, 208, 213
deserted by his first wife,
 117–118, 120–121, 160–163
early games and winnings,
 22–32
education of, 17–18
enters tournament billiards,
 32–46
and Mike Eufemia, 165,
 177–178
as executive host at Caesars
 (Atlantic City), 238–239
as a father, 93–94, 104, 113,
 117–118, 120–121, 157, 158,
 160–163, 172, 180, 235, 240
and Minnesota Fats, 216–220,
 223, 224–233, 236–238
final retirement from
 championship play, 115,
 214–215
first championship win, 82–92

Mosconi, Willie (*cont.*)
  first marriage of, 93–94, 104,
    113, 117–118, 120–121, 157,
    160–163
  first world championship
    tournament, 39–46, 62
  and Rags Fitzpatrick, 153–154
  and Jackie Gleason, 192–196,
    200, 201, 204, 205
  and Ralph Greenleaf, 9–10, 31,
    42–46, 47–56, 68–69, 74–75,
    79, 84, 90–92, 94–97,
    109–116, 145–150, 160, 170,
    214–215, 227
  Greenleaf Memorial Cup won
    by, 149
  hand accident of, 103–104
  and Willie Hoppe, 133–134,
    142–145, 176
  and *The Hustler* (movie), 191,
    192–206, 234
  in Intercity League tournament,
    76–92
  in Invitational Pocket Billiards
    Championship, 211–215
  in Kinston tournament,
    177–178, 181
  and Luther Lassiter, 159–160,
    168–170, 177–178
  and Onofrio Lauri, 80–84, 91,
    209–212
  in Legendary Stars competition,
    236–238
  and Jimmy Moore, 160, 165,
    167, 168, 177–178, 213, 237
  and Paul Newman, 196–205
  in 1930s tournaments, 39–77
  1950 title of, 141–142, 145
  1953 title of, 159–160, 163–164,
    170, 171
  in 1954 championship
    controversy, 164–172

physical appearance of, 65, 85,
    86, 148, 214, 222, 230, 242,
    243
  playing style of, 2, 43–45,
    48–51, 60–61, 63–66, 68,
    71–72, 75–76, 84, 85–89,
    96–98, 102, 104, 110, 114,
    121, 124–125, 129, 139–140,
    148, 150, 155–156, 164, 179,
    184, 231, 242
  and Andrew Ponzi, 67–70,
    80–83, 87, 94–97, 101–107,
    109, 126, 134–136, 145,
    149–150, 173
  pool hall owned by, 179, 184,
    186, 191
  press on, 81, 82, 83, 84–86, 89,
    110, 124, 130–131, 148, 160,
    162, 167, 181, 240
  pressure on, from competition,
    179–181, 184–185
  and Joe Procita, 80, 81, 82, 87,
    124, 165, 169
  records set by, 130, 136, 147,
    164–167, 177, 178, 214–215,
    245
  relationship with his father,
    1–10, 18, 22, 29, 32, 39,
    117–118, 189, 218
  as retired champion, 115, 209–214
  "retirements" of, 72–74, 93–94
  and Richard Riggie, 177–178
  and Erwin Rudolph, 43–45,
    63–64, 80, 82, 83, 87, 92,
    94–97, 171, 177, 178
  second marriage of, 157–159,
    160–163, 172, 185–189,
    200–201, 235, 238, 239
  speed of, 64–65, 86, 105, 114,
    130
  stroke suffered by, and recovery
    from, 182–191

as a television personality, 223,
224–233, 236–239, 240
temperment of, 66, 68, 75–76,
85–86, 96–97, 105, 126,
130–131, 148, 155–156, 163,
179–180, 186–188, 227
in three-cushion billiard
matches, 133–134
in Tournament of Champions,
94–98
in $20,000 Black Velvet
Challenge, 220–222
and Rex Williams, 220–223
and World War II, 92–94,
98–104, 108–109, 112–118,
120, 122, 124
Movies, pool, 42, 191–206, 215,
216, 217, 233, 234–235
Murphy, Cisero, 208, 212, 213
Murphy, Dan, 219

Nagurski, Bronco, 12, 21
National championships, 32,
33–34, 36–39, 62, 134,
141–142, 152, 154
National Football League, 123
Navarra, Ezequiel, 135–136
NBA, 123
Newby, Earl, 169
Newman, Paul, 196–205
Newsweek magazine, 85
New York Herald Tribune, 64
New York Yankees, 20
Nicklaus, Jack, 87
Nicknames, pool, 153, 212
Nine-ball, 28, 135, 159, 199, 200,
219, 231–233, 237
Nixon, Richard, 202

Object ball, 49–50, 87, 88, 125,
141, 142, 143, 222

O'Briens Academy (Syracuse), 79
Offense, 79, 88
Ohlson, Conrad, 110
One-pocket, 217, 219, 233
Origins of pool, 13–15
Ovington's Billiards (Brooklyn),
209

Palace Theater (New York), 13
Pelligrini, Bob, 238
Pennsylvania Hotel (New York),
62–63, 68
Perlstein, Snooks, 165
Peterson, Charley, 137
Philadelphia Arena, 170–171
Philadelphia Athletics, 3, 17, 19
Philadelphia Eagles, 238
Philadelphia Phillies, 3, 17
Pincus, Fatty, 27–28
Ping-Pong, 176
Pocket billiards, use of the term,
14–15, 40
Pockets, 24–25, 87, 131–132, 133,
140–141, 221
Ponzi, Andrew (Andrew
D'Allesandro), 8, 23, 24, 34,
43, 44, 63, 67–70, 71, 72, 76,
80–83, 87, 91, 92, 94–97,
101–107, 109, 126, 134–135,
139, 145, 149–150, 173
Ponzi, Charles, 106
Ponzi Game, 106
Pool:
in the 1920s, 2–15, 191, 206
in the 1930s, 21–77
in the 1940s, 76–140
in the 1950s, 141–191, 206
in the 1960s, 192–215
in the 1970s, 215–236
in the 1980s, 236–243
origins of the game, 13–15

Pool (cont.)
  popularity of, 103, 150–151,
    191, 206–207, 215
  terminology, 14–15, 40
  See also specific players and
    tournaments
Popularity of pool, 103, 150–151,
  191, 206–207, 215
Position, playing of, 49–50
Practice, 8, 98, 230, 239–240
Press, 13, 64, 81, 82, 83, 84–86,
  89, 91, 110, 124, 130–131,
  148, 160, 162, 167, 181, 217,
  219, 240
Pressure, 98, 179–181, 184–185
Prize money, 13, 21, 22–23, 39,
  57, 64, 77, 89, 97, 106,
  126–127, 140, 152, 166, 191,
  215, 218–220, 224, 231, 237
Procita, Joe, 76, 80, 81, 82, 87,
  124, 133, 136, 165, 169
Psychology, sports, 75
Puckett, U. J., 236, 237

Racism, 123
Rack, 87–88
Radio, 99
Raft, George, 85
Rail-first bank shots, 198
Ralph, Edward, 41
Rambow, Herman, 42
Ramsey, Herb, 67
Red Cross, 117
Riggie, Richard, 177–178
Roaring Twenties, 11–12, 15
Roosevelt, Franklin D., 100
Ross, Marty, 165–166, 168
Rossen, Robert, 192, 196, 205
Rotation, 221, 231–233
Rudolph, Erwin, 43–45, 63–64,
  69, 71, 76, 80, 82, 83, 87, 91,
    92, 94–97, 107, 129, 165, 171,
    177, 178
Rules and formats, championship,
  33–34, 39–42, 70, 134,
  138–142, 164–168
Russell, Charlie. See Mosconi,
  Joseph William
Ruth, Amelia, 146–147
Ruth, Babe, 12, 13, 17, 49, 86, 87,
  146, 183

St. Jean, Andrew, 35–36
St. Joseph's College (Philadelphia),
  188
St. Louis Browns, 100
St. Louis Cardinals, 19, 20
St. Moritz Hotel (New York), 200,
  201
Schaefer, Jake, 132–133
Schenley's Academy (Boston), 80
Scoring systems, 40–42, 67, 92,
  133, 140–142, 171–172, 223
Scott, George C., 200, 204, 205
Scratch, 78
Seaback, Charlie "Chick," 37,
  38–39, 43
Sebastian, Joe, 135
Sectional tournaments, 33, 36–37,
  62, 154
Seven-ball, 237
Sharif, Omar, 234, 235
Sharks, 29–31
Shaving points, 188
Sheraton Hotel (Philadelphia),
  219, 220
Shor, Toots, 192–195, 201
Short championship tournaments,
  138–139
Shutouts, 80
Sigel, Mike, 234
Sinatra, Frank, 196, 202–203

61-pool, 40
Slow-downs, 129–130
Slumps, 102–103
Smirnoff Beverage and Import
    Company, 220
Snooker, 221–223
Southern players, 141, 159
South Philadelphia Dance
    Academy, 5
South Philadelphia High School, 18
Spears, Edgar, 47
Spicer Manufacturing Corporation
    (Toledo, Ohio), 104
Spinks, Leon, 233
Sports:
    in the 1920s, 11–12, 15, 20
    in the 1930s, 18–77
    in the 1940s, 76–140
    in the 1950s, 141–191, 206
    in the 1960s, 192–215
    in the 1970s, 215–236
    in the 1980s, 236–243
Staton, William, 212
Stickball, 16
Stick bridge, 126
Storer, Clyde, 44, 45
Straight pool, 39–40, 41, 133, 159,
    221, 231, 233
Strand Academy (New York), 36,
    113–114
Strategy, 8, 40–42, 48–51, 66, 87,
    88, 98, 101–102, 127,
    129–130, 140–144, 164
Stroke, 2, 48–49, 74
Superior Billiard Parlor
    (Philadelphia), 179, 184, 186,
    191
Sutton, Willie, 26

Taberski, Frank, 8, 15, 43, 52–53,
    112

Tables, 24–25, 44, 123, 133, 134,
    137–138, 140–141, 176, 191,
    206–207, 216, 221, 240
    1960s remodeling of, 206–207
    size of, 140–141, 171
    snooker, 221–222
Talent, 87
Taylor, Eddie, 212
Television, 151, 175, 196, 218,
    219, 220, 223, 224–233, 236
    Mosconi on, 223, 224–233,
    236–239, 240
Tennis, 151, 175
Terminology, pool, 14–15, 40
Tevis, Walter, 203, 217, 218
Three-cushion, 133–134,
    135–136, 138, 142–145, 176,
    212, 219
Tilden, Bill, 12
Time magazine, 85, 130
Total-point tiebreaker, 92
Tournament of Champions (1942),
    94–98
Town Hall (Philadelphia), 90–92,
    126
Tozer, Dan, 91, 191
Travel, 57–60, 89, 118, 123, 149,
    158, 159, 179, 184
Trick shots, 59–60, 198, 220, 231,
    233, 239
Trophies, 241
$20,000 Black Velvet Challenge,
    220–222
Tyrrell, Peter, 170, 171

University of Michigan, 137
University of Minnesota, 137
University of Pennsylvania, 137
Ursitti, Charles J., 214, 225

Waldorf-Astoria (New York), 226,
    230, 231–232

Wanderone, Rudolf. *See* Fats, Minnesota
Washington, George, 14
Washington Senators, 100
West Side Story (movie), 205
Whitlow, Baby Face, 216
Wide World of Sports (TV show), 218, 224–233
Williams, Rex, 220–223
Williams, Ted, 83, 122
Willie Mosconi on Pocket Billiards (book), 190
Women players, 10, 206
Wood, Harry, 38
World championship, 8, 12, 13, 31–32, 33–34, 37, 39–42, 62, 71, 72, 76, 178–179
  of 1878, 15
  format and rules, 33–34, 39–42, 70, 134, 138–142, 164–168
  of 1910, 41
  of 1912, 41
  of 1919, 52
  of 1929, 38
  of 1932, 31–32
  of 1933, 39–44, 62, 106–107
  of 1934, 62, 107
  of 1935, 62–66
  of 1937, 67–69
  of 1938, 69–70, 72
  of 1939, 72–73
  of 1940, 76
  of 1941, 76–92
  of 1942, 94–98, 101
  of 1946, 99, 124, 126–127, 154
  of 1948, 134–136
  of 1949, 138–140
  of 1950, 141–142, 145
  of 1951, 145–146
  of 1952, 153–154
  of 1953, 157, 159–160, 170, 171
  1954 controversy, 164–172
  of 1963, 207–209
  of 1966, 211
World of Leisure, 239
World Series, 19
World War I, 11
World War II, 92, 93–94, 98–104, 108–109, 112–118, 120, 122, 124, 150, 152
Worst, Harold, 176, 212, 213

Ziegfeld Follies, 4

Stanley Cohen is a freelance writer whose previous books include: *The Game They Played*, about the college basketball scandals of 1951; *The Man in the Crowd*, a memoir of a lifelong fascination with the world of sports; *A Magic Summer*, a retrospective of the 1969 Mets; and *Dodgers! The First 100 Years*. Cohen previously worked as an editor and reporter for newspapers and magazines and as a teacher at Hunter College and at New York University, where he is a member of the Adjunct Faculty. He resides with his wife, Betty, in the Bronx and in Tomkins Cove, New York.